ASSERTIVENESS FOR MANAGERS

To Thelma, Alexandra, Edward (and Inca)
who, by reminding me of life's priorities, show me
what to be assertive about

ASSERTIVENESS FOR MANAGERS

Terry Gillen

Gower

First published in hardback 1992 by Gower Publishing
This paperback edition published 1994 by
Gower Publishing
Gower House
Croft House
Aldershot
Hants GU11 3HR
England

Gower
Old Post Road
Brookfield
Vermont 05036
USA

CIP catalogue records for this book are available from the British Library

ISBN 0-566-02861-1 (HBK)
      0-566-07613-6 (PBK)

Printed in Great Britain at the University Press, Cambridge

Contents

List of Figures and Tables   vii

Preface   ix

Your assertiveness profile   xi

Part One

1   **Introduction: reversing the domino effect**   3

2   **Recognizing behaviour**   8

3   **What makes us behave the way we do? – Positive self-talk**   24

4   **What makes us behave the way we do? – Early programming**   35

5   **What makes us behave the way we do? – Rights**   46

6   **Assertiveness and effective management**   66

7   **Assertive techniques**   72

Part Two

8 **Introduction**   97

9 **Reprimanding or criticizing a member of staff**   99

10 **Being reprimanded or criticized**   107

11 **Handling aggressive people**   118

12 **Handling submissive people**   129

13 **Handling resentment**   136

14 **Delegating an unpleasant task**   141

15 **Resolving conflict**   147

16 **Saying 'No' to a request**   154

17 **Handling work overload from your boss**   162

18 **Telling your team about tough targets**   169

19 **Giving praise**   175

20 **Being praised**   183

21 **Performing well in meetings**   189

22 **Talking to a poor listener**   195

23 **Seeking guidance from your boss**   204

24 **Reducing stress**   211

25 **Handling persistent sales people**   217

26 **Conclusion**   227

   Suggested reading   233

   Index   235

List of Figures and Tables

Figure 1	Assertiveness profile.	xv
Figure 2	Self-talk.	28
Figure 3	Effect of positive and negative self-talk.	30
Figure 4	Hierarchy of needs.	68
Figure 5	Situational leadership model.	69
Figure 6	Reprimanding or criticizing a member of staff: summary.	106
Figure 7	Being reprimanded or criticized: summary.	117
Figure 8	Handling aggressive people: summary.	128
Figure 9	Handling submissive people: summary.	135
Figure 10	Handling resentment: summary.	140
Figure 11	Delegating an unpleasant task: summary.	146
Figure 12	Broader field of vision.	152
Figure 13	Resolving conflict: summary.	153
Figure 14	Saying 'No' to a request: summary.	161
Figure 15	Handling work overload from your boss: summary.	168
Figure 16	Telling your team about tough targets: summary.	174
Figure 17	Giving praise: summary.	182
Figure 18	Being praised: summary.	188
Figure 19	Performing well in meetings: summary.	194
Figure 20	Talking to a poor listener: summary.	203
Figure 21	Seeking guidance from your boss: summary.	210

Figure 22   Reducing stress: summary.   216
Figure 23   Closed questions algorithm.   223
Figure 24   Handling persistent salespeople: summary.   226
Figure 25   Levels of assertiveness.   229

Table 1   Summary of aggressive, submissive and assertive
            behaviour.   13
Table 2   Links between events, content of our data banks,
            and our learned response.   213

Preface

Visit any works canteen, office dining room, bar or restaurant at lunchtime and, sooner or later, you will overhear conversations about people's managers – what makes the good ones good and what makes the bad ones bad. You will hear comments like 'The trouble is, he never listens', or 'You know where you are with her, she's firm but fair.'

On leaving the canteen, dining room, bar or restaurant, you may muse as to the high ratio of reported 'bad' managers to 'good' ones. You may also wonder how effective, in relation to their actual potential, those people are who work for the 'bad' managers: 30%, 40%, 50%? How much more effective could they be if their managers realized that along with every pair of hands a brain comes free.

This is the situation that started me thinking. A frequent remark at the end of an assertiveness programme is 'It's my boss who should come on this course.' And quite right too! Although assertiveness training has its roots in the clinical therapy given to people having difficulty coping with life's problems, on my courses everything I covered was congruent with effective management behaviour.

Concurrently, I found that on management programmes, input relating to management style and team-building was received more positively by those managers who behaved assertively, and not so well by those who behaved aggressively or submissively. There were also those managers who, despite receiving the message positively, lacked the interpersonal skills to put it into practice when the inevitable conflicts arose during exercises.

Consequently, I began to experiment, introducing assertiveness (without actually using the term) on management courses, and found many of its essential elements well received, provoking much thought, discussion and action.

To cut a long story short, having made the connection between assertiveness and effective management, I was asked to put my thoughts between the covers of a book so that they could be more widely available. Having done so, I want to express the usual, but nonetheless sincere, appreciation to everyone who has helped me along the way:

- Joy Ward for the speedy translation of handwritten scribble to neatly typed manuscript.
- Those professional people at Gower for their suggestions (and patience).
- My family, to whom this book is dedicated, for their understanding of my enforced isolation in the study.
- The countless people on my courses who have shared their experiences and feelings which contribute to what I hope is the practical nature of this book.

On several occasions, when people have heard that I was writing a book, they asked what is was about. My initial reply was that it was about assertiveness for managers. That was usually followed quickly by 'Well . . . about overall management effectiveness, really', and a few seconds later by '. . . and also about how better relations between people can contribute to organizational effectiveness.'

Subconsciously, I must be hoping for a wide readership! If lunchtime conversations on management are anything to go by, however, a wide range of people could benefit from reading it.

Terry Gillen

Your assertiveness profile

In reading this book, you may like a 'fix' on your own behaviour to see if you are aggressive, submissive or assertive. Most people use a mixture of all three behaviours. By completing the following questionnaire, you will be able to see what your mix is. The questionnaire is based on the characteristics of aggressive, submissive and assertive behaviour described in this book.

In responding to the following statements, please allocate 0, 1, 2 or 3 points to each question, according to whether it is

Totally untrue	0 points
Occasionally true	1 point
Often true	2 points
Totally true	3 points

Write your score in the box provided, and work quickly. It is your first reaction that you want to record. Try not to look back at previous answers – consider each question afresh. Don't flick forward to the scoring page, either.

1. I find it easy to take charge of a situation. ☐

2. I conform to accepted behaviour even if it is not what I would choose myself. ☐

3. The volume of my voice, when faced with confrontation, is about average. ☐

4. I can stare people out. ☐

5. I would feel vulnerable if I was suddenly put in charge of handling a crisis. ☐

6. I often wring my hands together when nervous. ☐

7. I often have to raise my voice to achieve results. ☐

8. I do *not* use sarcasm and ridicule to obtain my way. ☐

9. I believe that how people behave is up to them. ☐

10. I find it easy to put forward my viewpoint even when other people are trying to put forward theirs. ☐

11. Even if I do get nervous I rarely fidget. ☐

12. I am often critical of my own behaviour. ☐

13. I find it difficult to look people in the eye when there is a problem between us. ☐

14. I often wag my finger at people or jab it in their direction to emphasize a point. ☐

15. I believe that people *should* behave in certain acceptable ways. ☐

16. I can be very persistent and usually obtain my own way. ☐

17. The hesitancy in my voice makes me appear nervous. ☐

18. Even when listening to the views of other people, I keep sight of my own views. ☐

19. When people try and obtain *their* way by making me feel sympathetic towards them, I ensure they stay responsible for finding their own solutions.

20. I believe that being open about how I feel assists in achieving clear communication. ☐

21. If anyone tries to 'bully' me, I can give as good as I receive. ☐

22. I can use sarcasm to let people know what I think of them. ☐

23. I feel uncomfortable when people criticize me. ☐

24. When people try and force me to do something, I usually manage to achieve a compromise with which we are both happy. ☐

25. I rarely see the validity of people's criticisms of me. ☐

26. I tend to approach problems in a consultative and democratic manner. ☐

27. It would embarrass me to tell people how I really feel. ☐

28. I find it easy to let people put forward their views in preference to my own. ☐

29. If other people land themselves in difficulties; that is their problem. ☐

30. I find it difficult to stand my ground in an argument with someone else. ☐

31. I have learned a lot by listening to criticism. ☐

32. I feel easily intimidated by more forceful people. ☐

33. I believe that being open about one's emotions is a sign of vulnerability, so I rarely do it. ☐

34. I find it easy to relate to, and to feel responsible for, other people's problems. ☐

35. I find that standing my ground usually encourages the other person to come to a compromise. ☐

36. I will make eye contact with people, but not to such an extent that they are made uncomfortable by it. ☐

Now transfer your score for each question to the appropriate box and add the totals. (The remaining columns of boxes are for the questionnaires you give to other people.)

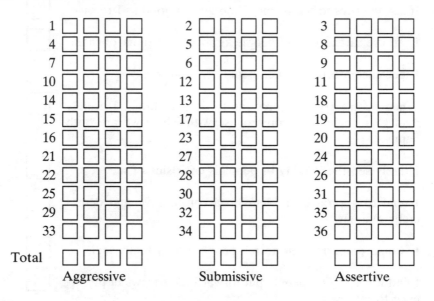

Now transfer your scores to the appropriate axes in Figure 1 to produce your 'assertiveness profile'.

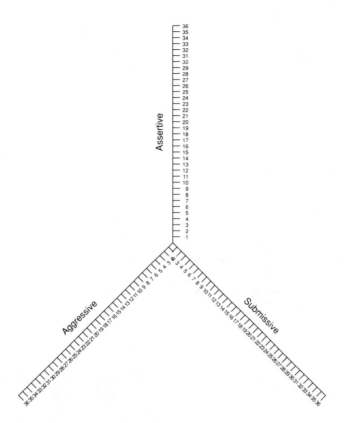

Figure 1 *Assertiveness profile*

In looking at your assertiveness profile, you will benefit from a twofold consideration. The first is, *'What shape is it?'*

Is it heavily skewed to the left, indicating that you are basically aggressive?

Is it heavily skewed to the right, indicating that you are basically submissive?

Is it set very low, indicating that you are rarely assertive but, instead, oscillate between aggressive and submissive behaviour?

Is it a centrally positioned equilateral triangle, indicating that you exhibit all three behaviours?

Is it the ideal shape – tall and thin – indicating that you are primarily assertive?

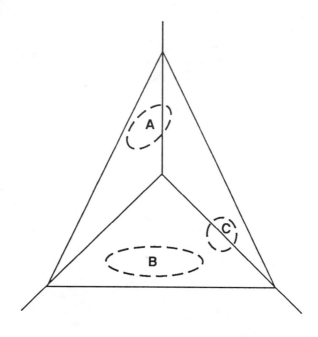

I have chosen this triangular representation of aggressive, submissive and assertive behaviour deliberately because it contradicts a common perception.

We know that aggressive and submissive behaviours are opposite extremes, and often think of them as being at either end of a continuum:

Aggressive ◄──────────► Submissive

As a representation of reality, this model has two flaws. The first is that it fails to reconcile in most people's minds the fact that they, and people they know, actually oscillate between aggressive and submissive behaviour; only some people are either/or. Second, it tends to place assertiveness as a kind of compromise position in the middle.

The triangular model represents reality more accurately. It shows assertive behaviour for what it is – a third option.

Take a triangle based on the maximum scores for each axis and you can probably visualize how people's actual behaviour would fit into it.
Person A is basically assertive, but becomes aggressive when pushed. Person B is never assertive, but responds to problems by being aggressive or submissive. Person C is total submissive. Looking at the shape of your profile will indicate into which part of the model your behaviour fits.

The first consideration, then, concerns the shape of your profile. The second concerns, '*What shape do other people think it is?*'

On the next few pages is another questionnaire. It follows the same pattern as the first, but is designed for other people to complete about you. I suggest you photocopy it several times and give it to your boss, a colleague and a subordinate. When they return the questionnaire to you, you can then plot the resultant profiles on the same axes, differentiating them with different colours.

You can then ask yourself several questions:

- In what way do I see myself differently from how they see me?
- Do my superiors, colleagues and subordinates have different views of me? In what way? Why?
- What is it about my behaviour that has led them to their conclusions? (You may want to talk to them about this, although I suggest you wait until you have read Part One. That way their answers will mean more to you.)
- Which aspects of my behaviour should I highlight and which should I suppress?
- What do I want to get out of reading this book?

A questionnaire about me

To:_____   From:_____

Date:_____

I am currently reading a book called *Assertiveness for Managers* by Terry Gillen. To help me obtain maximum benefit from the book, I am seeking feedback on how my behaviour is seen by others. I should be grateful, therefore, if you would answer the following questionnaire about me.

   In responding to the following statements, please allocate 0, 1, 2 or 3 points to each question according to whether it is

Totally untrue	0 points
Occasionally true	1 point
Often true	2 points
Totally true	3 points

Please write the score in the box provided and work quickly – it is your first reaction that will be most accurate. Try not to look back to previous answers but consider each question afresh.

1. He/she finds it easy to take charge of a situation.

2. He/she conforms to accepted behaviour even if it is not what she/he would choose for him/herself.

3. The volume of his/her voice, when faced with confrontation, is about average.

4. He/she can stare people out.

5. He/she would feel vulnerable if suddenly put in charge of handling a crisis.

6. He/she often wrings his/her hands when nervous.

7. He/she often raises his/her voice to achieve results.

8. He/she never uses sarcasm/ridicule to obtain his/her way.

9. He/she lets people determine freely how they behave.

10. He/she finds it easy to put forward his/her viewpoint, even when other people are trying to put forward theirs. □

11. He/she rarely fidgets when in a tricky situation. □

12. He/she is his/her toughest critic. □

13. He/she finds it difficult to look in the eye people with whom there is a problem. □

14. He/she often wags a finger at people or jabs it in their direction to emphasize a point. □

15. He/she tries to impose his/her 'rules' of behaviour on other people. □

16. He/she can be very persistent and usually obtains his/her way. □

17. The hesitancy in his/her voice makes him/her appear nervous. □

18. He/she listens to other people's views but does not lose sight of his/her own. □

19. If anyone seeks help by attempting to generate sympathy, he/she ensures they stay responsible for finding their own solutions. □

20. He/she is open in his/her communication. □

21. If anyone tries to bully him/her, he/she responds in kind. □

22. He/she uses sarcasm to get his/her way. □

23. He/she is sensitive to criticism. □

24. When forced with someone trying to obtain their own way, he/she is good at getting them to compromise. □

25. He/she does not accept criticism. □

26. He/she approaches problems in a democratic and consultative manner. □

27. I rarely know what he/she really feels or he/she is embarrassed if I do find out. □

28. He/she lets other people's views prevail in preference to his/her own. ☐

29. He/she does not help other people when they have a problem. ☐

30. He/she is easily out-argued. ☐

31. He/she listens to criticism. ☐

32. He/she is easily intimated by more forceful people. ☐

33. I rarely know what he/she feels; I think he/she feels sharing emotions is a sign of vulnerability. ☐

34. He/she is extremely understanding and takes other people's problems on board. ☐

35. He/she stands his/her ground, but is prepared to reach a compromise on a win-win basis. ☐

36. He/she makes eye contact, but not to such an extent that people feel uneasy. ☐

Thank you for responding to this questionnaire.

PART 1

Chapter 1

INTRODUCTION: REVERSING THE 'DOMINO EFFECT'

Whether you are talking about managing, leading, discussing, persuading, directing, appraising, counselling, selling or negotiating, it all boils down to one thing – *human interaction*.

In this chapter we will examine the importance of human interaction to managerial effectiveness, and how the quality of that interaction is affected by our values, attitudes, and beliefs. The chapter is entitled *Reversing the 'Domino Effect'* because of the repercussions of human interaction on business effectiveness.

At one time or another, most children have played with dominoes by standing them on end in a long line, knocking over the first one, and then watching with delight as each successive domino topples the next in line. A similar phenomenon happens in management, but it is not so delightful to watch. One thing goes wrong, and before you know it, a chain reaction occurs. This is the domino effect.

With dominoes, however, the effect cannot be reversed. You cannot pick up one domino and cause it to return the others to a standing position – but in management, you can do something similar. You can make a seemingly small change which starts off a *positive* chain reaction. That is the aim of this book – to enable you to make the small but elusive change which will produce significant and long-term benefits.

The thinking behind this aim is worth examining.

The world of management is becoming tougher and many companies are attempting to steal a march on their competitors by seeking to understand and provide what customers want – and therein lies a paradox. Despite an intense use of high technology, the impact of human interaction on commercial performance has never been greater.

Whether you are looking at someone serving a customer, the people from different stages in the production process addressing a quality problem or a manager encouraging staff to higher performance, you are looking at human interaction. Furthermore, the effect of that interaction will rest less on what was said and more on the manner in which it was said. The manner in which we interact depends on our attitudes, values and beliefs.

It has long been recognized that managers are the single greatest influence on people at work. Yet in many organizations, that influence is at best unhelpful, and at worst downright counter-productive.

A brief examination of management style theory will help here.

Most managers are familiar with the description of the two extreme management styles described by Douglas McGregor as Theory X and Theory Y. Managers exhibiting an X style of management base their actions on the belief that people are basically lazy, will avoid work and responsibility and are motivated by base desires. The resultant style is authoritarian. All power resides with the manager who, through close monitoring and the application of punishment and reward, manages to squeeze adequate performance out of the unwilling workers.

Managers exhibiting a Y style believe that work is natural to people and can be enjoyed; that people are motivated by feelings of team spirit, achievement and personal growth, and that they will soak up as much responsibility as their abilities and their employers will allow. The resultant style is democratic. Power is shared; people become self-motivating; rewards are psychological as well as material. People drive themselves to achieve the targets they helped set.

Although these theories have been extended by several people (such as Blake & Mouton and Tannenbaum & Schmidt), the basic concept is sound.

Its relevance to today's environment, however, lies less in the management actions it describes, and more in the beliefs on which it is based. The reason those beliefs are so important is based on the changing nature of authority at work. Workplace authority is derived from three main sources – status in the hierarchy; technical knowledge; and what can best be described as *personal credibility*. Only the last source is on the ascendancy.

Many organizations are developing leaner, flatter structures and devolving authority as low down the hierarchical structure as it can go. In tandem with these changes, the 'youth revolution' continues apace, reducing the respect that was traditionally reserved for figures of authority. The result is that grade and job titles no longer generate the respect they once did.

Similarly, increased use of modern technology has spread information ('power' in most organizations) making it as available as the nearest terminal, enabling people with keyboard skills to take and action decisions. Conversely, many 'blue collar' jobs are now far more cerebral than they once were, requiring judgment and discretion from levels of people who, at one time, were thought of primarily as order fodder. Technical authority is therefore no longer the scarce commodity it once was.

That only leaves the authority relating to your personal credibility – that isn't something your company bestows upon you, and neither is it something you pass an exam in. It is something other people *feel* about you. *Most of their judgements will be made on the basis of how you interact with them.*

Most managers interact with people every day. In fact, they spend 70–80% of their time doing just that. Interaction involves 'rules' – who is superior to whom, what subjects are alright for discussion, what is and what is not negotiable, what behaviour is expected and acceptable, etc. Where the 'rules' are clear and shared by both parties the interaction is usually straightforward. Where the 'rules' are uncertain or not shared by both parties, the interaction rarely turns out as satisfactory to all concerned. Wherever there is *change* the 'rules' become confused.

Consider the amount of change in today's workplace – flatter organizations, decentralized authority, small teams geared up for rapid response to customer-led developments, changing technology, obsolete skills, retraining and outplacement, to name but a few – and ask yourself if the 'rules' are becoming more or less stable.

It is at these times that our *coping mechanisms* are stretched to the full. Those people who cope well do so because their interaction with others is based on beliefs, attitudes and values which by providing a stable emotional base, manifest themselves in a style of interaction that is both efficient and which enhances their personal credibility, i.e. they behave assertively.

To summarize so far, managers have a tough job to do and the place where the domino effect is triggered or is put into reverse is in their interaction with others. The quality of that interaction is becoming more critical for two reasons. First, the changing nature of authority at work is placing more emphasis on managers' personal credibility, and second, the 'rules' governing the way in which we interact are less predictable than they used to be. This lack of predictability tests the way in which we cope with conflict.

This is where assertiveness has a lot to teach us. If you ask any manager to describe their best ever boss, their ideal colleague or the sort of staff they would like, the chances are they will produce a list of assertive characteristics such as confident, open and honest, not easily intimidated, sensitive to others, patient, calm, persistent, etc.

As a way of interacting with other people, assertiveness is totally congruent with the style of management increasingly sought in modern companies. So ask yourself, do you want to be the sort of manager who:

- motivates staff
- earns loyalty from staff
- enables staff to achieve good results
- earns the respect of colleagues

- is held in high esteem by senior management
- feels OK about him or herself

If so, you are ready to benefit from developing your assertiveness.

Before you begin, you may find the following 'signposting' useful.

The next chapter, *Recognizing behaviour*, examines aggressive, submissive and assertive behaviours, and how to recognize them. There then follow three chapters concerning *what makes us behave in the way we do*. They discuss the self-fulfilling prophecies that affect our behaviour, and show how *positive self-talk* can help make the process work for us rather than against us. They consider how the *early programming* we received as children affects our behaviour in adult life, and how the concept of *rights* is central to assertive behaviour.

A further chapter, *Assertiveness and effective management*, examines how assertiveness fits into accepted management theory. The final chapter in Part One looks at how assertiveness comes alive with several simple but effective *Assertive techniques*.

That chapter concludes what might be called the 'theoretical building blocks' of Part One. Having read it, you will be equipped to gain maximum benefit from Part Two – a selection of how assertiveness can assist managerial effectiveness in relation to seventeen issues typically faced by managers. A quick word of warning, however: it would be a falsely economical use of time to go straight to Part Two. It will mean much more after you have read Part One.

Finally, a couple of points about terminology. First, in many books on assertiveness, a variety of terminology is employed to describe different types of behaviour – assertive, aggressive, submissive, passive, non-assertive, and so on. I have adopted only three terms – aggressive, submissive and assertive. Second, while this book is aimed at managers, they too have different names used to describe them – team leader, supervisor, controller, manager, director, and so on. I have used, therefore, one catchall – the boss!

I hope this simplified terminology will help.

Workout sheet

Many of us have a great capacity to accept things the way they are, to postpone making changes even when we know those changes are the right thing to do, or even to make excuses absolving ourselves from the responsibility for our situations. The following questions will help you identify those situations where assertiveness could help. In answering them, please remember that they are all aimed at your interaction with other people.

1. Do people ever get the better of you by using bullying, sarcasm or emotional blackmail? In what sort of situations?

2. Do you find yourself being overapologetic, blaming yourself or feeling that other people, generally, are better than you? What sorts of situations trigger these reactions?

3. Do you ever find that you feel bad about yourself or about someone because you spoke more harshly than you meant to? What sort of situations are you thinking about?

4. Do you regularly feel uneasy before a meeting, interview or conversation which you think might prove difficult? Please provide some examples.

5. Do you regularly find yourself feeling impatient with other people? Again, in what sorts of situations?

6. In what way is your organization changing? How does that change manifest itself in people situations? How do you feel about that?

7. What sort of work situations make you feel uncomfortable, before, during or after the event?

8. In what sort of work situations do you make people feel uncomfortable either before, during or after the event?

9. In what sort of work situations involving other people would you like to improve your performance?

10 In what ways would your boss, colleagues and staff like you to alter your behaviour?

Chapter 2

RECOGNIZING
BEHAVIOUR

In the last chapter we established the importance of human interaction to business success. In situations where we feel psychologically uncomfortable we frequently resort to our natural reaction of fight or flight.

So although human interaction is necessary to business success, it can also leave us feeling psychologically uncomfortable. An angry customer, an unco-operative colleague, a critical boss or an awkward member of staff can cause problems for the best manager, never mind the rest of us. As many of us have *learned* during childhood, to make the connection between a difficult situation and our fight or flight response, we do so automatically, even though we are now adults and our verbal problem solving skills are adequate to cope.

In this chapter, we begin the process of examining how our internal responses are manifest in behaviour so that, by the end of it, you will

- have a framework of terminology to use through the rest of this book;
- be able to recognize other people's behaviour, and categorize it as aggressive, submissive or assertive;
- improve your self-awareness by understanding more about your own behaviour.

Recognizing as aggressive someone who persistently slams doors, thumps tables and threatens other people is quite easy. Similarly, recognizing as submissive someone who sits quietly with hunched shoulders and downcast eyes while someone unjustly criticizes him is also quite easy. But look at the following dialogue from a weekly meeting, and ask who is being aggressive, submissive and assertive:

'OK,' said Bill who was chairing the meeting. 'The next item on the agenda is Monthly Returns.' He turned to John, the Company Account-ant. 'This is your item, John, so perhaps you would like to introduce it.'

John cleared his throat and shifted in his seat. 'Yes, thank you, Bill. Yes, right . . . the Monthly Returns. Well . . . as you know they are supposed to be in by the 5th of the next month and many are coming in a little bit late.' John flashed his eyes around those assembled at the table and then returned them to his papers.

Bill filled the ensuing silence. 'Is that everyone's returns, John, or only some? And how late is a little bit late!' he asked calmly.

'Well it's mainly Sales, actually', replied John. 'Usually about two weeks late.'

Bill turned to Phil, the Sales Manager, and raised his eyebrows to signal to Phil that he would welcome a response.

Phil let out an impatient sigh and rolled his eyes towards the ceiling. 'C'mon Bill. You've just given us the toughest targets we've had in a fourth quarter. I'm on at my people every day to bring in business; how can I push them to fill in forms as well?'

'What exactly is the problem,' pursued Bill, 'The amount of information required or the timescale within which it is required?'

'It's both,' blurted Phil. 'I've told Accounts. My people are up to their ears. But they don't listen. Typical accountants. As long as they've got lots of forms to chase they're happy while we work 16 hours a day to pay their salaries.'

'It isn't our fault,' stated John, 'We're under pressure too, you know. Since we were taken over by Amalgamated Holdings we've had to provide lots of additional information. Your trouble,' he continued, pointing a finger in Phil's direction. 'is that you think the world revolves around Sales Department.'

Bill held up a hand for silence. 'This is getting us nowhere fast. How would you feel if we spent the next ten minutes examining what goes into these forms, where else the information could come from and how it could be collected more easily? Then at least we'll know what kind of problem we are dealing with.'

Well, how did you categorize the characters? Phil was generally aggressive throughout. His dismissive attitude to another department's problems and his sarcastic generalization about Accounts were all indicators of his feeling of superiority.

John began submissively. He was physically nervous and his voice hesitant. He was also reluctant to come to the point, so he waffled until pressed by Bill. He also tried to pass the blame on to the parent company. Phil's comments must have touched a nerve, though, because John ended up responding in kind to Phil.

Bill was always assertive. It was obvious that he was chairing the meeting, yet at no time did he force anything on anyone. He sought information, and consistently brought the conversation back from an emotional to a rational level. In the end he was the one who proposed a way out of the conflict with which they could all agree.

Much of the behaviour in this example was fairly subtle, yet could be just as effective in hindering efficient interaction as if it was extreme and obvious.

Recognizing aggressive, submissive and assertive behaviour is easier if you keep in mind some basic definitions.

Aggressive people want to win, even at the expense of others. While that attitude is acceptable and even desirable in sport or selling, when you either win or lose to the competition, in most other aspects of life it is unproductive because of the underlying attitudes from which is springs.

Aggressive people believe that they have rights and other people do not; that what they have to say is more important than what other people have to say; that their contribution is more worthy than anyone else's. Consequently, it is generally alright for them to 'win' over other people by speaking more loudly, interrupting them, bullying, using sarcasm, patronization or intimidating body language such as leaning over people or excessive eye contact.

Such people tend (at least overtly) to be very sure of themselves. They use 'I' excessively, state what *they* want to the exclusion of others, are highly critical and quick to blame, and frequently adopt a 'full frontal' stance.

Such a stance is quite unusual in most of us. People rarely stand with head, shoulders, hips and the angle between their feet all pointing directly at the other person. It can be quite intimidating. (It is a stance normally associated with gun fighters or fist fighters as they face one-another displaying their bravado.) Similarly, they often try to appear bigger than they really are by standing erect, puffing out their chest with hands on hips, folding their arms across their chests, etc.

They are, of course, according to their own definition, usually correct in what they do. Hence, in their conversations with others, they often use authoritarian words like 'should' and 'ought', and frequently deliver suggestions or requests as if they were orders. If they do lose their temper, it is usually the other person's fault for having made them do so. They feel disdain for people whom they maltreat, and resentment for those who are also aggressive but better at it than they are. In short, if everyone else would simply do as they were told, life would be much easier.

Submissive people are the opposite. Their prime concern is to avoid conflict, even at the expense of themselves. While the avoidance of conflict is often desirable, sometimes there is no alternative. In fact, there are two points to make about this definition. First, the key phrase in it is *even at the expense of themselves*. Submissive people are not only reluctant to stand up for themselves, they will avoid placing themselves in situations where they have to do so. Second, submissive people experience conflict where many other people do not even notice it. Their sensitivity to conflict is very finely tuned, primarily because of their underlying beliefs about themselves.

They believe that other people have rights and they do not; that what they have to say is not important; that their contribution is less valuable than other people's. For example, 'It's only a suggestion and it's probably not a very good one . . .'

Submissive people experience conflict more frequently than the rest of us and, because of their low self-esteem, try and avoid it in a variety of ways. To begin with, they tend to speak softly, allow other people to interrupt them, get upset when criticized, and are easily intimidated.

Much of their body language stems directly from the adrenalin released into the blood stream as part of the fight or flight response. Adrenalin increases the respiration rate, with the effect that submissive people often have to draw breath before the end of a sentence. It increases the amount of oxygenated blood flowing through the muscles, thus making submissive people fidgety. It makes the soles of the feet and palms of the hands sweat, causing them to subconsciously rub their hands together.

Submissive people tend to be unsure of themselves, so they exhibit a good deal of self control ('I ought' and 'I must do this'), self-criticism ('I wish I wasn't so useless at this') and self-flagellation ('Nothing ever goes right for me'). Unlike aggressive people who attempt to make themselves appear larger than they are, submissive people try and appear smaller. They hunch up, tightly cross their legs, put their knees together or clasp their hands in their laps. They wrap an arm around or fold their arms across their stomach to 'protect' the vulnerable parts of their abdomen. They 'hide' behind a hand covering their mouth.

According to their own definition, they are not as correct as other people. They are therefore quick to agree. They reduce their 'exposure' by going along with the majority, and by avoiding eye contact. Their gaze is usually down.

They will also attempt to 'defuse' a potentially conflicting situation by making the other person feel sorry for them, or they will 'defer' conflict by beating around the bush and not being straight with people, particularly when making a request or wanting to refuse someone else's request.

A final characteristic of submissive people is that they usually feel bad about themselves. They feel bad if they refuse someone else's request, and bad if they accept it knowing they should not have done so. They feel selfish if they stand up for themselves, and ashamed if they do not. Sometimes the frustration can build up to such an extent that they lose their temper and retaliate (giving a very good impression of aggression), usually in response to a fairly benign request – and subsequently feel guilty for having done so! In short, life would be a lot easier if it was a nice warm bath.

Assertive people are entirely different. They are quite capable of standing up for their rights, but they do so in a way that also helps other people stand up for theirs. They do not avoid conflict as submissive people do, nor do they revel in it like aggressive people. They simply address it in a way that is fair to both parties. They feel that what they have to say is just as important as that which others have to say, and that their contribution is just as valuable (no more so, no less so) than that of other people. They seem to have an inner confidence or reassurance which enables them to state openly what they want or how they feel, and to resolve conflict by constructing a mutually acceptable compromise.

Much of their body language stems directly from this calm self-assurance. They frequently appear relaxed, they make plenty of 'open' movements – for example, outstretching their hands, palms uppermost. They are attentive and keen to enquire – for example, finding out why you feel their request will cause you a problem. While they will often look for compromise, they can also be very persistent and very firm if they feel someone is trying to win at their expense.

They are straightforward. They will agree and disagree, accede or refuse honestly, not evading the issue, and they will do so with good eye contact and a tone of voice which supports rather than undermines what they have said.

A summary of these behaviours is given in Table 1.

So, how do these behaviours manifest themselves in managerial interaction? First, let us consider how one particular problem would be tackled by aggressive, submissive and assertive managers. We shall then go on to look at a range of typical management problems together with typically aggressive, submissive and assertive responses.

Table 1 *Summary of aggressive, submissive and assertive behaviour*

	Aggressive	Submissive	Assertive
What they think	Everyone else is inferior	Don't upset people	People deserve respect
	People should be more like me	I need others' goodwill	We all live by different rules
		I'm inadequate	
			People and their behaviour are two separate things
	People should behave as I think they should	I lose, you win	I feel alright
	I win/you lose		We both win
Verbal characteristics	Raised volume	Quietly spoken	Medium volume and pace. Steady pitch
		Weak voiced	
	Rapid speech	Hesitant speech	
	Should, ought and other authoritarian words as instructions to others	Should, ought and other authoritarian words as self-regulatory instructions	Emphasis on key words usually factual rather than personal Expressive of facts rather than emotions
	Tone of voice displaying sarcasm, criticism, ridicule, etc	Tone of voice undermines conviction	
		Frequent justifications and permission-seeking statements Frequent sighs	
Non-verbal characteristics	Finger wagging, finger pointing/ jabbing and similar threatening, impatient and authoritarian gestures	Handwringing, fidgeting, frequently shifting posture when under pressure	Encouraging/ attentive movements Gestures support words being said
	Stern face Extremes of expression	Changing facial expression to match that of the other person	Facial expression supports communication otherwise neutral/ attentive
	Excessive eye contact	Minimal eye contact	Good eye contact 50–70% of time
	Full frontal 'Expanding' posture	'Shrinking' posture Closed posture Protective gestures Distance from other person	Open posture
			Comfortable distance according to the circumstances

Table 1 *Concluded*

Tactics	Generally dismissive of others Self-centred Interrupts	Inconspicuous Quick to agree	Attentive to others Listens
	Put-downs, sarcasm, ridicule, exaggeration, generalizations Critical of person Autocratic Suggestions/ requests given as orders Abrupt Uses questions to threaten Bullying	Takes criticism personally/as proof of self-depreciation self-flagellation Rambling Reluctant to get to point Indirect communication: 'There's a lot of work today', meaning 'I'd like some help please' Cop out statements 'I'll try . . .' 'If only', 'I wish I could . . .' Avoids decisions, hides true feelings	Criticizes behaviour, not person Accepts valid criticism and learns from mistakes Factual/rational Authoritative States wants, feelings etc., openly Questions to discover others' feelings
	Allocates blame to others	Accepts blame Blames self	Looks for solutions

Situation

A manager has a young staff member responsible for compiling two sorts of statistical information. The first is for a monthly Directors' Pack, distributed to all Board members and other senior officials five working days before every Board meeting. The second is in response to one-off requests for information from departments within the company. Although the subject matter is the same in both cases, the former is routine and now well within the staff member's capabilities, while the latter is novel and challenging. Consequently, the staff member is allowing the one-off requests to take priority over work for the monthly Director's Pack, with the result that for the last two months the manager has had to help with its production and, even so, missed the deadline. The manager has been heavily criticized by his boss over the timeliness of the Pack, and so has decided to tackle the staff member about it.

Aggressive

Manager: . . . and another thing, I'm becoming sick of always having to bale you out on the monthly Directors' Pack. I want it done on time this month, OK?

Staff member:	'I'm sorry, boss, it's just that the number of one-off requests I'm getting is growing all the time, and things have just become a bit late.'
Manager:	'Look, it's up to you to manage your time.'
Staff member:	'But everybody wants everything yesterday, and most of the requests come via you anyway and you delegate them to me.'
Manager:	'Are you saying you don't like the way I run things here?'
Staff member:	'No, boss.'
Manager:	'Good, or otherwise, you might find yourself looking for another job. Next month the Pack had better be on time, or else.'

Submissive

Manager:	'Hello. I can see you're a bit busy but I was wondering if I could have a quick word with you.'
Staff member:	'Yes, if it's quick. I've got a rush job on for Marketing Department.'
Manager:	'Oh yes, only a moment. It's about this wretched monthly Directors' Pack. There's been . . .'
Staff member:	'That thing? It's not due until next week.'
Manager:	'Yes, I know. It comes around with monotonous regularity doesn't it? Yes, well . . . one or two people have said that they'd like us to stick to the agreed deadline . . . if at all possible. Messes up their schedules if they don't get it on time. That sort of thing.
Staff member:	'Oh, really?'
Manager:	'Yes, so I was wondering if you could possibly give it a bit more priority this month.'
Staff member:	'OK, but I have got a lot on this week.'
Manager:	'You will try, though, won't you?'
Staff member:	'Yes OK boss.'
Manager:	'Oh good.'

Assertive

Manager:	'I'd like to talk to you about the monthly Directors' Pack. It's been late for the past two months despite the fact that I've helped. Previously you've always produced it on time. Why is it now late?'
Staff member:	'It's not the Pack that's the problem, boss, it's all these one-off requests from other departments. There's more than there used to be and so they take up more time.'
Manager:	'They're squeezing the time available for the Directors' Pack?'
Staff member:	'Yes, that's exactly it.'
Manager:	'Why are you giving them priority?'
Staff member:	'Well . . . they've usually got pretty tight deadlines, and I always think I can catch up the time later, and then along comes another one so I never do.'
Manager:	'OK. I know it isn't easy when you are in demand. Let me ask you, though, which do you feel is the more important part of your job?'
Staff member:	'All of it really . . . No, I suppose it's got to be the Directors' Pack . . . It's just so boring. It's routine, easy . . . there's no challenge left in it for me.'
Manager:	'Let me make sure I understand you. Your fame as a supplier of statistical information has spread so you now find yourself with more requests than before. You give more priority to those requests than to the Directors' Pack because of the more urgent deadlines and because you find them more satisfying.'
Staff member:	'Yes, that's exactly it.'
Manager:	'OK I need to make it plain to you that the Directors' Pack has to take priority. It cannot be late again . . . I see you're not too happy about that.'
Staff member:	'But how do I make time for everything?'
Manager:	'That's usually impossible. We all have to take decisions on priorities, and occasionally say 'No' to someone, or at least suggest an alternative arrangement to them. Let me make a suggestion. Why don't you list the steps you

	need to take to compile the Directors' Pack then come to see me this afternoon with your diary, and we'll jointly schedule in your tasks and discuss what to do about any requests from other departments whose deadlines may prove tricky?'
Staff member:	'That would be a great help. I'd also like to discuss something else with you.'
Manager:	'What's that?'
Staff member:	'I've categorized all the requests for statistical analyses that we've had in the last six months. There are several consistent themes. With subscriptions to the right databases we could produce the information in half the time.'
Manager:	'Bring that too and we'll see if we can make case for the expenditure – right after we've sorted out the Directors' Pack.'

Our aggressive manager has succeeded in alienating and frustrating an otherwise productive member of staff. Managers like that in our example normally see themselves as superior to their staff (and not just in terms of the organization structure). They see staff as people who need to be coerced into performing, and generally incapable of self-generated thought. Even if we give the benefit of the doubt to the example manager and assume a certain amount of 'recoil' from the criticism just received from his or her boss, the effect on the staff member is probably the same. The Pack may be produced on time from now on, but at a ridiculous and unnecessary cost in terms of motivation, job satisfaction, loyalty, and so on.

In terms of behaviour, we could see that the dialogue was patronizing, sarcastic, critical, and abrupt. In short, a real contrast to the submissive example.

The submissive manager has failed abysmally. Such managers usually see their role as running a happy ship, smoothing out trouble, and placating more demanding personalities. They attempt to avoid conflict by minimizing issues and postponing potential disagreements by not actually coming to the point. They frequently know what needs to be done, but fail to address the problems directly. Consequently, problems remain unresolved only to surface at a later date. Their credibility as managers is minimal.

The assertive manager in the example has clearly scored a success. The staff member is under no illusions about the priority that must be given to the Directors' Pack and feels as if the manager is helping resolve a problem, thereby boosting the manager's credibility in the eyes of the staff member. Finally, the staff member has volunteered a way of providing a better service to the department's internal customers.

Yet the manager's behaviour was simple and straightforward. He or she asked a number of questions to get to the bottom of the problem, concentrated on the behaviour that needed changing, not on the staff member's personal qualities, and twice checked his or her understanding of the staff member's situation. Yet at the same time, he or she addressed the issue firmly and squarely.

Such behaviour usually comes from people who are relatively sure of themselves; confident but not arrogant. At the same time, however, they are prepared to listen, to obtain information before passing judgment; to stick to their guns or compromise whichever is appropriate. They are prepared to involve other people, not as passive observers and recipients of orders, but as parties of equal value to the situation. This respect for one's fellow people only comes when it is counter-balanced by a healthy respect for oneself.

Here are a few more managerial situations to further your appreciation of how aggressive, submissive, and assertive behaviours are manifest at work.

Situation

Tackling a staff member who has recently started being persistently late in the mornings.

Aggressive

Abrupt. Judgmental, probably jumping to conclusions as to the reason for the lateness. Possibly sarcastic and patronizing. Threatening, e.g. 'I'm fed up with the way you're always coming in late these days. You'd better ask Santa Claus to bring you a new alarm clock for Christmas 'cos there's no room for stragglers in my department.'

Submissive

Unwilling to tackle the matter directly; refers to it obliquely or gradually. Minimizes the problem. Shows signs of discomfort, e.g. 'I hope you don't mind me mentioning this, but I can't help but notice that your timekeeping hasn't been quite as good as it used to be, if you know what I mean. I was wondering if you could possibly make a little bit extra effort. Helps with the image of the department, that sort of thing, you know.'

Assertive

Straightforward. Points out change in timekeeping standards. Neutral tone of voice to avoid any hint of accusation. Concentrates on behaviour, not personal characteristics. Specific, not general. Enquiring, e.g. 'I've noticed that for the last week you've been coming in later than usual, after our normal start time. I'd like to talk to you about it, please. Is there a problem?'

Situation

Asking a staff member to take on an unpleasant one-off task.

Aggressive

Ignores staff member's feelings and opinions. Dismissive attitude. Possibly discourteous, e.g. 'I want this done by close of play Tuesday and no bellyaching about it.'

Submissive

Puts off the 'confrontation' until the very last minute. Long-winded introduction. Over apologetic, e.g. 'I know you're not going to like this. I'd do it myself only I've got a lot on at the moment. I'd ask someone else if I could, but to be honest, I was wondering if you would possibly do it.'

Assertiveness

Direct, open and honest. Shows empathy. Asks, does not tell. Prepared to compromise. Checks staff member's feelings, e.g. 'I know this is an unpleasant job but on this occasion I'd like you to do it. At the next team meeting I'd also like you to present proposals for sharing it around the whole team, including me. How do you feel about it?'

Situation

Leading a team meeting to resolve a fall off in quality.

Aggressive

Dictatorial. Uninterested in others' opinions. Accusing. Absolves self from blame, e.g. 'Now listen you lot. I don't know what you think you're playing at but quality stinks. It never used to and I've no intention of presiding over sloppy workmanship. So pull your socks up and *don't let me down, OK?*'

Submissive

Unable to maintain focus on central issue. Easily sidetracked by staff members who want to shift blame elsewhere. Over-apologetic, e.g. 'Well . . . other managers have begun to notice that our quality isn't . . . er . . . all that it used to be . . . Yes, I know, they don't really understand our problems . . . I'm sorry to keep on, it must seem as if I'm nagging, but . . . er . . . I'm afraid we really must try harder.'

Assertive

Addresses the problem directly. Not interested in blame. Firm in maintaining focus and keen to share responsibility for a solution, e.g. 'OK, so that's the situation. Our quality has fallen off causing problems in both Production and Marketing. What I suggest we do is specify the problem in detail and then generate as many potential solutions as possible. How do you feel about that?'

Situation

Hit with a serious problem requiring an *immediate* team response.

Aggressive

Shouts, overreacts, makes staff feel vulnerable, e.g. 'For crying out loud, it's always me who has to bail other people out when they screw up. God it makes me furious. John, you contact the suppliers and find out what the hell they're playing at. Bill you get yourself organized and stop production. Sally you drop whatever you're doing and get everything back from Despatch – *and no foul ups!*'

Submissive

Feels helplessly vulnerable which shows in lack of decisiveness and panic. Raised pitch of voice, nervousness. Unclear communication e.g. 'Listen everybody, please. There's a bit of a problem. Something's gone wrong with the product and we need to . . . er . . . sort it out. I think we need to stop production and . . . er . . . stop all deliveries. Oh and . . . er . . . I think it might be a good idea if someone contacted the suppliers.'

Assertive

Calm, but urgency shows in body language. Communicates firmly and clearly. Specific language, e.g. 'Everybody, please pay attention. We have a serious problem. Quality Control has found abnormally high traces of lead in the finished product. We need to stop production and stop any despatches reaching customers. Sally, go to Despatch, stop them sending anything out and see if they can recall anything that's on the road. Bill, see the Production Manager, explain the problem, and ask him to stop production immediately. John, 'phone your contact at the suppliers and ask her to come over straight away. I'll contact Quality Control and find out more details. I'd like us to reconvene here in 30 minutes when I should have more information. Any questions? OK go to it.'

Much of the time it is the tell-tale, and normally obvious displays of body language that indicate whether someone is behaving aggressively, submissively or assertively. Although such indicators have been omitted from these examples, the type of behaviour being illustrated is still fairly obvious from the tactics alone.

Aggressive managers are generally dismissive of others and self-centred. They interrupt, use put-downs, sarcasm and unwarranted generalizations to get their way. Their coercive approach usually achieves results in the short term but at the long-term price of switching off their staff rather than switching them on.

Submissive managers are so keen to avoid conflict that they are reluctant to come to the point or to be open and frank. They leave matters unresolved, avoid decisions, and employ evasive statements like 'I'll try'. Their readiness to avoid conflict by agreeing makes them very malleable.

Assertive managers address issues openly, honestly, and with an enviable economy of words, without being abrupt. They involve others, actively encouraging them to volunteer their views and feelings. They know how to turn a criticism into a learning opportunity. When the situation demands they can give direct orders, but do so in a way that stimulates rather than intimidates.

You know where you are with an assertive manager. They are straight with people and involve others whenever possible. They tend to be rational, and use sound reason and fact rather than emotion to reach a solution. They are firm but fair.

So by now you should be familiar with the terminology in use throughout this book to describe aggressive, submissive, and assertive behaviour. You should also be able to recognize and categorize other people's behaviour, but above all, you will hopefully know a bit more about how your behaviour is probably perceived by others. You can pursue that theme in the following workout sheet. When you have examined in more detail how you behave you can then move on to the next chapter to consider *why* you behave as you do.

Workout sheet

If you have not already completed your Assertiveness Profile you will benefit from doing so. Otherwise, these questions will indicate whether you tend to be aggressive or submissive:

1. Do you often see situations in terms of win/lose?

2. Do you often feel superior or inferior to other people?

3. Do you say 'should' and 'ought' often when talking to other people?

4. Do you use many 'shoulds' and 'oughts' when talking to yourself?

5. Do you make suggestions sound like orders?

6. When agitated, do you frequently have to draw breath before reaching the end of a sentence, or feel fidgety?

7. Do you often feel unsure of yourself?

8. Do you agree with the majority to avoid conflict?

9. Do you find it difficult to come to the point when disagreeing with someone or delivering bad news?

10. Are you tolerant towards other people, but able to stand up for yourself?

Chapter 3

WHAT MAKES US BEHAVE THE WAY WE DO – POSITIVE SELF-TALK

So far I have described how the changing nature of work and of attitudes towards authority at work are calling for more *assertive* managers as opposed to their aggressive or submissive counterparts.

I have shown in examples how aggressive and submissive behaviours manifest themselves in styles of management which are, at best, unhelpful and at worst plain counter-productive, yet how assertive managers achieve that elusive combination of high concern for both people and production.

Assertive behaviour is worth cultivating. It leads to a management style more appropriate to today's environment; it gives us a more professional image; it helps us achieve better results in the 70–80% of our time that most of us spend with other people; it also helps reduce levels of stress, and improves our confidence and self-esteem.

In this chapter we tackle the question, 'What makes us behave the way we do?' This is one of these questions where the more you know, the more complex and 'if and but'-dependent the answer becomes. I shall answer it, therefore, in as straightforward a manner as I can, including only that subject matter which I know from leading assertiveness courses contributes to learners' understanding – of both the subject and themselves.

As the answer to the question 'What makes us behave the way we do?' is fairly lengthy, I have divided it into three chapters. By the end of them you will appreciate

- the impact of positive self-talk;
- the significance of our early programming;
- the concept of Rights and its application to the workplace.

This chapter concerns positive self-talk.

The effect of positive self-talk

We need to begin this section with a simple statement.

The outcome of any situation depends upon the way people behave.

This may sound like a statement of the obvious but it is surprising how many times people ignore it.

Ask anyone how they *should* behave to achieve a given outcome, and they will probably be able to tell you. Ask them how they behaved the last time they encountered such a situation, and they may well describe behaviour which is actually counter-productive.

The problem is a simple one – *we tend to behave by default rather than by design*. We then compound the felony by *retrospectively justifying* our behaviour. We act as if we have been victims of fate or circumstance, or as if our behaviour was genuinely beyond our control.

How many of these statements sound familiar?

'People like that always make me lose my temper.'
'I'm useless in those types of situation.'
'I'm here to obtain results, not treat people with kid gloves.'
'What's the point in disagreeing? My boss is a law unto himself.'
'Well that's this company for you. No one tells you anything.'
'I always become nervous when I'm put on the spot.'

As a result, we absolve ourselves from responsibility for the consequences of our behaviour, and so miss a vital point – we tend to gear up our behaviour not to what we want to happen, but more to what we *expect* will happen.

You see, very few situations are entirely new to us. We have probably encountered them, or something like them, many times. Add to this statement the fact that our brains have an amazing *recognition capability* and you have a recipe for potential problems.

Let us concentrate on this recognition capability of the brain for a moment. It is frequently our saviour. On the road, we *recognize* potential danger signals from the movement of traffic or pedestrians, and react accordingly. We notice when someone in an argument is about to lose their temper and back off. We 'detect' that a vendor is about to be less than fair and withdraw our offer. This ability to rapidly survey a situation, check for something like it in our data banks, and react accordingly is essential for our survival. On occasions, however, it can be counter-productive.

It makes us jump to conclusions, stereotype people, and generally exhibit a consistent pattern of behaviour in reaction to certain types of situation. In short, it reinforces our current behaviour, and makes it more difficult for us to change our behaviour, even if it is not what we want.

We recognize a situation, check our data banks, see that we usually lose our temper, have to coerce the other person, feel nervous or inadequate and, not surprisingly, do the same again. That is what I mean by gearing up our behaviour according to what we expect will happen which may not be the behaviour we would select if we were starting from scratch, rather than simply checking our data banks to see how we normally behave in such situations. All of which begs the question 'What is it that makes us *expect* a heated exchange, a feeling of discomfort, to lose our temper, or to suddenly feel inferior?'

The phenomenon we experience is known as *mind set* – if we set our mind to think positively, the outcome is more likely to be positive; if we set our minds to think negatively, the outcome is more likely to be negative. A simple example illustrates the point.

Most people have, at some time, watched athletics on television and are familiar with the weightlifter chalking his hands, staring purposefully at the weights in front of him as he paces up and down psyching himself up.

If we could actually hear him, we would be astounded if we heard him muttering, 'By God, that looks heavy. I'm going to look a real fool when I drop that.' His chances of successfully lifting the weight would be approaching zero. Similarly, a high jumper who psyched herself up by saying, 'This is crazy. I've never jumped that high in my life' would inevitably fail to clear the bar.

Instead, they set their minds to success. The weightlifter tells himself he's going to throw the weights through the ceiling, and the high jumper tells herself that she can fly.

Engaging in such positive self-talk does not give them guaranteed success. It simply gives them a better chance. Conversely, negative self-talk gives them guaranteed failure.

The link between positive self-talk, positive expectation and positive behaviour is a real one, and is deliberately employed by sportspeople. Much research has been done on how sports people get themselves ready for peak performance. It seems to make no difference whether you are looking at boxers, runners, tennis players, golfers, swimmers or mountaineers, they put as much emphasis on mental preparation as on physical preparation. Many biographies of sports people illustrate how, compete as they might, some would never win until they *believed* they could.

I have stressed this point not to suggest that with the right attitude you can become Chief Executive next year, but to illustrate the *significance* of positive self-talk.

Our actions are like a heat-seeking missile. (For those readers who have never come across such a thing, a heat-seeking missile is usually employed in air-to-air or ground-to-air combat. It 'senses' and follows the heat from an aircraft's exhaust. No matter which way the aircraft turns, its attempts at evasion are useless because the missile follows the aircraft's exhaust faithfully until contact is made.) The 'heat' that our actions follow are our dominant thoughts.

The word 'dominant' is important. It has been said that while the capacity of our subconscious mind is virtually infinite, our conscious mind can only handle one thought at a time. This one-thought-at-a-time feature means that you can successfully substitute positive self-talk for negative.

Let us summarize so far. When faced with a situation we check our data banks to see what sort of situation it is and how we normally behave in it. We then gear up our behaviour according to our expectation of what will happen, rather than what we would like to happen. If we wished, we could intervene and substitute negative self-talk with positive (despite our data banks) which, while not guaranteeing success, would at least give us a sporting chance.

At work we do not always have the time to psych ourselves up like athletes, because the event to which we are reacting might occur suddenly. An angry customer, for example, might trigger a thought process of 'if only these customers knew what we had to put up with in here! It's a miracle they get the damn product on time as it is – and now all this one wants to do is nit-pick. God, it makes me angry.' Or, a department that persistently fails to send the figures they have promised, might trigger a thought process of 'Oh no, I've checked every item of post and those figures still haven't arrived. This will be the third time I've had to bother the Sales Manager, and he'd always losing his temper. Why do I always get the rotten jobs. I'd better plead as hard as I can.'

In the first example, the individual is going down a thought process that is leading to aggression. The exchange is likely to be heated, with no satisfactory outcome for either of them. In the second example, a busy manager is about to be bothered yet again by an overapologetic moaner and is unlikely to give priority to a reminder about the promised figures.

Yet in both examples the outcome could be entirely different if the people concerned set their minds to a positive outcome. For example, 'Customers don't become upset for nothing; they either have, or think they have, a valid reason. We might be a bit chaotic in here, but all customers deserve good service. And anyway, I don't want to make my job more difficult than it already is so let's find out why this customer is upset'. Or 'Perhaps when I requested the figures before, I didn't explain clearly enough that they're for a report to the Chairman. This time I had better be much more precise and confirm the deadline.'

What happens has been outlined diagramatically in Figure 2.

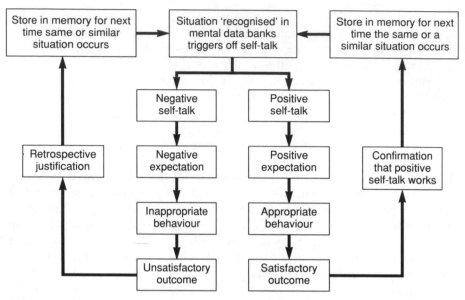

Figure 2   *Self-talk.*

It makes sense, therefore, to keep our self-talk as positive as possible.

The concept of self-talk is easy to ignore or even ridicule because it is not always easy to recall such 'conversations' we have with ourselves. In response to this comment I would make two points. First, that self-talk happens incredibly fast. While we speak out loud at about 165 words a minute, we can think at literally *thousands* of words a minute. They happen so fast we may not even notice them in the heat of the moment.

Second, we are learning beings. Once we have learned to associate a certain expectation with a certain situation we can make the connection automatically, effectively bypassing the need for self-talk. In this capacity, the brain acts as an efficient tape recorder.

Tape recorders, as we know, can play back as well as record. What is played back with our cerebral tape recorder, however, is less factual and more emotional. For example, most people have experienced the phenomenon of, say, turning on a radio and hearing some music they associate with a particularly memorable holiday, a romance or formative teenage years (or, if they are lucky, all three!), and for a moment they re-experience the emotions prevalent at the time.

Now think back to our descriptions of aggressive, submissive, and assertive behaviour. What childhood tapes are replayed when your boss stands in front of you wagging a finger? Childhood feelings of resentment at unnecessary discipline, anger at unjust criticism, inadequacy at having disappointed an authority figure, or what?

One thing is certain. The resultant self-talk could easily be irrational, or contain wild generalizations or excessive exaggerations:

'This is always happening to me.'
'No-one ever listens to my suggestions.'
'It's always me who gets the worst jobs.'
'I never get any breaks.'
'Life is so unfair.'
'I just can't cope with this.'

An example of the effect of positive and negative self-talk is given in Figure 3.

Reading the nicely boxed example in Figure 3 makes it all look neat and easy. In real life, of course, so many things are competing for your attention that thinking time is unmercifully squeezed. That, however, is no excuse for reaching for the usual support of 'It's OK in theory but I can't change my personality, can I?'

Whether you can or cannot change your personality is a question that would no doubt keep psychologists amused for hours. It is also a question that is beside the point, because to behave assertively you don't *have* to change your personality – only your behaviour and thoughts.

The good thing about behaviour and thoughts is that they are learned, and anything that has been learned can be *unlearned* and replaced with something else. Think about it. No-one is born feeling jealous, guilty, ashamed, angry, unworthy, incapable, competitive, or bad tempered. All these characteristics are *learned*, and while it might take a lot of effort to unlearn them and replace them with more rational thoughts, they can at least be controlled.

There are two steps towards learning to control them. The first is to simply be aware of them and to understand the harm they can do to us and those around us. The examples given overleaf should help you in achieving that awareness. So, too, might a little inward reflection to consider if you are basically positive or negative. Here is an example. If you have a terrible car journey home during which you persistently have to avoid other road users, do you feel stressed, arrive home in a mood, tell your spouse and children all about the road hogs, have a rotten evening and blame it on the other road users? 'If only there weren't so many idiots on the road, I'd still be in a good mood when I get home.'

Alternatively, after such a journey would you feel relieved to arrive home in one piece and say to yourself, 'Yes. If I *can* stay calm when these idiots cut me up on the road I'll still be in a good mood when I get home.'

It all depends on whether you are prepared to accept responsibility for being in charge of yourself. Imagine two people driving to the same meeting. They do not know one another, and are travelling in separate cars

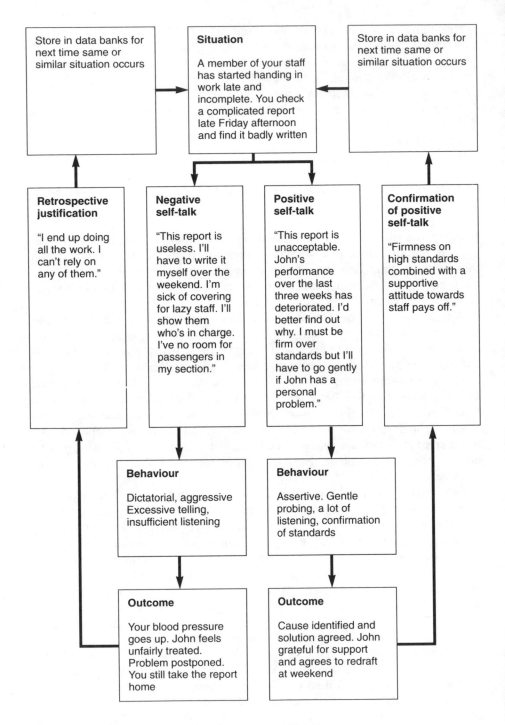

Figure 3 *Effect of positive and negative self-talk.*

within a few hundred yards of one another in the outside lane of the motorway. They have allowed plenty of time for the journey, and are progressing at a good pace.

Half a mile ahead a lorry jack-knifes. No one is hurt, but that side of the motorway is brought to a standstill. Neither of our drivers has a car 'phone, and neither knows how long the holdup will be.

As the delay continues one driver becomes more and more upset. He fumes, curses, shouts obscenities at the unknown cause of the holdup, asks the gods why it always happens to him, and so on. The other driver assesses the situation, peers at the long line of stationary vehicles ahead and behind, and realizes that he is going nowhere and that there is nothing he can do about it. He turns off his engine and reads the two professional magazines he thought he would not have time for, and then glances at the book of poetry he keeps in the glove compartment for just such emergencies.

Forty-five minutes later the traffic is on the move again, and the two executives eventually arrive at the meeting. Both are half an hour late. Both apologise. But one is cool, calm and collected, and the other is as taut as a tightly coiled spring. Whose fault do you think it is, his or the lorry driver's? In my view, one driver owned the problem while the other blamed it on someone else, because *the problem was not the traffic jam it was the way he reacted to it.*

It is a blessing to all us James Bond fans that Ian Fleming made his hero a positive thinker. Imagine the scene – 007, clad in scuba suit, is swimming along underwater when he is attacked by two enemy agents. After a nerve tingling fight he manages to despatch them, but not before one has cut through the pipe from his compressed air cylinder.

Undaunted, he clenches between his teeth the fountain pen Q gave him (which is really an auxiliary supply of compressed air). Within 30 seconds he is attacked by a shark, which he manages to finish off with another gadget from the MI6 laboratories.

But his troubles are not yet over. He is just about to enter the airlock of the mini-submarine when a huge octopus grabs his legs. In less than a minute the entire movie screen is filled with octopus ink and severed octopus tentacles.

The next scene shows our resourceful hero emerging from the submarine airlock. He unzips his scuba suit to reveal a white tuxedo, bow tie and perfectly pressed dark trousers, and along comes a curvaceous young lady with the obligatory shaken-not-stirred Martini.

If James Bond was not a positive thinker he would greet the lady with, 'For crying out loud, the ruddy enemy agents in the sea tonight. And sharks, I've had it up to here with sharks, and if I meet one more octopus . . .' The film, of course, just would not be the same.

Are you a positive thinker? If you were given a glass filled half way with your favourite drink, would it be half full or half empty? Would your staff and colleagues call you a positive thinker?

Look at the following statements, and ask yourself which person you would rather deal with:

Person A	*Person B*
These traffic jams are going to give me an ulcer.	That was a long delay but at least I got some reading done.
Well, I'm not sure if I've got time.	Today is impossible but I could meet you at 4 o'clock tomorrow.
You misunderstood me. You're just not listening.	Sorry, perhaps I haven't expressed myself clearly enough.
Well that's Office Services for you; a real bunch of cowboys.	Give me all the details and I'll speak to Office Services about it.
We're no worse than anyone else.	How would you like to see it done?
No one tells you anything in this place.	I'll find out.

Most people would chose Person B every time.

Please bear in mind why positive thinking is so important to assertive behaviour. Negative thinkers think negatively about themselves (usually submissive), and about other people (usually aggressive). Positive thinkers find it easy to see the 'half full' side of a situation, and see the logic in someone else's viewpoint, or the strengths in a below par employee:

Negative Self-talk	*Postive Self-talk*
I do wish the boss wouldn't shout at me like that.	I must stay calm when the boss becomes angry and get him to be precise about what I've done wrong.
If she makes a mistake like that again I'll severely reprimand her and make no mistake about it.	That's a serious error. I'd better find out quickly why it happened, and whether I have a communication, training or disciplinary issue on my hands.
That's a rotten job. I'll give it to Jenkins. He's too big for his boots.	Can any of my team benefit from this job?
Some people are never satisfied. You work all day to finish a report and all they do is find fault in it.	Expecting praise and receiving criticism is never pleasant, but the criticisms may be valid and will make me a better report writer.
I'll never get promoted. My face doesn't fit.	I would like to know the objective criteria for promotion.
I didn't mean to yell at Sally. If only I didn't have such a temper.	I've upset Sally and myself – time to apologise.

Some final comments – positive thinking is not a case of having rosy thoughts and hoping that life will turn out well. It concerns *being in charge of you*. People who think this way achieve more because they see opportunities; they are better people to be with because they shun pessimism; they enjoy a more stress-free existence because feeling out of control is one of the most stress inducing states there is.

How do you rate so far? You may find it worthwhile to consolidate this chapter with a workout sheet before moving on to look at the impact of our early programming.

Workout sheet

1. Look back over some situations where either you or the other person felt psychologically uncomfortable. Could you have achieved a better outcome by behaving differently?

2. What kind of things do you say to yourself before, during and after such situations?

3. To what extent do those sayings exaggerate, generalize or do a disservice to you or the other person?

4. How would you describe your dominant thoughts – positive or negative, half full or half empty?

5. To what extent are you in charge of yourself, or are you like the negative person in the traffic jam?

6. Give some examples of your negative self-talk, and then write a positive replacement.

Negative self-talk   *Positive replacement*

Chapter 4

WHAT MAKES US BEHAVE THE WAY WE DO? – EARLY PROGRAMMING

In reviewing the previous chapter, certain points stand out:

- We frequently behave by default rather than by design.
- The 'default behaviour' is the result of our capacity to 'recognize' a situation and check our data banks to see, on the one hand, what sort of situation it is, and how we normally behave in such situations.
- We often persist in inappropriate behaviour, or in behaviour we would prefer to change because of our tendency to retrospectively justify our actions.
- This retrospective justification can have two effects. First, 'absolving' us of responsibility for the way we have just behaved. Second, confirming the information that is in our 'data banks'.

The term 'data banks' has been chosen deliberately. Think of the characteristics of computer data banks. They can store vast amounts of information and allow rapid access. They can take information originally input for one purpose and use it for another. They also have less useful characteristics, however. Computerized information tends to attract a validity all of its own. If it is on a computer printout, it *must* be correct! Second, very few people critically evaluate what they have stored on computer until the data banks are full and they have no choice but to dump some of the unwanted and outdated information to make room for more.

This incentive does not arise in regard to our mental data banks because of the infinite capacity of our subconscious mind. We therefore accumulate a great deal of information. Some of it is essential, some of it is outdated, and some of it is downright counter-productive to positive self-talk and assertive behaviour.

There is a further feature of the 'data bank' analogy which is worth mentioning. Information in a data bank is usually worthless until it is used in some way. The way in which it is used depends on the design of the computer program. If the program is poorly designed, the information will not be used well, and *vice versa*. If the program defines a certain character-istic as bad as opposed to good, or worthless as opposed to worthy, or permanent as opposed to changeable, that is the way the information will be interpreted.

So in addition to the information technology equivalent of GIGO (garb-age in, garbage out), we can also suffer from spurious programming. In effect, far from serving *us* like an obedient robot, we begin to serve it! We become the servant of our programming as *it* instructs us. We rarely if ever question this situation because we do not just regard the programming as unchangeable, we regard it *as us*.

In this chapter, therefore, we are going to give our data banks and programming a reappraisal. As a result of reading it you will be able to begin the process of segregating the bits you find useful from those you do not, but above all, distinguishing between *the real you* and all the rubbish that has been stuffed inside your head since you popped out of the womb.

That may sound like an amazingly bold statement, and one which may tempt some readers to skip the next few pages on the basis that they are mature thinking adults. If you come into that category, I implore you to read on, thinking about it in context. In the first chapter I explained why I believe that effective human interaction is more important to business success than ever it was in the past. While in the womb, you had a predominantly solo existence. Once you were born you had to adapt to a gregarious existence. And where did you learn how to adapt? In your family. There is significant evidence that what you are now is a result of what you learned in your early, formative years from those around you.

Children do most things for the sake of someone else. They do what parents encourage because it results in praise, and avoid what parents discourage because it results in punishment.

Children also experiment with behaviour to discover from their parents (and often older siblings, and later school teachers) what is acceptable and what is not, what is rewarded and what is actively discouraged. They also experiment with feelings, and learn that some meet with indifference and disapproval, while others are approved and encouraged.

In this way, children learn certain 'rules of the road' from their parents by which they adapt from a solo to a gregarious existence. As a psychologist friend once put it to me, 'Children live in a world dominated by two things

– giants and rules. And it's the giants who make the rules and the giants who apply them – usually haphazardly and inconsistently.'

Many of the rules are sensible:

- 'Wash your hands after you've been to the lavatory.'
- 'Don't touch the oven, it's hot.'
- 'Don't cross the road without looking.'
- 'Don't talk to strangers.'
- 'Don't run down the stairs.'

and so on.

A lot of rules are not rules at all, just preferences:

- 'Don't talk with your mouth full.'
- 'Always fold up your clothes before you go to bed.'
- 'Tidy away your toys after you've finished with them.'
- 'Don't answer me back.'
- 'Do as I say instantly.'
- 'Big children don't cry.'

Some of the rules are open to misinterpretation and generalization:

- 'You're too young.'
- 'That's too difficult for you.'
- 'You can't do it.'
- 'You're stupid.'
- 'You're very naughty.'
- 'You wicked child.'
- 'You're too emotional.'
- '*Anything* you want, darling.'
- 'You're the most beautiful child in the whole wide world.'

They become descriptions of *you* rather than the *behaviour* you have just exhibited.

This is one way in which parents begin the process of filling their children's heads with rubbish. We do not distinguish between rules, preferences and observations of behaviour. Another way is to have a *restraining* rather than an *empowering* influence on them. For example, we often mean and say totally different things:

We mean	*We say*
Hold that glass carefully, please	Don't drop it
Keep your balance	You'll fall

Please do it this way next time   Don't let me catch you doing that again

You'll pass your exams if you plan   You're going to fail your exams
your revision and stick to it

The restraints we put on our children are not only common, they are usually loud and clear, while the empowering influences are uncommon and usually so diluted they escape unnoticed.

Here are two examples of conversations I have had with my seven year old daughter, together with the 'rules' I am imposing. Although both conversations have taken place at one time or another, I have written both so that you can make an appropriate comparison. The situation is that she is having difficulty doing a sum for school homework.

Example 1

Me:	'Hi, Alex, what's up?'
Alex:	'I can't do this stupid sum.'
Me:	'Why not?'
Alex:	'I'm useless at sums. It's not fair.'
Me:	'Well have another go.'
Alex:	'It's no good, I can't do it.'
Me:	'Well let me show you how.'
Alex:	'But I still won't be able to do it.'
Me:	'Well, look, I'll do it so that you don't get stuck.'

Example 2

Me:	'Hi, Alex, what's up?'
Alex:	'I can't do this stupid sum.'
Me:	'Why not?'
Alex:	'I'm useless at sums. It's not fair.'
Me:	'Would you like to have another go and show me what you're doing?'
Alex:	'It's no good, I *can't* do it.'
Me:	'Oh dear. We'd better cancel your horseriding and swimming lessons then.'
Alex:	(with horror) 'Why?'
Me:	'Because twelve months ago you could neither swim nor ride a horse.'
Alex:	(with indignation) 'But I *learned* how, didn't I?'
Me:	'So you can *learn* how to do things?'
Alex:	'Yes.'
Me:	'But twelve months ago, had I asked if you could swim

	or ride a horse, and if you were in the mood you're in now you'd have said, 'No, I cant'. You see 'can't' is a forever word. Whose decision is it if you *can't* do something or if you *can learn* how to do it?'
Alex:	'Mine.'
Me:	'So what shall we do about this sum?'
Alex:	(with enthusiasm) 'Daddy, will you show me how to do it?'
Me:	(sitting alongside Alex but ensuring she is the only one holding a pencil) 'I'd love to.'

In the first example, I had taught my daughter that:

- her view of her arithmetical ability is accurate
- demonstrating inferiority generates sympathy
- sympathy makes problems go away
- someone else will 'fix it' for her.

The effect is that she will internalize these 'rules' about herself and about what is an acceptable way of coping with a problem.

In the second example, I had taught her that:

- she is capable of learning
- trying to generate sympathy will not make someone else 'fix it' for her; she has to own the problem to prevent it from surfacing again later
- she is capable of fixing it
- admitting that you do not know how to do something and seeking positive help is legitimate behaviour.

In the first example I have restrained my daughter, and in the second, I have empowered her. In the first she feels bad about herself (despite having achieved what she wanted), and in the second she feels alright about herself. Feeling alright about yourself is not an undisputed birthright – it requires 'permission' from your parents.

The third way in which we parents fill our children's heads with rubbish is the most sinister. It concerns the techniques of manipulation we use to control their innermost emotions. Here is an example:

Child:	'Mummy can I go out and play?'
Parent:	'Have you tidied your room yet?'
Child:	'Not yet.'
Parent:	(in disbelief) 'Well, what on earth have you been doing up there?'
Child:	(with downcast eyes) 'I don't know, Mummy.'

Parent:	(with hands on hips) 'I told you to tidy it up. Why haven't you?'
Child:	'I don't know, Mummy.'
Parent:	'What do you mean you don't know?'
Child:	(still with downcast eyes, now fiddling with fingers) '. . .'
Parent:	(standing over child, wagging finger) 'When I tell you to do something, you go and do it. Is that clear?'
Child:	(looking ashamed) 'Yes, Mummy.'
Parent:	(with mock signs of despair) 'I work my fingers to the bone for you and what gratitude do I get? None, that's what. I don't know why I bother I really don't. Go and tidy it up at once.'
Child:	'But, Mu . . .'
Parent:	(with steely glare, jabbing finger in child's direction) 'And don't you dare come down until it's finished.'

In this example the mother has just taught her daughter that there is something wrong with her if she does not have a reason for her behaviour, that she should feel guilty for making her mother work so hard with no gratitude, and that being bullied is very unpleasant. Here is a second example which shows an assertive way of handling the same situation:

Child:	'Mummy, can I go and play?'
Parent:	'Have you tidied your room yet?'
Child:	'Not yet.'
Parent:	'Then why do you want to go out?'
Child:	'I can hear the others playing in the street.'
Parent:	'Then you can play with them as soon as you've tidied your room.'
Child:	'But Mummy, they might be gone by the time I've finished.'
Parent:	'Yes they might, but I'd still like you to tidy your room.'
Child:	(in a sulk) 'It's not fair. No one else has to tidy their rooms before they go out and play.'
Parent:	(kneeling to be closer to child's height) 'I can see you feel it's unfair that I've asked you to tidy up when you want to be out playing, but I've asked you to tidy up already this morning. So you can go and play as soon as you've tidied up.'

In this example the mother has acknowledged her daughter's feelings, shown her that manipulative comparisons will not work, and that she (the mother) intends to persist. The child may not like having to tidy up before she goes out to play but, unlike the child in the first example, she probably feels alright about herself and her mother.

There are several common manipulation techniques that we learned from our parents and so 'teach' to our children:

1. *We stand in judgment of them*
    We apply our giant-like rules of what is right and wrong, appropriate and inappropriate, acceptable and unacceptable to them and their actions.
2. *We make them feel stupid or inadequate*
    We castigate them if they cannot provide a valid (*in our terms*) reason to justify their behaviour. We criticize *them* when we should be criticizing their behaviour.
3. *We instil a belief that they should feel bad if they do not want to own our problems*
    We transfer our problems to them. For example, 'Do you have to make that noise? Can't you see I've got a headache?' or 'If you don't eat your breakfast I'll be late for work.'
4. *We demonstrate our disapproval if they change their minds*
    Most parents have gone through the routine
       'Do you want peas?'
       'No, I don't like peas.'
       'You always used to.'
       'I don't like them now.'
       'Don't be silly. You eat them.'
5. *We show them that mistakes are something to feel bad about*
    This technique is applied in two ways. First, by chastizing children for making a mistake (that is, being a small person, still learning how to coordinate, still learning the social graces, etc.), and second, by defining a mistake in terms of our 'reality' and not theirs.
6. *We imply that we will withhold our love or goodwill if they do not do things our way*
    By words and body language, even kind caring parents withdraw the one thing on which all children depend. The messages are clear: 'Do things according to my rules or you're on your own' – 'Good children do not tempt others to withdraw their goodwill.'

These manipulation techniques makes us feel very uncomfortable, and even stressful. Their effect is not only to fill our data banks with a bit more rubbish, but to trigger off the two coping mechanisms most readily available to us as children – fight or flight.

So, unpalatable though it may sound, a significant influence on our self-talk is the programming we acquired as a young child. As we come to terms with a gregarious existence, we look up at the all-powerful giants in our lives. We know we feel alright when they are pleased with us, and not alright when they are displeased with us. We accept their 'rules', as we understand them, and experiment with behaviour seeing what response it induces from the rule-making giants.

All too often that response is a restraining influence rather than an empowering one. When this is the case it helps to fix our self-image as someone who:

- will try . . . and almost make it
- isn't quite sure if the ability is there
- would succeed, if only . . .
- definitely could not do it

That self-image stays with us into adulthood. It has more to do with what we believed about ourselves as children than what is possible today as adults. Much of it is based on our fight or flight response to conflict, and not on our verbal problem solving skills. It is just as much a problem for older people (adults) at work as it is for younger people (children) at play.

This early programming tends to influence our adult years in three main ways. First, it can provide us, in association with our self-image, with a pre-conscious *life plan*. This is an overall restraint or enabling permission that puts boundaries on what we feel we are capable of.

According to many psychologists, we all have one. They are rarely obvious to us, but if you like you can try a quick experiment. Answer the following question: 'What happens to people like you?' Examples of responses I have heard are:

'. . . almost made it.'
'. . . make sure they get what they want'
'. . . fall between two stools'
'. . . always give other people priority'
'. . . enjoy life to the full'

The second way in which early programming influences our adult years is by showing us a *preferred way of communicating* with other people.

There are those who have a pronounced *judgmental* concept of life. They demonstrate thought processes, feelings and behaviours adopted from similar, influential authority figures. The behaviour is characterized by imperatives (do, don't, ought, should, never), ethics (good, bad) and *prejudices*. Their voice is typically condescending or authoritative. They use parental finger wagging liberally. They are judgmental and moralistic. They tend to be very authoritarian and critical of those who do not conform to their view of how people *should* behave.

As a boss, such people are disasters. They are either forever finding fault or criticism in you or your performance, or they are so overly concerned with your welfare that you feel smothered. While, at times, we all need guidance or are grateful and reassured when someone is concerned for our welfare, their behaviour tends to induce either rebellion or steadfast compliance to the safety of the 'rules'. Neither of which is useful in today's world of leaner, flatter, customer-oriented, quality conscious organizations staffed by decision making problem owners!

While there are those people who have a pronounced judgmental concept of life, there are others who have a dominantly *spontaneous* and *felt* concept of life. They are very expressive, showing feelings, attitudes and behaviours reminiscent of childhood, some of which can be undesirable (self-pity, sulking, stubborn, dependent, irresponsible, etc). Their voice is frequently whining or defiant, placating or apologetic. Gestures and expressions show helplessness, sullenness, interest or glee! They will show attitudes like strict compliance, shame or hurt.

Working with them is not easy. When things are going well their fun-loving nature can be an asset, but their spontaneity means that they are changeable and emotional. As with children, they operate to a different logic and are comparatively self-centred. As a boss, colleague or subordinate, therefore, they can be difficult to handle.

Finally, there is another category of people who have managed to distance themselves from both the judgmental and emotional sides of their nature. They process information from their environment *rationally* and *systematically*. Consequently, they are firmly rooted in logic.

They have a thoughtful, practical approach to problems in which they gain information, weigh up alternatives, and make an unemotional evaluative decision. Such people solve problems, resolve conflicts and make decisions. Compared with the judgmental and spontaneous types of people, this logical bunch sound great.

The drawback is that they are working only in one sort of reality, in which concern, emotions and fun can easily be forgotten – and these factors are just as important to effective interaction.

To one extent or another, all three types exist in each of us. We all have the rules handed down from authority figures (usually parents), the childhood tapes recorded during our formative years and the ability to think things through rationally. We can use the above descriptions to *question* how we interact with other people and determine if we have the three types in the right balance or if we need to make changes:

- Do you become very critical of other people because they are not behaving how, in your judgment, they should behave?
- Do you do things for other people because that way you know it will be done 'correctly'.
- Do you think that other people are stupid because they become emotional or cannot see the logic of your argument?
- Do you avoid responsibility or hope that someone will take the initiative to shield you from exposure?

An affirmative answer to any of these questions may signal a need to rebalance your thoughts, feeling and styles of interacting with others to avoid being seen as aggressive or submissive.

The final way in which our early programming influences our adult years is by giving us a view of our *rights* compared to the rights of other people.

The concepts of rights is central to assertiveness, and is also fundamental to the way in which managers interact with their superiors, colleagues and subordinates. We therefore devote the next chapter to rights, but pause first to consolidate what we have just covered.

On emerging from the womb we began adapting to interacting with others, and our data banks began accumulating information. Much of that data is of questionable validity. First, because much of it relates to a time when our verbal problem solving skills were underdeveloped, which made us rely exclusively on our fight or flight response; a significant proportion is therefore outdated. Second, because the programs used to retrieve, assess and present the data are often faulty due to the rules they contain. We learn our rules as children from authority figures, usually parents but also older siblings and school teachers. Because, as children, they seem to us like all-powerful giants, most of what we do we do because of the response we get from them. The rules we learn from them are often more restraining than empowering, and dictate our entire self-image which comprises our life plan, our preferred way of communicating, and our rights.

Workout sheet

1. Think of three situations in which you experience conflict (either actual or potential) with someone else. What 'rules' are you each following? Are they essential 'rules' or just personal preferences?

2. In what ways do you criticize *people* when it is their *behaviour* that has upset you?

3. In what ways arc your restraining your staff by moaning or saying how difficult things are?

4. What 'rules' about yourself have you internalized? In what ways do they make you inferior or superior to other people? In what situations do they make you 'right' or 'wrong'?

5. Consider situations that typically annoy or upset you. How would a seven year old child feel in those situations? How does that compare with your own feelings?

6. How do you feel and react when people
    *   stand in judgment of you
    *   try and make you feel stupid or inadequate?
    *   attempt to get you to 'own' their problems?
    *   use 'logic' against you?
    *   criticize you for a 'human' mistake?
    *   try emotional blackmail on you?
    Are those feelings and reactions productive or counter-productive?

7. What happens to people like you? Is that the way you want it to be? Does it make you feel alright about both yourself and about other people? How would you like things to be different?

8. How do you prefer to interact with other people – using your 'rules', spontaneously or using cold logic?

Chapter 5

WHAT MAKES US BEHAVE THE WAY WE DO? – RIGHTS

At the end of the last chapter the point was made that *the concept of rights is central to assertiveness and also fundamental to the way managers interact with those around them*, so this chapter begins with an explanation of that statement.

Let us use an analogy. Have you ever gone into a shop to buy something and been greeted with all the right customer care phraseology? 'Thank you for calling in, how may I help you?', etc., but still felt as if you were an inconvenience to them because you spotted the tell tale signs of impatience, irritation, or just couldn't-care-less mentality. Similarly, have you ever bought anything from a shop that has no customer care graces or glib phrases, but to which you remain a loyal customer because they behave as if they *value* your custom? The point is a simple one: the outward manifestations of customer care mean nothing unless they are built on the appropriate attitudes and beliefs.

Similarly with assertiveness. It is worthless to be familiar with the techniques of assertiveness if you do not believe you can make them work; there is no point in even trying to behave assertively if you do not know what to be assertive about. The concept of rights is the foundation on which your assertiveness stands.

So too with management. Referring back to Chapter One, the way in which you manage will reflect your beliefs about people at work – not the beliefs you vocalize, but the beliefs that manifest themselves in practice. Here is an example: do you believe in consulting with your staff? If you answered 'No', ten out of ten for honesty. If you answered 'Yes', please go to the next questions:

- List three important issues on which you have consulted them in the last six months.
- Did you gather their reactions to your decisions, modify your decisions according to their views, persuade them to modify their decisions to accommodate your views, or delegate the decisions to them in total?
- How often do you consult with them?
- How often do they consult with you?
- Do you still feel that you *really* believe in consulting with your staff?

In other words, there is no point in 'believing' something unless you can *prove* it in practice. The road to Hell, they say, is paved with good intentions.

Whether your focus is on being more assertive, managing more effectively, or both, a central issue is the concept of rights, because they reflect so accurately the beliefs you have about yourself and about other people.

We begin this chapter by looking at the place of rights in basic assertiveness theory, then widen it to look at rights in general. Finally, we look at rights at work, particularly in relation to the efficient utilization of human resources. By the end of the chapter you will be able to:

- reappraise some of the fundamental beliefs you have about yourself and other people;
- appreciate how an understanding of rights
  - leads directly to the techniques of assertiveness
  - lends itself to a management style and management actions synonymous with managerial effectiveness.

Assertiveness training has its origins in clinical therapy given to people who have difficulty in coping with life's problems and conflicts – or more precisely, in coping with the people who cause those problems and conflicts. It provides them with tactics for resisting the manipulation techniques of others, but first enables people to feel comfortable about using them. Hence the assertive rights originating in early assertiveness theory stem directly from, and present a mirror image to the manipulation techniques described in the last section.

For example, the main manipulation technique from which all the others grow is that people stand in judgment of us. They apply their rules to our behaviour to determine what is right or wrong, appropriate or inappropriate, acceptable or unacceptable. They could bully us into behaving the 'right' way, imply that there is something wrong with us if we do not behave the way we 'should', or they could try and induce feelings of sympathy, inadequacy or guilt if we behave in a way with which they do not agree. So:

- You 'should' want to have Sunday lunch with your mother-in-law every weekend, or feel guilty if you do not;
- You 'should' want to move on in your job, putting career before family, or feel out of place or unusual if you do not;
- You 'should' avoid showing your emotions or risk being labelled 'childish' if you do show them;
- You 'should' avoid disagreeing with your boss to avoid rocking the boat and being the odd one out;

and so on. You 'should' agree with all these rules – unless you believe you have the right *to be the ultimate judge of your own thoughts, behaviour and emotions.*

At this stage I feel it is worth re-establishing our focus. I am not advocating an anarchistic or Bohemian existence where we engage in some kind of behavioural free-for-all. I am saying that:

- when you were young, authority figures taught you how to behave, think and feel;
- those rules are probably now internalized in your programming;
- consequently, when other people attempt to impose their rules on you, there is a danger that
  - you will feel bad about yourself because your behaviour was not what it 'should' have been
  - you will feel bad about yourself because you have behaved the way they wanted which was not the way *you* wanted
  - you will resent their attempt at imposing their rules on you;
- you may trigger similar feelings in them if you attempt to prescribe the way they 'should' behave in an attempt to manipulate them.

Let us take an example. Two managers are working on a joint project. Both are competent managers. Manager A has a young family and attempts to balance work and family by careful prioritizing and scheduling. Manager B is hungry for promotion, and tries to submit work well ahead of deadlines by burning the midnight oil. Here are three alternative conversations:

Alternative one

Manager B: 'Hi, John. About this project.'
Manager A: 'Yes, Bill. What about it?'

Manager B:	'If we really put in the hours this week we can crack it over the weekend and get the report in a week early.'
Manager A:	'What's the problem? Everything's on schedule. It'll be ready a week Monday exactly on target. What's wrong with that?'
Manager B:	'Nothing's wrong with it, John. But that's OK for the losers around here. We can really score some points by getting it in early.'
Manager A:	'Evenings and weekends are bad enough when something's late but not just to get it in early.'
Manager B:	'What's the matter with you? Don't you want promotion?'
Manager A:	'I'll get promotion my way, thanks. I'm not working my socks off just so you can be the boss's blue eyed boy. So get lost!'

Alternative two

Manager B:	'Hi, John. About this project.'
Manager A:	'Yes, Bill. What about it?'
Manager B:	'If we really put in the hours this week we can crack it over the weekend and get the report in a week early.'
Manager A:	'Oh, I, sort of . . . had plans this weekend.'
Manager B:	'Work comes first, you know that.'
Manager A:	'Yes but, I kind of promised the kids.'
Manager B:	'What's the matter, don't you want promotion?'
Manager A:	'Of course I do but. . . .'
Manager B:	'Good that's settled then. I'll see you in the meeting room around seven.'

Alternative three

Manager B:	'Hi, John. About this project.'
Manager A:	'Yes, Bill. What about it?'
Manager B:	'If we really put in the hours this week we can crack it over the weekend and get the report in a week early.'
Manager A:	'Why is it important to you that it goes in a week early?'
Manager B:	'Promotion. It doesn't come to those that wait you know. You've got to be in there – shining.'
Manager A:	'I understand your keeness Bill, but I prefer to stick to the original schedule.'
Manager B:	'What's the matter with you, John, don't you want promotion?'
Manager A:	'I'd be delighted with it. I just don't see it resting on getting the report in a week early.'

Manager B:	'You may not want promotion, John, but that's no reason to screw up my chances.'
Manager A:	'No it isn't but, as I said, I don't see it resting on getting the report in a week early, so I prefer to stick to the original schedule.'
Manager B:	'So you won't help?'
Manager A:	'I'll give you all the help I can – but as per the original schedule.'
Manager B:	'So I'll see you next Tuesday then?'
Manager A:	'That's right, next Tuesday.'

In the first example, Manager A has clearly resented Manager B's assumption that B's 'rules' also apply to A, and has responded aggressively. Manager B has presented A with a problem, and A has responded with the fight response.

In the second example, we get the impression that A has also resented B's assumption that his rules are the 'right' ones for everyone. This time, however, the problem has triggered A's flight response, and A has preferred to avoid the conflict by giving in (and, it should be noted, by creating two more problems. One with his wife and children, and one with himself because he is bound to feel guilty at disappointing them).

In the last example, Manager B tries very hard, but because A is the judge of his own behaviour he feels neither resentment at B's attempted imposition nor an uncomfortable urge to let B win at his expense. Consequently, because he does not feel psychologically threatened, his response is to use his verbal problem solving skills. Manager A has stood up for himself, and Manager B knows that if he wants to influence A in the future he will stand a better chance if he uses sound reason and fact.

Let us take another example. We sometimes attempt to manipulate people by making them feel stupid or inadequate. We castigate them too if they cannot provide what we regard as a valid reason to justify their behaviour. Furthermore, we criticize *them* when it is their *behaviour* that has upset us.

This technique is very popular amongst impatient parents. As children do most things because of the response it gets from parents, this technique can be combined with an adult's physical height advantage to great effect.

Parent:	'Steve, have you done your chores yet?'
Child:	'No. . . .'
Parent:	'Why NOT!'
Child:	'I don't know.'
Parent:	'I asked you half an hour ago to finish them. Why haven't you done as I asked?'
Child:	'I don't know.'
Parent:	'What do you mean you don't know?'

Child:	'. . . . .'
Parent:	'What are you, STUPID or something?'
Child:	(to himself) 'I must be.'

The truth is that as children live life in a spontaneous manner and to a different set of 'rules' to grown ups, poor Steve probably got sidetracked by something quite innocent, like watching a spider build a web, the patterns chalk can make on a chalkboard, or his latest colouring book. He now knows for sure whose rules are the 'valid' ones and, as parents are 'never wrong', that he must be pretty stupid for not learning that in the first place. Given this treatment persistently he has also learned a legitimate way of interacting with others, so that when *he* becomes a manager. . . .

Steve:	'Paul, have you finished the proposal for Universal Electronics yet?'
Paul:	'No, I'm still doing the one for High Tech Tools. You gave me that one first.'
Steve:	'But the one for UE is for more money. It needs to go in tonight's post.'
Paul:	'Oh, I didn't know.'
Steve:	'Isn't it obvious. For crying out loud, have I got to tell you everything?'
Paul:	'. . . . .'
Steve:	'What are you, STUPID, or something?'

The truth (as I see it) is that we all have the right *to be treated with respect as intelligent and valuable human beings.* My IQ may be above average for the population at large, but I am definitely 'stupid' compared with Einstein. On the other hand, I have never been 'stupid' enough to forget to wear my socks, or 'stupid' enough to have to check my telephone number in the telephone directory as Einstein did! Neither can I perform many of the brilliant arithmetical, musical and artistic feats of many *autistic* children. (Stephen Wiltshire, for example, is severely autistic, yet can see an architecturally complex building for only a few minutes then later draw it from memory accurately to the smallest detail.)

Given this right, no-one can ever insult you again *without your permission*! Paul may not prevent Steve from attempting to manipulate him by calling him stupid, but he doesn't have to retaliate. But it is tempting. . . .

| Paul: | 'No I'm not stupid, neither am I bloody mentally telepathic. If you want to change things for crying out loud tell me. OK?' |

Neither does he have to feel inadequate. But it is a soft option. . . .

Paul:	'Sorry Steve. I guess I didn't think' (and to himself) 'Why do I keep getting it wrong?'

All he has to do is respond using his verbal skills. . . .

Paul:	'No I'm not. I'll get onto the UE proposal now and make special arrangements for its despatch. Will this arrangement on proposal value equalling proposal priority stand in the future?'
Steve:	'No. Only for the next month or so until the cash flow's back to normal.'
Paul:	'OK, just as long as I know.'

To illustrate the point I have made Steve's behaviour extreme and obvious. He could, however, have used a more subtle form of manipulation. Usually referred to as a *put-down*, it comes in the same category of attempting to manipulate you by unnecessarily belittling you.

Put-downs come in many forms, from a despairing exhale of breath combined with eyes rolling upwards, to patronizing remarks and all-embracing generalizations. Once again, it is up to you if you give them 'permission' to affect you:

Example	*Possible response*
It's OK, Sally, *I'll* sort it out. Don't you worry your pretty little head about it.	I'm not worried and I *am* capable of sorting it out. I just need the guidance I came to see you about in the first place.
That's typical isn't it. All you people want to do is find the obstacles.	Whether it's typical or not I can't say. The only reason to identify the obstacles, however, is so that we can plan to overcome them.
Well that proposal is just plain rubbish.	In what way, exactly?
Surely you're not daft enough to think that will work.	It's a suggestion. Have you a better one or can you explain rationally where mine falls short?
If I were *you* I'd kick a few backsides.	Thank you, but I prefer to tackle the problem the way I think best.

Put-downs include describing you in emotional terms, stereotyping you, sarcastically doubting you, making decisions on your behalf, patronizing you, and so on. The liberal use of put-downs is a cheap and ineffective substitute for tough management often favoured by managers of little substance.

Another common form of manipulation is to make someone feel responsible for our predicament when in reality they are not. Here are some
examples:

Sister 1:   'Can I borrow your blue dress tonight?'
Sister 2:   'Well I wanted to wear it myself tonight.'
Sister 1:   'But you always let me borrow it.'
Sister 2:   'I know but I want to use it tonight.'
Sister 1:   'But I'm seeing Frank tonight and I just don't have a
              decent dress. Not to meet his folks in.'
Sister 2:   'I want to wear it.'
Sister 1:   'It's not fair. I'll have a terrible evening and his parents
              won't like me. It's all your fault.'

It is a technique with which users attempt to generate sympathy and so
achieve their aims through emotional blackmail. As such it is a favourite
of submissive managers:

Manager: 'Susan, I know you have a lot on at the moment, but we
              need to finish the report for Marketing Department by
              Friday.'
Susan: 'Friday! That's more than a week ahead of schedule. No
              way.'
Manager: 'I know it'll be tight, but I have promised.'
Susan: 'It won't be tight, it'll be impossible without working
              round the clock.'
Manager: 'Well the Marketing Manager was rather insistent.
              Apparently the Chief Executive is very interested in the
              results.'
Susan: 'I still can't work around the clock.'
Manager: 'But you're the most experienced in the team. Don't let
              me down, Susan. If I have to go back and change it now
              what will he think of me?'

Powerful stuff this emotional blackmail, primarily because, as children, we
were responsible for just about everything. A child is the centre of his or
her universe and parents are omnipotent. Put those two facts together and
if a parents tells you, firstly, that you are responsible for their predicament
and, secondly, that unquestioning co-operation is a worthwhile trait, you
are susceptible to this manipulation technique. Susceptible, that is, until
you believe you have the right *to determine for yourself whether or not you
are responsible for someone else's predicament.*

A related manipulation technique is to demonstrate our disapproval if
someone changes their mind. The dinner time example about peas in the
last chapter may sound flippant, but it is not. The child may have no other

reason than 'fancy' for no longer liking peas, or it could be something to do with the fact that young children seem to have an exaggerated and oscillating sense of taste. Either way, the parent is teaching the child, firstly, that it is 'wrong' to change your mind for a reason that does not satisfy the parent and, secondly, that if you do not have what the parent will regard as a good reason, it is acceptable to invent one.

How do we carry over this response into adult life?

Example one

Phil:	'Joyce, I have a peak workload coming up soon. Can you help me out with some staff as usual please?'
Joyce:	'Well I hadn't planned on it this time round.'
Phil:	'Hey c'mon Joyce you always help me out.'
Joyce:	'Yes, I know. It's just that this time. . . .'
Phil:	'What's the matter Joyce, you haven't suddenly changed your mind have you?'
Joyce:	'No, of course not. It's just that. . . .'
Phil:	'Good, I knew I could count on you.'

We begin the conversation with the best of intentions, but as soon as we think of having to 'admit' that we have changed our minds for a reason the other person may not find acceptable, all the old tapes get replayed and we capitulate.

Example two

Tom:	'Let me have your calculator, please Andy.'
Andy:	'My calculator?'
Tom:	'Yes, the one you always lend me.'
Andy:	'The battery's gone.'
Tom:	'That's OK, I have a spare.'
Andy:	'The square root function isn't working.'
Tom:	'That's OK I don't need that function.'
Andy:	'Someone else is using it.'
Tom:	'But I can see it on your desk.'
Andy:	'I'm using it for dictation.'
Tom:	'But you can't use a calculator as a dictation machine.'
Andy:	'You can if you don't want to lend it to somebody!'

A flippant example, but deliberately so to illustrate a point. Rather than just saying to Tom 'Sorry, Tom, but I worry when people use my expensive calculator so I prefer not to lend it out anymore.' Andy feels a need to invent excuses that he hopes Tom will accept to account for his having changed his mind about lending out the calculator. There are three potential outcomes to this example.

1. Tom gets the calculator.
    Andy feels bad about Tom getting the calculator, but worse about himself for lending it.
2. Tom does not get the calculator.
    Andy feels bad about Tom for making him invent excuses, and bad about himself for lying to Tom.
    Tom feels bad about Andy for being devious.
3. Tom does not get the calculator.
    Andy feels alright about Tom for asking to borrow it, and alright about himself because he has been honest with himself and with Tom. Tom maybe feels that Andy's reason is 'odd', but respects Andy for being straight.

The third outcome is only possible if Andy believes in a fundamental right – *to change your mind, satisfying only yourself that your reason is valid and whether a reason need be communicated to the other person.*

A final comment about this right. As organizations become flatter and more open, people feel more at ease to speak up and say what is on their minds. Consequently, it is not difficult to envisage a situation when 'suddenly' members of your staff or colleagues own up to wanting to cease going along with something they have apparently accepted (but actually resented) for a long time. Are you going to acknowledge their right to do so, are you going to feel hurt, hard done by, or retaliatory? Or are you going to respect their right and discuss their concerns openly, honestly and assertively?

The next manipulation technique is surely one of the most devisive and counter-productive for a modern manager – making people feel bad about mistakes. I am not suggesting that we actively encourage mistakes, other than in exceptional circumstances. (For example, every time I fly I hope the pilot made all his mistakes in the simulator.) What I am suggesting is that, as a simple matter of work variation, mistakes *will* happen and that to make people feel bad about them, or worse still bad about themselves, only encourages them to avoid trying or to sweep mistakes under the carpet.

But let us look at what we mean by a mistake, where this manipulation technique arises, and also how its effect on self-esteem can be devastating.

By 'mistake' we mean someone else not doing something *our* way, to *our* standards, or to *our* rules. That is, their 'mistake' exists in terms of our judgment – not in actuality. A 'mistake' is not universal. Several people may share your rules and so agree with your reality. Nevertheless, a mistake is a matter of judgment.

You start making mistakes as soon as you are born – normally from both ends at once! Babies do that kind of thing, however, so it is within the 'rules'. Unfortunately, as you grow, the rules become less accommodating. Three year olds are so alive to everything that goes on around them that they get distracted and 'take too long' over their meals. They don't appreciate the niceties of adult protocol, and ask 'embarrassing' questions at social gatherings, like 'Why has Daddy's boss got such a big nose?' They lack the verbal skills to communicate 'clearly', the dexterity to manipulate 'accurately', and (thank God) the maturity to take everything 'seriously'.

Consequently, according to *our* rules and *our* judgment, they make mistakes. As if that was not bad enough, we react all too often by belittling them, showing our displeasure, withdrawing our love, or letting them know that according to our judgment they have got it wrong. In the land of giants, children are inferior beings, and their self-esteem is dented repeatedly with each new 'mistake'. In other words, they are 'punished' for being three years old, five years old, seven years old, etc. Is it any wonder, therefore, than when we become giants ourselves we try to avoid mistakes on the one hand, and on the other come down hard on those 'junior' to us who make them? The result is tragic and wasteful. People perform below par just to avoid making mistakes.

As a manager, how do *you* 'reward' mistakes? With a put-down or with a coaching session?

Good managers know that if their staff are human they will make mistakes and if they are trying hard they will make even more. They know that a wholly negative and judgmental attitude to other people's mistakes encourages them to delegate upwards, to throttle back, and to conceal their errors. They know that while mistakes are, at best, inconvenient they are so much worse if their learning potential remains unsalvaged. They know that, even though they too will make mistakes, they will not allow that fact to threaten their self-esteem, nor will they be afraid to admit to them. In short, they award themselves and everyone else the right *to make mistakes*.

A final manipulation technique is to imply that we will withhold our love or goodwill unless the other person does things our way. Again, the origins go back to childhood when we depended on and valued parental love more than anything else. We learned early on how unpleasant it could be when Mummy or Daddy withdrew that love, and so avoided tempting them to do so.

This cause and effect between our non-co-operation and feeling uncomfortable persists as we grow. One of the most common tactics of emotional blackmail in seven year olds is 'I won't be your friend any more.' Our tendency to avoid 'making' others withdraw their love or goodwill is accentuated by our regard for co-operation.

Once again, I am not suggesting that assertive people do not co-operate. They do. I am pointing to the fact that there are times when we co-operate even though we wish we would not, solely to avoid the conflict of having to say 'No.' In those circumstances, the driving force that makes us co-operate is the deeply rooted fear of causing someone to withdraw their goodwill. The result is that we feel 'used' if we co-operate, and guilty if we do not. It is a common fault of submissive managers who believe that they can only manage with the active goodwill of others, and that the availability of that goodwill is wholly dependent on the manager being 'nice' and 'co-operative'. The result is that such managers are easily taken advantage of, find it difficult to request help themselves, and find it traumatic to reprimand or criticize someone.

This state persists until people realize they have a right *to be independent of the goodwill of others*, and that if a relationship is only going to work on the other person's terms (which usually means at your net expense) then it probably is not much of a relationship anyway. In fact, relationships of any substance tend to be strengthened when both parties behave assertively. That way they are open and honest, and their relationship is based on mutual respect and understanding.

So far, then, we have discussed several rights:

1. To be the ultimate judge of your own thoughts, behaviour and emotions.
2. To be treated with respect as an intelligent and valuable human being.
3. To determine for yourself whether or not you are responsible for someone else's predicament.
4. To change your mind, satisfying only yourself that your reason is valid, and whether or not you need communicate a reason to the other person.
5. To make mistakes.
6. To be independent of the goodwill of others.

How do you feel about those rights? No doubt you can think of exceptions when you would choose not to invoke them (after all, you have the right *not to exercise a right*), but can you really deny any of them?

A further point to make about them is that rights also carry responsibilities. For example, if you accept the right to make mistakes perhaps you should also acknowledge the responsibility to 'own' them. If you wish to act independently of the goodwill of others, can you legitimately use such emotional blackmail yourself? If you want to be your own ultimate judge, are you going to raise your tolerance threshold where others are concerned?

Here are a few more basic human rights you may wish to consider, together with some background comments.

To use emotion rather than logic to make some of my decisions

Why not? What is so inferior about intuition, gut reaction or good old-fashioned childlike spontaneity that it always has to be subordinated to logic?

Logic is an adult phenomenon. It was applied to us as children by our parents to 'prove' we were wrong. If we could not rationalize our desires in terms acceptable to their logic, we must have been wrong.

Accepting this right means you need never again feel inadequate or awkward about saying 'I don't know *why* I want to do it. I just *feel* like doing it. Why do you find that so odd?'

To admit I do not know or do not understand something

Again, our early programming makes us feel 'not alright' and inadequate when someone is deliberately trying to trap us using their logic. As soon as we invent a reason – 'Gotcha!' – we have fallen into their trap. You can simply sidestep their trap by saying 'I don't understand. Why don't you explain it to me as you see it, then we'll see how I feel about that.'

To not care that I am imperfect
To be myself

While most of us are keen to improve, we often succumb to a manipulation technique that makes us feel bad about our imperfections, and hence susceptible to someone else's view of how we 'should' be. Thus we give up our right to be our own judge.

In countering this manipulation technique, it helps to realize that only God is perfect. If you strive to be perfect, therefore, you will only fail and thus condemn yourself to permanent frustration and a never-ending feeling of failure.

So in response to this manipulation technique, we often make up excuses, attempt to rationalize our behaviour, or retaliate by pointing out to the other person how they fall short of how we think *they* 'should' behave. Far better to:

- accept any truth that there might be in their observation but not let it upset you. If you want to, you can then discuss it rationally;
- explain that, to you, it is alright or that you have other priorities.

Incidentally, people who accept these rights generally make themselves impervious to sarcasm.

To say what I want or how I feel
To stand my ground
To be listened to
To be treated as an equal
Not to allow other people to do my thinking for me unless I feel
alright about it

I have grouped together these rights because they are very similar. One of
the greatest faults of submissive people is that they start off saying what
they want but give in at the first hint of resistance from the other person.
Similarly, one of the greatest faults of aggressive people is that they make
it difficult for other people to stand their ground by not listening to them.

Hanging on to these rights makes you less susceptible to the commonest
form of bullying (not being listened to), and makes *you* listen to others
more – a well respected trait.

To put myself first on occasions

In gregarious societies, co-operation is encouraged. Unfortunately, for many
people, the result is that they do not vocalize their desires and feelings. As
a result, their desires do not go into the melting pot, and they never receive
consideration, so they persistently subordinate themselves to other people.

The solution is to give yourself some airtime so that what you want gets
considered along with what everyone else wants and, occasionally, to be
'selfish'. Carve out a little private time, put yourself first now and again,
and stop being a doormat.

To stand up for my rights
Not to stand up for my rights

This seeming contradiction requires explanation. First, having rights means
nothing unless you do something about them. (Remember the manager
who 'believes' in consultation but who never consults?) Rights have to
manifest themselves in your behaviour, or they are worthless.

Putting them into practice, however, may mean *taking risks* with your
behaviour. You may be seen to be 'different' from how you normally are;
you may experience opposition from other people, and so on. Acknowledging the right to stand up for your rights may well be of immense psychological support.

Similarly, you may recognize that, at times, discretion is the better part
of valour, yet feel a dilemma in that you 'should' stand up for your rights.
But if your boss is in a rage, or if your own temper is about to explode,
it may not be the best time to try out your new found skills of assertiveness.
So do not be assertive *and do not feel bad about it*.

So there you have a description of rights as a foundation to assertive behaviour. Do you agree with them? Do you agree that they also apply to work? After all, people do not stop being human beings when they sign a contract of employment. At work, rights exist in three basic categories – legislative, procedural, and cultural.

The category where problems arise is usually the cultural area. It is here that 'rules' are not written but rely on agreements between and assumptions about people. This is where the way you manage and the way you allow yourself to be managed depends upon:

- where you are on McGregor's X-Y continuum (see Introduction)
- your self-image
- your preferred style of communicating with people
- your view of your rights and of other people's rights
- how those beliefs manifest themselves in practice

In short, the way you manage depends on whether you are aggressive (you have more rights than everyone else), submissive (you have fewer rights than everyone else), or assertive (you share a well-balanced view of rights).

Here is a list of rights compiled by managers who have attended my assertiveness courses:

- To express my opinion
- To have my suggestions and opinions listened to
- To be kept informed about matters that affect me
- To be consulted on matters that affect me
- To receive relevant and timely information
- To receive clear communication
- To seek clarification
- To be given explanations
- To have a fair and acceptable workload
- To have co-operation from others
- To say 'No' to something that is not my responsibility
- Not to be treated unfairly because of a mistake
- To appropriate training
- To appropriate coaching
- To appropriate counselling
- To know what is expected of me and how I'm being judged
- To receive regular and constructive feedback on my performance
- To receive fair and consistent treatment
- To understand clearly my areas of responsibility and my authority levels
- To have a suitable and safe working environment conducive to high productivity
- To agree my objectives and performance standards

- To do my job my way once the 'essentials' have been agreed
- To determine my subordinates' objectives if they cannot agree them
- To have staff and colleagues complete work to agreed timescales and standards
- To constructively criticize the performance of staff, colleagues and superiors where it prevents me from doing my job properly
- To reprimand staff where necessary
- To set performance standards
- To competence in other people
- To receive encouragement and support from my boss
- To have support from colleagues and staff
- To *enjoy* my work

Well, how do you feel about these rights? How many do you already accept? How many will you share with other people? How many are contradictory to the current culture in your organization or department? How many would be out of place in modern lean, flat, green, customer led, quality conscious and results-orientated organizations?

To illustrate the place of assertiveness in organization effectiveness, I have provided below two examples from my own experience of leading assertiveness courses and of combining it with aspects of organization development.

Example one

This example is a scientific organization employing 9 000 people. It was subject to a massive cultural change exercise to facilitate its move from a Government funded, Civil Service linked establishment to a profit making business. One aspect of the culture change was the replacement of the annual confidential staff report managers wrote on their staff with an open appraisal delivered by reporting managers face-to-face with the member of staff concerned. My role was to enable reporting managers to acquire the attitudes and skills necessary to make the new appraisal system work.

Part of my input was on assertiveness. At the end of it, participants compiled a list of rights for both reporting managers and the staff members being appraised (see p. 62).

For managers who were accustomed to a closed, confidential reporting system these rights were almost revolutionary. Many of them had been concerned that delivering criticism, for example, would cut off the staff member's co-operation, and so had mentally prepared to water down or avoid such sections. Many had thought that to allow staff members to criticize the way they were managed would severely undermine managers' authority.

Rights Relating to Appraisal Generated by Reporting Managers

Reporting Manager's Rights	*Staff Member's Rights*
Basic human rights plus	Basic human rights plus

• To control the overall pace and direction of the discussion	• To sufficient preparation time
• To constructively criticize, reprimand or discipline staff member	• To a boss who admits his/her mistakes
• Not to be 'blackmailed' by staff member's reaction to criticism	• To fair and consistent treatment
• To be listened to and have views considered	• To an opportunity to respond openly to criticism
• To disagree with staff member	• To reasons and explanations for manager's opinions
• To honesty from staff member	• To criticize the manager
• To give instructions to and make requests of staff member	• To be listened to
• To co-operation from staff member	• To honesty from the manager
	• To choose not to answer unreasonable or personal questions
	• To feel alright after the discussion

It was only after addressing their fundamental beliefs about people at work, and about their own self-image and anxieties and how they would show up during an appraisal interview, that they realized just what their rights and responsibilities were! Feedback after the first round of interviews has been extremely positive. The appraisal interviews are addressing real issues; where nerves are touched, matters are handled with sensitivity; many managers are so encouraged by the enhanced manager/staff relationships that they make regular appraisal part of their management *modus operandi*.

Example two

The second example comes from the Customer Relations Department of a large motor manufacturer. Individual workload had increased due to a headcount reduction in the department and a spate of quality control problems in a new plant. The mounting in-trays and unremitting telephone calls had left their mark on staff.

Standards were deteriorating, teamwork was a thing of the past, and morale was rock-bottom, despite plans to alleviate the problems (e.g. better software, greater use of standard letters, transfer of some 'goodwill' budget to dealers and temporary influx of experienced staff to help shift the backlog).

I was brought in to reaffirm in the Customer Relations Department the standards of customer care the manufacturer was promising in its advertising, to change negative into positive thinking, and to rekindle the teamwork that used to exist. Three *interlinked* modules were prepared, on customer care, assertiveness, and team-building. After the assertiveness module the participants compiled the following list of rights *and responsibilities*. The reason I have included the list as an example, even though none of the participants was a manager, is as follows.

I frequently encounter managers who recoil in horror at the thought of their staff being 'given' rights such as being consulted or making mistakes. They fear that the flood gates of anarchy will be well and truly opened, and that the days of their authority will be numbered. It is my experience, however, that the converse is true, and that the responsibilities people accept make them better workers, better team members, more flexible and more creative. So, what do you think?

Rights and Responsibilities Generated by a Demotivated Customer Relations Department

Rights	*Responsibilities*
• To a role and job that is described accurately	• To prompt that description • To execute it to maximum ability • To 'own the problem'
• To enjoy my job	• To motivate myself • To tackle unpleasant tasks with equal enjoyment to the pleasant tasks
• To be accepted and valued as I am	• To 'open-up' • To be frank and honest
• To have an environment conducive to work	• To work properly and efficiently and to make the best use of what is currently available
• To have the tools necessary to do my job	• To make management aware of my needs • To make the best use of currently available tools
• To receive help and co-operation from others	• To actively offer my help and assistance to my fellow team members • To guide and coach new team members
• To express my views	• To volunteer opinions • To generate ideas and be innovative in my approach to problems
• To get on with the job using my own judgment	• To be thoroughly up to date with policy • To respond positively when asked to be flexible to achieve team objectives

Hardly the thin end of the anarchy wedge, is it?

This brings us to the end of the section on rights, and so this is an appropriate place for a summary. As I said at the beginning, the concept of rights is central to assertiveness and to the way managers manage. Reviewing your rights helps you reappraise the content of your data banks and the programs that are in them, and to sort fact from fiction in terms of what you believe about yourself and other people. It provides a base from which to repel the manipulation techniques people employ, both wittingly and unwittingly, and a way, finally, of replacing your fight or flight response with your verbal problem solving skills.

An expression of rights is an expression of beliefs – what you believe about yourself and about other people. What you believe, you will expect – and you may rest assured that it will come to pass.

As you have the right to choose your own thoughts and not be bound by any opinion of you (including your own), there is no reason other than inertia why you should not set your sights very high in terms of health, happiness, love, understanding, peace of mind and prosperity – unless, of course, you are already doing so.

Workout sheet

1. How do you feel about this section on rights – all statements of the highly obvious, food for thought, or a stimulus to the profound reappraisal of your data banks?

2. If you are a parent, which of your children's rights are you ignoring? How does that compare with how you manage your staff?

3. In what situations are your rights being ignored? By whom? What would you like to do about it? Will that cut across their rights?

4. In what ways do people try and manipulate you? What are your rights in those situations?

5. In what situations are you ignoring the rights of others? What would they like you to do about it? Does that cut across your rights?

Chapter 6

ASSERTIVENESS AND EFFECTIVE MANAGEMENT

In each of the preceding chapters an element of assertiveness has been described, and some examples of that element in practice have been given and related to the world of work. In this chapter I want to relate assertiveness to management once more. At the end there is another workout sheet so that you can concentrate on your own way of managing. To begin, though, it is worth summarizing some essential background about the way in which we behave.

When problems arise, we frequently behave by default rather than by design. Default behaviour is usually an adult version of our fight or flight instinct and the associated behaviours we learned as a child.

The behaviours are the result of a search through our mental data banks to see what sort of situation it is and how we normally behave in it. The information within our data banks is usually accepted unquestioningly, even though it may be the result of unreasonable manipulation techniques employed by parents, older siblings and other authority figures. Consequently, we may have a warped view of our rights – the foundation on which our approach to other people and situations is built.

In other words, what you believe about yourself and about other people has a significant impact on the way you manage.

Consequently, aggressive managers put people down, disregard their views, and are intolerant of mistakes and of those who deviate from the way in which people 'should' behave. They undervalue the potential contribution that can be made by staff, and treat people as order fodder. As a result, resentment towards such managers increases, and commitment to and concern for the task decreases. People's creativity and responsibility for results is gradually stifled.

Submissive managers spend so much time trying to avoid conflict by being 'nice' and compliant that they are easily put upon. They accommodate and accept unpleasantness as the price of winning co-operation from others. They tend to deny their own strengths and lose the courage of their convictions. Instead they attempt to achieve their aims by generating sympathy or gratitude. The 'rules' they emphasize concentrate on maintaining smooth relationships, and not on standards of performance. Cynicism towards them increases, and productivity deteriorates.

By contrast, assertive managers are clear about their purpose, and have the confidence to be steadfast in its pursuit. They involve others and help their staff accept their share of ownership of company objectives. Their staff know what is expected of them, and feel supported in their attempts to perform. Consequently, they are flexible, creative and output orientated.

Where does this body of assertiveness knowledge fit into accepted management theory? Right in the middle. Take Douglas McGregor's Theory X and Theory Y. Theory X beliefs are that people are basically lazy, will avoid work, shun responsibility and need coercing and bribing if they are to perform, sounds very descriptive of an aggressive manager. Theory Y beliefs are that people can enjoy their work if they feel involved in it, are willing to be treated as mature partners, are capable of self direction and responsibility, are totally congruent with an assertive manager's view of basic human rights.

Take Maslow's work on a hierarchy of needs, from physiological needs, through security, a feeling of belonging and self-esteem to self-actualization, shown in Figure 4 (see p. 68).

We know that submissive people suffer from low self-esteem, and that many of the manipulation techniques examined in the section on rights are based on the manipulator's low self-esteem, or are designed to dent the self-esteem of the one being manipulated, and possibly also affect their feeling of security.

Conversely, assertive management has a positive affect on those areas. Involving people, treating them with respect and dignity, not making them feel inadequate or guilty, acknowledging their 'rules' as well as ours; all have a positive affect on people's feelings of security, belonging and self-esteem.

Consider Frederick Herzberg's analysis of motivators and demotivators, which points clearly to the positive effects on performance of job enrichment tactics – involving people by consulting with them and treating them as intelligent human beings by devolving authority to them. Speculate on the sense of achievement such tactics instil in people. Review the two examples given in the last chapter and consider the positive effects on both motivation and performance of clear thinking on rights.

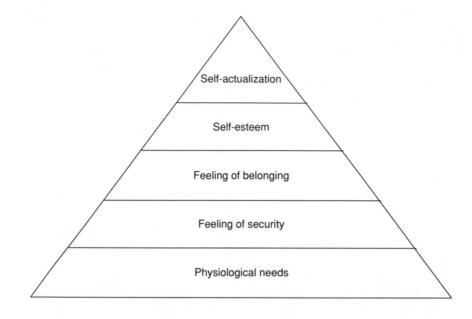

Figure 4   *Hierarchy of needs*

Look at the work of Tannenbaum and Schmidt. Their situational leadership model describes how successful managers combine attention to the
task (defining objectives, planning activities, specifying roles, etc.) with
attention to people (building working relationships and providing socio-
emotional support) in one of four combinations (shown in Figure 5).
The combination such managers select depends upon four main factors –
the complexity of the task, the risk of the task going wrong, the consequence
of it going wrong, and the ability of the team to handle the task.

Irrespective of the risk involved, an aggressive manager would probably
prescribe in detail how the task 'should' be done, thus ensuring it is devoid
of learning potential and any sense of achievement in completing it.

Submissive managers will be so concerned about the risk that they will
probably adopt a high people/low task style in an attempt to make themselves and their staff feel alright about it. As they have failed to specify
objectives and procedures, however, the task is likely to faulter, resulting
in panic measures to try and save the day.

Assertive managers due to their sensitivity to other people, will be flexible.
They will probably begin with a high task/low people style so that everyone
has the *security* of knowing where they stand. They will then move to a
high task/high people style, giving maximum attention to both results and
people's comfort, *sense of belonging*, and *esteem* (learning and achievement).

Consider what management theory says about team-building. If a group
of people are to maintain a high level of productivity, two kinds of needs

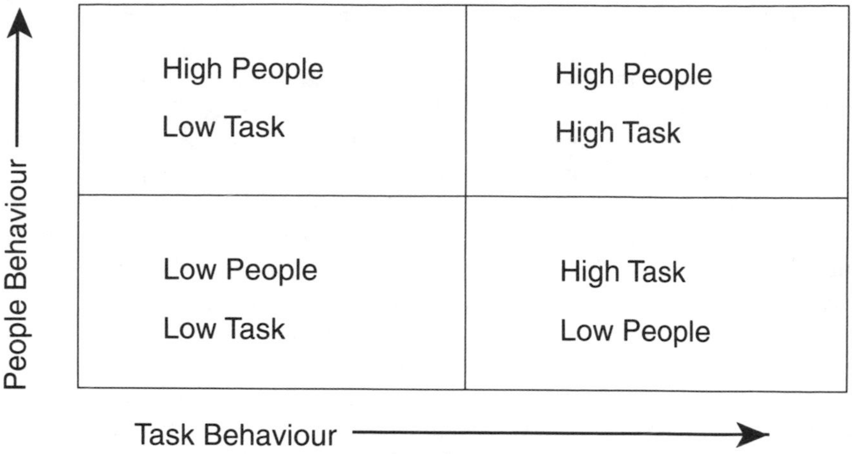

High People Low Task	High People High Task
Low People Low Task	High Task Low People

People Behaviour →

Task Behaviour ────────→

Figure 5 *Situational leadership model.*

have to be satisfied – what it takes to complete the task in hand, and what it takes to strengthen the team feeling. What people say and do, therefore, can be categorized in three ways:

- whether it relates to the task;
- whether it relates to group maintenance;
- whether it contributes to neither of the above, and may even be dysfunctional.

Look at the following behaviours:

Task behaviours	*Group maintenance behaviours*	*Dysfunctional behaviours*
Initiating ideas	Encouraging	Interrupting
Initiating solutions	Standard setting (behaviour)	Not listening
		Negative criticism
Initiating progress	Summarizing feeling of the group	Seeking sympathy
Standard setting (task)	Mediating	Special pleading
		Seeking personal approval
Seeking information		Misplaced humour
Seeking opinions	Relieving tension and anxiety	Playing politics/ scoring points
Giving information		
Giving opinions		
Elaborating		Withdrawal
Co-ordinating		
Summarizing		
Testing for consensus		

Assertive managers, feeling alright about themselves, are happy to initiate ideas, solutions and progress, but they also involve people in decision making. They seek information from their team members, and check how people feel about tasks, rules, standards and timescales. They give information and share their own thoughts, feelings and opinions. They mediate where there is conflict, and check for consensus before moving on.

Aggressive managers are happy to initiate things as well, but do so in a way that excludes their staff. They rarely check people's feelings, and are quick to interrupt, criticize and play off one side against the other.

Submissive managers may initiate things, but without conviction. They check people's feelings, but allow the negative ones to dominate. They are unduly accommodating on adverse reaction to standards, and use sympathy, praise and approval-seeking in an attempt to 'buy' co-operation. Their humour is used less to relieve other's tension and more to relieve their own anxiety. They may even 'withdraw', allowing others to dominate the proceedings.

As you will have gathered by now, it is my view that assertiveness theory has a significant place in what we know about management. It is totally consistent with what we know about motivation, management style and teambuilding. *Its main contribution, however, is the prominence given to the beliefs we have about ourselves and other people.* Just like the shop assistant who does not really mean 'Have a nice day', managers who do not truly believe positive things about themselves and other people will always achieve less than they and their staff could achieve given an *assertive* management style.

Workout sheet

1. If your staff were writing your obituary, what would they say? How does that compare with what you would like them to say? How does it compare with the section on rights?

2. To what extent do you make and 'police' the rules in your area, bend to pressure from your staff, or *agree* the 'rules' with them?

3. What effect do you have on your staff members' feelings of security, belonging and self-esteem?

4. To what extent does working with you give staff a positive sense of achievement?

5. To what extent do you vary your people and task orientation according to the situation? How do your staff feel about that? What effect does it have on output?

6. How many of your behaviours would people classify as dysfunctional?

7. In what ways do you need to change the way you manage people to encourage them to better performance?

Chapter 7

ASSERTIVE TECHNIQUES

Having given your 'data banks' a spring clean and looked at how assertiveness fits into accepted management theory, you may well be thinking 'OK, but what do I actually *do* to be assertive?' That is the purpose of this chapter, to introduce assertive techniques that can be used individually or in combination to help you stand up for your rights, and to acknowledge the rights of others.

The techniques themselves illustrate how rights can manifest themselves in practice. They will be illustrated in more detail in relation to specific situations in Part Two. This section, then, serves as both a culmination of Part One and an introduction to Part Two.

Each of the techniques is described below by showing how it relates to assertive rights and the problems to which aggressive and submissive people are prone. A word of warning, however. Be prepared to feel a little uneasy about some of the techniques as you read about them. On their own some of them sound odd, to say the least – a bit like listening to one member of a barber shop quartet, or one instrument of an orchestra. Their power and their beauty will become evident when you see them combined.

1. Negative assertion or agreement

How do you usually react when someone criticizes you? Do you retaliate in the same manner, feel annoyed that someone is trying to change the way you do things, feel bad about them, or feel bad about yourself?

Criticism is a common form of attack because people do not always say what they want or how they feel in a straightforward manner. They have learned either to 'go in hard' or to approach a problem obliquely with snide or double-edged comments. In response to this type of attack, fight or flight is common.

Example (spouse criticizes your long working hours)

'It's not fair. You're always working. I *never* manage to do what I want to do. You're just plain selfish.'
   'I'm selfish?!? You're a fine one to talk. What about the times you. . . .'

or:

'It's not my fault. I'm sorry. It's just that. . . .'

In this example, both responses are inappropriate because they leave the real problem – the spouse's *concern* over your working hours – unaddressed.

Negative assertion would be appropriate in both examples. It is often described as 'verbal judo'. In judo, you rarely counter with force, but gain advantage by using your opponent's weight and momentum against them. So you roll with the punch, as it were, by *agreeing* with the other person.

It recognizes that, if you really are your own ultimate judge, it is your decision if you let the criticism affect you. Continuing the martial arts analogy for a moment, I once mentioned this technique to a black belt Karate instructor. He said it reminded him of how a bar room bully once tried to pick a fight by taunting him about karate and how, when he refused to accept the challenge, the bully tried to punch him. My conversation with the karate expert went like this:

'My God, you didn't kill him did you?'
'No'
'You put him into hospital then?'
'No'
'You must have given him a severe bruising then.'
'No'
'Well what did you do?'
'Every time he threw a punch at me I moved out of the way. After he'd fallen over three or four times, he got very embarrassed and ran out.'
'But didn't you want to hit him?'
'No. I *know* I can defend myself. I don't have to keep proving it.'

Relate this conversation to assertiveness. It's up to you if you retaliate or feel hurt by a put-down, so why not surprise the other person by just 'moving out of the way':

'Get you. What did you do, sleep in those clothes?'
'They are a bit crumpled.'

When people on my courses hear this suggestion they usually express doubts about my sanity, so I give a demonstration, asking a volunteer to criticize my clothes. The conversation usually goes like this:

'That tie you're wearing is revolting.'
'I suppose it is.'
'I don't know how you have the nerve to wear it.'
'Neither do I.'
'And those shoes! My grandfather had a pair like that.'
'They are old-fashioned.'
'And your suit is so absolutely boring.'
'So it is.'

This conversation goes on for about a minute during which I maintain a neutral tone of voice, an expressionless face and about 90% eye contact with my 'attacker'. It normally ends up with the volunteer turning to the group in exasperation saying 'This is crazy. I'm having *no effect* on him whatsoever.'

I then ask one question and make one statement. The question is 'Which one of us will give up first?' The volunteers always say that they will give up first, and they will not try it again. The statement I then make is 'Yes, and we're both as unharmed as if I was a black belt Karate instructor!'

The example of criticizing my clothes has a serious message. It is serious in that it illustrates that my volunteers have a right to their opinions. *To them* my tie might well be revolting, my shoes old fashioned and my suits boring. They have a right to their opinions just as I have a right to have a different opinion. They have also learned that such attempts at goading me do not work.

The example concerning working hours is more profound, but the same technique can be used. The spouse's statement effectively contains two parts – 'You're working X hours' and 'I think X hours is too long.' So, with the overall aim of

- remaining assertive yourself
- sidestepping the attempt at emotional manipulation
- attempting to get your spouse to behave assertively (saying what it is about your working hours that is causing concern, but doing so openly and honestly)

why not agree with *the first part* of what was said?

'I *am* working long hours at the moment.'

This simple response will help you stay calm, avoid emotional retaliation from you, and prompt your spouse into continuing the conversation assertively, especially if you combine it with *Fogging* or *Probing*.

2. Fogging

The term 'fogging' is an apt description of this assertive technique. Think what happens when you are driving along and you suddenly enter a bank of fog. You immediately slow down. But do you damage the fog? Does *it* harm you? As you enter the fog bank, does a chunk of fog equivalent to the size of your car spurt out the other side? You have no affect upon *it*, but it has a major affect on *you*.

As a technique, it helps counter some of the common faults of aggressive and submissive people when faced with criticism – counter-attack, allocation of blame to someone else, profuse apologies, self-flagellation, etc. It ensures that you listen to focus on what is being said rather than what you *think* is being implied. It counters any attempt at manipulation, and leaves you free to form your own judgments.

All you do is reflect back to the other person, either *verbatim* or paraphrased, what they have said to you. The effect is twofold. First, it enables you to 'stay out of it' emotionally and, if appropriate, to check your understanding of what you have just heard. Second, it prompts the other person to clarify, justify, or shut up!

So, in response to my critical volunteers, the conversations often go like this:

'That tie you're wearing is revolting.'
'You don't like it?'
'Like it? I hate it. I don't know how you have the nerve to wear it.'
'You feel I'm very courageous to wear it.'
'No, not courageous, stupid.'
'You feel only a person of limited intelligence would wear a tie like this.'
'No, not someone who is stupid. Someone who isn't afraid to upset other people by the way they dress.'
'So I don't mind upsetting people.'
'Yes. . . . no. . . . I mean. . . .' (To the rest of the group) 'I don't believe it, he's done it again!'

Although these conversations are humorous illustrations of the technique, look at how we are getting more and more specific, and consider

- first, how someone attempting a put-down would react. They would probably say to themselves 'I shan't try that again.'
- second, how it might benefit our example of the spouse and the working hours:

> 'It's not fair. You're always working. I *never* manage to do what I want. You're just plain selfish.'
> 'You're concerned about the long hours I'm working.'
> 'Well of course I'm damned concerned about it. I hardly ever see you these days.'
> 'Work *is* taking up a lot of time these days.'
> 'You're either at work, or you've brought it home or you're too tired to go out. We don't see our friends any more.'
> 'You don't like the reduction in our social life since I got promotion.'
> 'No, it's nice having the extra money, but I still want us to have our social life together.'
> 'So you'd like us to get the best of both worlds.'
> 'Yes'
> 'I agree, let's work something out.'

The conversation has become more rational, less heated, and more solution-orientated.

The final technique in the 'verbal judo' category is Probing.

3.   Probing

The probing technique puts you more on the offensive by exercising your right for clear communication. For example:

> 'That tie you're wearing is revolting.'
> 'What is it about my tie that you dislike?'
> 'It's so old-fashioned.'
> 'What is it about old-fashioned ties that you dislike?'
> 'Well. . . . I just think that people should dress fashionably that's all.'
> 'Why do you think that people should dress fashionably?'
> 'Because. . . . if. . . . (To the group) I'd rather have a go at the karate black belt.'

Probing helps desensitize you to criticism and to stay detached. It sends a clear signal to the other person that their remark has had no effect, and that it is up to them to justify themselves by providing relevant information, to examine the basis on which their judgments are made, or to back off.

Where there is a problem, it can get to the heart of the matter quickly – with two provisos! First, body language, particularly tone of voice, has to range from neutral to concerned. If not, the other person may resent the interrogation and misinterpret your motives. It is therefore usefully combined with two assertive tools, *self-disclosure* and *signposting*.

'Self-disclosure' means just that – telling someone something about yourself, such as 'That concerns me', or 'I feel uncomfortable when you speak that way', etc. It brings feelings and worries out into the open because it is only in the open that they can be resolved. It also is a good defence as most manipulators do not know how to handle it. You will also find that bringing such feelings into the open has a more positive effect on your self-esteem than 'inventing' excuses. 'Signposting' means telling the other person which way you are going in the conversation; whether you are about to ask a question, summarize, point out an exception, etc. It avoids simple misunderstandings. For example, 'Exactly what you do mean by that remark?' could be interpreted as 'Who the hell do you think you are talking to me like that?' Alternatively, it could be interpreted as the more benign, and signposted 'I fear I may have misunderstood your remark, could you be more specific please?'

So, returning to the working hours example, the conversation could go like this:

'It's not fair. You're always working. I *never* manage to do what I want. You're just plain selfish.'

'It bothers me that you feel that way. What is it about my working that upsets you?' (self-disclosure, probing)

'We never go out any more. We used to have a good social life and now every time I suggest going out you say you have work to do.'

'I am working a lot lately I know. But let me check, would you rather I hadn't taken the promotion?' (negative assertion, signposting, probing)

'Of course not. It's a good move and the extra money's nice but it's all work and no play and that's no fun.'

'I feel that too, at times. Given the fact that I'm still getting to grips with the job, what would you like to see happen?' (self-disclosure, probing)

'Why don't we reserve, say, two evenings a week so that we can play tennis at the club and then see a few friends in the bar afterwards. That still leaves you a lot of time to get the new job organized.'

The second proviso is that you use the correct type of questions. *Open questions* encourage the other person to talk. They are useful generators of information. For example:

'To what extent does this cause you a problem?'
'Why is that important to you?'
'How do you feel about that suggestion?'

They usually begin with 'How', 'What', 'Why', and they encourage the other person to participate.

They can cause the other person to rethink their views, and uncover real problems which the other person may have preferred to conceal. Above all, they open sensible dialogue.

Closed questions are those which can be answered with a simple answer like 'Yes' or 'No'. They do not generate discussion, but primarily serve to check something. For example:

'When did this first begin?'
'Have you checked that recently?'
'So what you're saying is. . . . Is that correct?'

Used properly, probing helps involve the other person, generate relevant information, and uncover problems. It also helps you stay relaxed and 'detached', and encourages the other person to express themselves more assertively.

So far we have looked at three techniques – negative assertive, fogging, and probing – which I described as a kind of verbal judo. They place a barrier between what the other person is saying and what you are feeling. As such, they enable you to respond with minimal effort while remaining emotionally detached. We now look at three more assertive techniques which are especially useful where you are initiating the interaction rather than simply responding to someone else.

4.   Broken record

The broken record technique is very useful for people who lack persistence, or who cannot resist responding to someone else's questions even though they know that the questions are designed to paint them into a corner. It stems from your rights to

- say what you want or how you feel
- stand your ground
- stand up for your rights

It also guards against your fight or flight response and the inevitable emotional repercussions. It helps you be persistent, to stick to the point, to stay calm and to stay confident – all of which have a beneficial effect on your self-esteem. All you have to do is keep repeating what you want *for as long as it takes*. Here is an example that many people have experienced – the doorbell rings mid-morning on a sunny Sunday. You open it and there stand two religious missionaries about to try and save your soul by converting you to their way of thinking. You know from past experience that if you start a conversation with them it will last an hour. You want neither the conversation nor the wasted hour. Often, people get rid of the missionaries by being nice to them, or by lying ('I've got something on the stove'). Even though they feel bad about themselves afterwards, the only recognized alternatives are to stand there talking for an hour, or to be rude to them. Using the broken record technique the conversation is over amicably in less than a minute.

You:	'Good morning'
Them:	'Good morning. We're from the such-and-such church and would like to talk to you about the world's problems. Don't you feel that mankind is running out of answers?'
You:	'Thank you for calling but I prefer not to talk right now.'
Them:	'But don't you feel concerned at the amount of starvation and aggression in the world?'
You:	'Yes but I prefer not to talk right now.'
Them:	'But if you're concerned, surely you've thought that there must be a solution somewhere?'
You:	'Maybe, but I still prefer not to talk right now.'
Them	'Oh . . . well . . . thank you for your time anyway.'
You:	'You're welcome, 'Bye.'

The result is that you feel alright about them because they have not wasted your time. You feel alright about yourself because you stood up for your rights. The chances are that the missionaries also feel alright about you because you were not rude to them, you did not lie to them, and you did not waste *their* time.

A friend of mine once used the broken record technique to great effect with his boss. He felt very bad at having been 'passed over' for promotion. Every time he broached the matter, his boss managed to fob him off. As a result, he felt very resentful towards his boss and negative about his job. Consequently, to use his words, he 'hid in the organization for a year not making much contribution.' After attending an assertiveness course, he decided to tackle his boss again. The conversation went like this:

Paul:	'I'd like to discuss with you the criteria for promotion to the next grade.'
Boss:	'Not that again. We've been over this before and I've told you – if you were suitable you'd have been promoted by now.'
Paul:	'I know, but that still doesn't tell me what the criteria are, so I'd like to discuss them.'

Boss: 'Paul . . . the matter's closed. There's no point in going on about it.'

Paul: 'I agree there's not. That's why I'd like to be clear in my mind about the promotion criteria.'

Boss: 'Paul. I'm trying to write a report for the Chairman. I haven't got time now.'

Paul: 'I appreciate that but I still want to discuss the criteria with you.'

Boss: '. . . . Oh. . . . look, stop by at three o'clock I'll be free then.'

The conversation took place and lasted for three hours. Paul did not get promotion. What he did get, however, was a clear idea what the promotion criteria were, and how he compared against them. He also learned more about the 'downside' of promotion, and decided he would cope better where he was. He also built a much better working relationship with his boss that has persisted to this day.

5.   Pointing out a discrepancy

We all know the situation – we assumed, believed or agreed that something would happen a certain way and, sure enough, it happens a different way. All of a sudden we are on the spot – do we do something about it and risk conflict, or do we leave it to avoid 'making a fuss' and end up feeling put upon.

Example

You have drafted a long and complicated letter which must go out in tonight's post. You have agreed with the typist that it will be ready at three o'clock to allow time for amendments. It is now half past three and there is still no sign of the letter.

The aggressive response is not only going straight to the point, it also carries huge overtones of blame:

'Where the hell's that letter. Have I always got to chase you for work?'

The submissive response is to sit and do nothing, but worry until perilously close to the postal deadline and then approach the typist:

'Hi. It's only me. I know you're very busy and I hate to be a pest but I was . . . er . . . just wondering if . . . er . . . there was any sign of that letter . . . getting awfully close to the postal deadline and there . . . er . . . might be the odd amendment or two.'

The assertive response, however, is straightforward and factual:

'Jenny, my letter to Universal Electronics. We agreed three o'clock and it's now three thirty. Is there a problem?'

This approach makes no apologies and casts no blame. It simply points out an actual or a perceived discrepancy:

- this is what we agreed. . . . this is what happened,
- this is what I expected. . . . this is what you did,
- this is how you usually do it. . . . this is how you did it,

and then opens the way for the other person to respond. In our example, the response could be anything from a problem such as the word processor being down, another manager jumping the queue, or the typist having forgotten. At least then you would know how to handle the situation.

6. Pointing out a consequence

The final assertive technique is the 'heaviest'. If delivered in anything other than a factual, neutral tone, it could easily be perceived as an aggressive threat because you are pointing out what will happen/what you will do/ what someone else will do, etc., if the situation persists.

To illustrate the care with which consequences have to be pointed out, you may like to try this exercise. Say each of the following sentences out loud three times:

- first, as if you are giving a close friend some humble and gentle advice
- second, as if you are making a factual statement to someone you have only recently met
- finally, as if you are attempting to threaten someone you dislike who cannot retaliate.

  - 'If these mistakes continue, the company will review your employment.'

  - 'Unless you adopt a softer tone with your staff you'll have a riot on your hands.'

  - 'If one more item goes missing I'll have the matter investigated by the police.'

Notice how, for each of the three sentences, your voice becomes harder and you emphasized different words as you progressed from the first to the third version. Hence the degree of care necessary with this technique.

Another aspect of care with this technique concerns timing – when you use it. Using it as an opening remark will be seen as aggressive no matter how carefully you pitch your voice. It is a last resort.

Here is an example in which two managers are charged by their boss to work together on a report. The deadline is fast approaching. Manager A has worked as per the agreed schedule, but Manager B is leaving it too late with the result that the report will miss its deadline:

Manager A: 'I'd like to talk about our report. I'm concerned that we are going to miss the deadline.' (self-disclosure)

Manager B: 'Look, I'm busy right now.'

Manager A: 'Yes, I appreciate that, but I'd still like to talk about our report.' (broken record)

Manager B   'And I'd like to get on with this. Can't it wait?'

Manager A: 'I'd like to talk about it now.' (broken record)

Manager B: 'OK, fire away.'

Manager A: 'When we were given the task, we agreed a schedule. Your part of the report is behind schedule and I'm concerned that we'll miss the deadline.' (pointing out a discrepancy, self-disclosure.)

Manager B: 'Look, at the moment I'm up to my ears. All you want to do is make matters worse for me.' (attempted manipulation)

Manager A: 'It may look that way, but we have a joint deadline and I'm concerned that we are going to miss it.' (negative assertion, broken record, self-disclosure.)

Manager B: 'It just isn't possible to do it now.'

Manager A: 'I understand it may be difficult and I'm prepared to help, but if we can't reach a compromise I'll have to see the boss to explain why the report won't be in on time.' (pointing out a consequence.)

Even with this build up, the consequence has to be pointed out carefully, as a night-follows-day occurrence, to avoid sounding like a threat. One final point – if having pointed out the consequence, it fails to trigger the required response, you have no viable option other than to carry out your promise.

Assertive tools

Earlier in this chapter I described two assertive tools (self-disclosure and signposting) which can be used to facilitate your assertive communication. Here are three more.

Basic assertion

Stating clearly, concisely and usually without justification, what you want, what you think or how you feel.

Empathy

Letting someone else know that you can and do appreciate their position while taking care not to come across as patronizing or condescending.

Workable compromise

Recognizing that imposing your will on someone else or achieving your aims at the expense of other people is the cornerstone of aggressive behaviour. Being assertive means letting other people stand up for their rights too, even helping them to do so, and that may require a compromise with which both parties feel comfortable – a win-win outcome. In achieving a *workable* compromise, you give your own self-respect priority treatment, and settle the conflict on real rather than spurious issues or who happens to be the most successful manipulator.

Here is a summary of what we have covered so far in this chapter:

Technique/Tool	*What is it*	*Useful when*
Negative assertion	Agreeing with the other person's comment or with the truth in what they have said	You want to sidestep a barbed comment, show such comments or tactics have no effect on you, refocus the conversation onto a rational level
Fogging	Reflecting back what the other person has said, possibly paraphrased into more rational/factual or less emotive terms	You want to resist the temptation to become emotionally involved. You want to show that put-downs have zero impact on you. You want to let the other person do the work in the conversation

Probing	Asking open questions (why, what, how, etc.) to encourage the other person to be more specific	You want to avoid responding or counter attacking. You want to put the onus on the other person to justify what they have said. You want to move the conversation from an emotive to a rational level
Broken record	Repeatedly stating what you want, what you think or how you feel	When you need to be persistent. When you want to avoid 'playing their game' or 'falling into their traps'
Pointing out a discrepancy	Drawing someone's attention to a difference in current from expected circumstances and inviting them to comment/respond	When the situation is not as you expected but you want to avoid jumping to conclusions (or being perceived that way) as to why
Pointing out a consequence	Drawing someone's attention to the inevitable outcome of the current state of affairs	As a last resort, you have to draw the line
Self-disclosure	Sharing what you think or how you feel	You wish to demonstrate trust and openness. You feel it appropriate to explain the feelings/ thoughts behind your actions. You wish to make it plain that feelings and emotions are legitimate subjects for discussion
Sign-posting	Letting the other person know what sort of communication (questioning, summarizing, proposing etc.) you are about to make	You feel a need to • clarify the communication process • stress that you are communicating openly

Basic assertion	Saying what you want, what you think or how you feel, usually without justification	At the start of a conversation, or when your views are in danger of being ignored
Empathy	Showing that you can and do appreciate the other person's situation	You suspect the other person may feel hard done by. You wish to pre-empt an objection from them.
Workable compromise	Agreeing a way forward which may not be what either of you wanted originally, but is what you can both accept	You can only move forward by mutual agreement. The matter is significant, and requires both of you to bring it to a successful conclusion. Future relationship requires a 'win/win' solution

With this summary in mind, let us see how the techniques can be combined to produce an impressive display of assertiveness.

Example one

Bob is a young assistant bank manager who lives within walking distance of the branch where he works. The branch is understaffed and, as Bob lives so close, the manager frequently 'asks' him to come in on his days off to cover for people who are unexpectedly absent. Although this usually results in Bob cancelling his personal arrangements at short notice, he has never had the courage to say 'No' to his boss, even though he would dearly love to. Consequently, he not only feels put-upon, but also regards himself as weak – until he receives some assertiveness training and decides he has a right to put himself first on occasions.

Bob is about to enjoy a well deserved day off when the telephone rings:

Bob: 'Hello'

Manager: 'Bob, it's Mr Jones here. I'm sorry to bother you on your day off, but Janice has just called in sick so I need you to cover for her. Can you come straight away please?'

Bob: 'I'm sorry to hear that Janice is sick, Mr Jones, but I won't be able to cover for her today.' (empathy, basic assertion)

Manager: 'Why not? What's so important that you can't come in?'

Bob:	'I have personal plans for today, Mr Jones, I'd be disappointed with myself if I cancelled them so I'm afraid I won't be able to come in today.' (basic assertion, self-disclosure, broken record)
Manager:	'Well . . . why can't you just postpone them? What's so critical about doing them today?'
Bob:	'Today is the day I've arranged to do them, so I won't be able to cover for Janice today.' (broken record)
Manager:	'This is really leaving me in a spot, Bob.'
Bob:	'I know it won't be easy, Mr Jones, but, as I said, I can't come in today.' (empathy, broken record)
Manager:	'This isn't like you, Bob.'
Bob:	'No, it isn't.' (negative assertion)
Manager:	'I've always been able to rely on you in the past.'
Bob:	'You have. I've always been very reliable.' (fogging)
Manager:	'Does this mean I won't be able to count on you in the future?'
Bob:	'I don't know. We'll have to see how I'm fixed on future occasions. But, as far as today goes, I can't cover for Janice.' (basic assertion, broken record)
Manager:	'Well, I guess we'll just have to get by. It's lunchtime that bothers me, we get so busy on a Friday.'
Bob:	'Tell you what Mr Jones, I'll be passing the bank at lunchtime. If you don't mind me coming in dressed casually I'll come in between one and two, but I can't handle any more.' (workable compromise, basic assertion)
Manager:	'Bob, that would be a great help. I'd be very grateful if you could. From one to two would get us over the busy period. Come in dressed how you like.'
Bob:	'From one to two, then. See you later.'

It was clear from this conversation that Mr Jones began by ignoring Bob's right to a planned day's vacation. At the first sign of resistance, he resorted to bullying. When that failed he tried emotional blackmail. It is to be hoped that Mr Jones learned that he could no longer take Bob for granted, nor simply order him about, but that results would be more easily achieved by treating Bob with the respect and dignity that had been missing hitherto.

Bob learned that he could stand up for himself; that he did not have to justify himself to anyone unless he thought it appropriate to do so; and that he was not personally responsible for the predicament in which Janice's sickness absence had placed Mr Jones.

Example two

Jean is a recently promoted manager. The position to which she has been appointed puts her in charge of 20 manual production workers. A fellow manager seems to have decided to take Jean under his wing. At first his attention and input were welcome, helping Jean quickly become familiar with her new duties, but now Jean fears that Paul sees himself as a permanent father figure whose role is to protect this fragile fledgling from the rough tough world of production.

Paul sees Jean in the works canteen and joins her with his lunch tray:

Paul:	'Hi, Jean. May I join you?'
Jean:	'Sure.'
Paul:	'So how's things?'
Jean:	'Pretty good. Production's up for the third successive month, absenteeism's down and I managed to sack that waster, Hubble, with no repercussions from the union.'
Paul:	'Great. So my suggestions on handling the union guy worked then?'
Jean:	'With some "personalisation", yes.'
Paul:	'Good. Hey, I heard some of your guys using some pretty blue language yesterday. Want me to have a quiet word with them?'
Jean:	'No, that's OK. My father was a sailor. I can swear in three languages.' (basic assertion, self-disclosure)
Paul:	'The production quotas come in next week. I've been thinking how you can sell them to your people.'
Jean:	'That's thoughtful of you, Paul. I don't like to turn down advice, but I'd quite like to try this one on my own.' (empathy, self-disclosure, basic assertion)
Paul:	'Hey, c'mon, Jean. These guys can be pretty difficult, you know.'
Jean:	'I know that. I'm getting used to them and they're getting used to me. We're gradually building respect for one another, but if they think I'm just firing someone else's bullets I'll lose credibility. I'd prefer to avoid that.' (self-disclosure, basic assertion)
Paul:	'I'm not sure you know what you're letting yourself in for.'
Jean:	'How do you mean?' (probing)
Paul:	'These guys can be pretty awkward, you know?'
Jean:	'In what way?' (probing)
Paul:	'They don't like anyone changing production quotas.'
Jean:	'The quotas will apply to all six production teams.'
Paul:	'Yes but you're the only *female* production manager.'

Jean:	'My being female makes a difference?' (fogging)
Paul:	'Of course. These guys don't want to be bossed about by a woman.'
Jean:	'They resent having a woman manager?' (fogging)
Paul:	'Yes . . . No . . . I don't know. I haven't heard anything, as such.'
Jean:	'So you're assuming that there may be a problem but you've seen no evidence of one?' (probing)
Paul:	'Yes.'
Jean:	'Paul, I'm grateful for your concern and for the advice you've given me over the last six months. However, I'm concerned that you feel I need so much looking after just because I'm female. I believe I can handle the new production quotas.' (empathy, self-disclosure, basic assertion)
Paul:	'I . . . I..don't know what to say. I didn't realize you felt that way. I'm sorry. I'll eat my lunch on another table.'
Jean:	'Perhaps I didn't say that very well. Let me explain. I value your advice. I just feel competent enough to manage my way. Why don't I tell you how I plan to introduce the new production quotas and you see if you can pick any holes in it?' (signposting, broken record, workable compromise)
Paul:	'Yes. That sounds like a good idea.'

In this encounter, Paul learned that his fatherly protection was seen as patronizing, and that Jean was not prepared to continue their relationship on that basis. Jean learned that severing the relationship would be like throwing out the baby with the bath water – she would lose a source of beneficial advice. Through careful use of assertive techniques, she was able to switch the relationship onto a more acceptable footing.

One of the problems with written dialogues is that aspects of body language have to be inferred. Yet a change in voice pitch and emphasis on different words can completely change how a sentence is received. An assertive intention can be received as aggressive if a voice is too abrupt or as submissive if the voice is too soft and hesitant and eyes are averted to the floor. I want to conclude this section, therefore, with a few comments on body language.

Body language accounts for a substantial part of what we communicate because so much of the information reaching our brains does so through the sense of sight. In other words, much of our communication is received visually. The problem is that we put most of our effort into organizing and delivering the *words* we use. Our body language is left to 'fend for itself' and, as a result, tends to come out 'unedited', communicating what we *really* feel. Where body language is synchronized with what we are saying it supports our verbal communication. Where it is not synchronized with our verbal communication it may even contradict it, because people more readily believe what they see rather than what they hear.

Clearly, if body language is so important it makes sense to use it to *support* what we want to communicate, and to positively influence other people.

Before we begin, however, I should stress that what follows is aimed at North Europeans and North Americans. When dealing with people from countries or cultures different from these, the meaning of body language may change. Those changes can be very subtle.

While the facial manifestation of basic emotions such as sadness, happiness, surprise or fear is fairly universal, consider some of the following differences:

- Malaysians smile effusively in the belief that it facilitates an harmonious relationship. Indonesians smile when giving bad news to someone in an attempt to assuage the hurt.
- Bulgarians and Greeks say 'No' by nodding their heads – something North Europeans understand as 'Yes'. They say 'No' by shaking theirs – something which someone from southern India would understand as 'Yes'!
- The Japanese tend to avoid eye contact as a sign of deference. The British resume eye contact at the end of their input to signify that it is the other person's turn to talk. Americans tend to maintain eye contact whether talking or listening as a sign of assertiveness. Saudis peer into your very pupils to gauge your innermost feelings whilst astutely hiding behind dark glasses.
- A Vietnamese will signify respect and humility by directly facing you, looking you in the eye and folding his arms across his chest. A North European does the same thing to signify aggression.

Add to these mannerisms differences in the meaning of gestures and you have a recipe for confusion. (A thumbs up sign in Britain, for example, shows that you are very pleased with something. Make the gesture to a northern Greek and he may well hit you.) If you travel widely, therefore, or work with people from different cultures, remember that what follows may only apply to North Europeans and North Americans.

Body language breaks down into six main categories – posture, gestures, face, eyes, tone of voice, and proximity.

Posture

Posture concerns the overall bearing of the body. It comprises the angle of the head, shoulders, hips and feet, direction and angle of inclination and position of arms and legs.

In general, people who feel comfortable with a situation and with themselves raise their head and look openly at you. They may lean back slightly
indicating that they are relaxed, or lean forward slightly to indicate attent-
iveness.

Gestures

People use their hands and arms in a variety of ways. Some gesticulate
frequently, and others hardly at all. Points worthy of note are

- arms can be used to signify self-protection and defensiveness when
  they are folded tightly across the abdomen; or they can be held down,
  with hands clasped casually together, to signify relaxation;
- hands can be used to hide behind, covering part of the face; they can
  be used to demonstrate openness and honesty by showing open palms;
  they can be used to cut the air aggressively to emphasise points;
- fingers can be used to jab the air pointing to *you*; they can be used
  to wag at someone like a school teacher talking to a naughty pupil;
  they can be wagged threateningly like a stick.

Face

The face is the most expressive part of our bodies. The areas around the
eyes and mouth are the most expressive. Raised eyebrows and an 'O'
shaped open mouth signifies surprise, but raised eyebrows and an open
smile indicate real pleasure; knotted eyebrows and downturned mouth signify sadness, while knotted eyebrows and tightly pursed lips signify displeasure. There is hardly a single emotion that does not show in the face
in such a way as to be instantly recognizable by someone else.

Eyes

Although the eyes are part of the face, they are important enough to
warrant specific mention.

Eye contact is crucial to assertiveness. Avoiding eye contact is a *learned*
avoidance response to conflict. It give us an immediate, if only temporary,
reduction in anxiety. Eventually it becomes habit forming. If we avoid eye
contact we can give the impression that we are shifty, lacking in confidence,
or disinterested. If our eye contact is too intense we appear aggressive and
threatening. If our eye contact is immediate and moderate (about 50–70%
of the time) we give an entirely different impression. We are effectively
saying, 'I mean what I say; I feel OK about the situation.'

Tone of voice

Tone of voice is an important aspect of our communication. If it is too quiet and hesitant people will infer nervousness on our part. If it is too loud, too fast and abrupt, people will infer impatience, and so on. Whenever possible, you should pay attention to

- volume, so that you can be heard;
- pace, so that you sound enthusiastic, concerned, relaxed, and so on, as appropriate;
- pitch: a low, slow monotone can make you sound bored; a high, rapid voice delivered in fits and starts will make you sound nervous. Pitch therefore needs to be moderate and varied.

Proximity

The message we give by the proximity we adopt is dependent on whether the situation is business, social or intimate.

Problems arise primarily when people feel their personal space is being 'invaded'. When they are expecting a business interaction, for example, and the other person enters their intimate zone – a favourite bullying tactic of aggressive people.

With regard to our assertive techniques and tools, therefore, there are certain aspects of body language to practise and others to avoid.

Technique Tool	What to practise	What to avoid
Negative assertion	Neutral expression Neutral tone of voice Eye contact Open posture	Bored expression Condescending tone Eyes rolled upwards Protective posture
Fogging	Neutral expression Neutral tone of voice Eye contact Relaxed posture	Expression of disbelief Sarcastic tone Know-it-all look
Probing	Inquisitive or neutral expression Emphasis on factual words Moderate eye contact Relaxed, open posture	Accusing expression Emphasis on personal words Excessive eye contact Invasive or arrogant posture

Basic assertion Broken record	Neutral expression Emphasis on key words Eye contact Open, relaxed posture	Signs of impatience or anxiety Vocal hesitancy Evasive looks down Aggressive or submissive posture
Pointing out a discrepancy	Concerned expression Emphasis on factual words Eye contact Relaxed posture	Pained expression Accusing tone or hesitancy Excessive or no eye contact Invasive or protective postures
Pointing out a consequence	Neutral expression Emphasis on factual words Eye contact Neutral posture	Impatient expression Emphasis on personal or emotive words Excessive eye contact Aggressive gestures and proximity
Self-disclosure	Concerned expression Neutral voice Eye contact Open gestures	Anxious expression Whining tone Evasive looks away Protective gestures
Empathy	Concerned expression Warm voice Eye contact Open posture	Excessive concern/ dismissive expression Excessive warmth/ rapid speech No eye contact Dismissive or protective gestures
Workable compromise	Genuine expression Neutral tone of voice Eye contact Relaxed posture	Impatient/resentful expression Condescending or hesitant tone Closed/protective posture

The best way to start learning about body language is to become more observant. Watch people interacting in business, socially, at play, on television, and so on, and ask yourself what is happening, what are they feeling, which aspects of their body language are helpful to the conversation and which are unhelpful? Become more aware of yourself. What are you doing with your body when you are worried, anxious, concerned, amazed, impatient, happy and sad? The three keys to effective body language are awareness, sensitivity, and practice.

We have now not only come to the end of this chapter but, when you have completed the following workout sheet, you will also have come to the end of this part of the book. In it, I have attempted to show why the way we interact with one another at work is crucial to business success and that, if managers use their skills of interaction to enhance their personal credibility, they will put the 'domino effect' into reverse. The way managers interact (their management style) is an outward manifestation of their attitudes, values, and beliefs.

Ask most managers what they believe about themselves and their staff and they will come up with some sound comments. Ask them to cite evidence to support what they have said, or watch them in practice and you will probably see more aggressive and submissive behaviour than you expected.

Having read so far, you should be more aware of your own behaviour, the attitudes, values and beliefs on which it is based, and how those attitudes, values and beliefs came to be there in the first place. You should have also considered your rights and those of other people, and determined some of the changes you can make to acknowledge them, using the assertive techniques and tools described above.

Part Two will help you in that process by examining a range of managerial situations and describing how to handle them assertively.

Workout sheet

1. How do you usually react when someone criticizes you?

2. How easily do you get to the bottom of the criticism?

3. When you have a 'difficult' conversation with someone, who does most of the talking, you or them?

4. To what extent do you naturally ask questions? To what extent do you jump to conclusions, finish a sentence for someone, or 'know' what they are thinking?

5. To what extent would people describe you as persistent?

6. To what extent do you tend to ask closed questions or open questions?

7. Do you find that threats work well for you, or could you not make a threat to save your life?

8. Can you point out a consequence or a discrepancy to someone without it sounding threatening?

9. To what extent would people describe you as empathetic?

10. How often do you feel that people misunderstand what you are saying?

PART 2

Chapter 8

INTRODUCTION

Once you have read the section on assertive techniques and tools, I hope you agree with me that assertive people are good at:

- sidestepping someone else's attempts at influencing them by manipulation (negative assertion, fogging, probing)
- emotionally detaching themselves from criticism (negative assertion, fogging, probing)
- focusing on real issues (fogging, probing)
- acknowledging and being open about their feelings (self-disclosure)
- listening (fogging, probing)
- seeing the other persons viewpoint (fogging, empathy)
- communicating clearly (basic assertion, broken record, signposting)
- standing their ground (broken record)
- being objective and not jumping to conclusions (probing, pointing out a discrepancy)
- resolving conflict (workable compromise)
- if they need to, letting the other person know the consequences of their behaviour (pointing out a consequence).

I hope you also agree with me that these are desirable characteristics in most people, and *essential* characteristics in a manager. Most staff respect managers who listen, give consideration to them, are firm but fair, know where they are going, consult and involve, and give regular feedback and praise. Most senior managers like their direct reporting managers to give voice to their views and opinions, to not take orders passively, to be honest about problems, to accept responsibility for mistakes, and to seek guidance when they need it.

Taking these characteristics as our guiding stars, in this part of the book, we examine a range of typical management situations.

The situations selected are those which managers on my assertiveness courses refer to most frequently as causing problems. You may want to read them all. Alternatively, you may want to use this part of the book as a reference section referring to situations as and when necessary. My suggestion, however, is that having identified those situations in which you want to be more assertive, you start with those as part of a planned and deliberate development programme.

The situations referred to in this part of the book are:

1. Reprimanding or criticizing a member of staff
2. Being reprimanded or criticized
3. Handling aggressive people
4. Handling submissive people
5. Handling resentment
6. Delegating an unpleasant task
7. Resolving conflict
8. Saying 'No' to a request
9. Handling work overload from your boss
10. Telling the team about tough targets
11. Giving praise
12. Being praised
13. Performing well in meetings
14. Talking to a poor listener
15. Seeking guidance from your boss
16. Reducing stress
17. Handling persistent sales people

Each situation tends to follow the same format – a description of why the situation can cause problems, with examples, guidelines on how to handle the situation assertively, with examples, and finally, a rapid reference summary.

Chapter 9

REPRIMANDING OR CRITICIZING A MEMBER OF STAFF

Think back to when you were of the sort of level and in the type of situation of your staff. How did you feel when someone more senior reprimanded or criticized you? Hurt, guilty, resentful? Or glad the matter had been brought to your attention? How does that compare with how your staff currently feel when you reprimand or criticize them? Is that how you want them to feel?

In this chapter, reprimanding and criticizing are taken together, because the differences between them are quite small. They tend to be differences of magnitude and formality but their effects are similar.

What managers want is good performance from their staff, and so spot 'improvement areas'. Staff, on the other hand, want their boss to see them in a good light, and so naturally focus on the favourable aspects of their performance. They can become defensive about problems, externalizing faults (that is, blaming something or someone else). These different perspectives contain ample scope for misunderstanding.

Most managers know that people tend to work better in a climate of approval rather than one of criticism. A climate of approval empowers them to get on with the job, and to stretch their performance. A climate of criticism restricts their performance either through a feeling of resentment or through fear of making mistakes, or both. Hence, there are two main faults when reprimanding/criticizing.

The first is to criticize too hard. It usually arises where managers think that macho management is the order of the day. They confuse toughness with directness and become far too abrupt. Another cause is where managers would prefer to avoid the confrontation but, recognizing that there is no alternative, psych themselves up too much and criticize too harshly.

They recognize their own rights to manage, to expect acceptable performance from staff, and to point out when performance or behaviour is below par. Unfortunately, they ignore all the staff member's rights. Their self-talk reveals this one sided approach:

'Poor performance has to be stamped out before it spreads.'
'Show any sign of weakness and these people will take advantage of it. Well that's not going to happen to me.'
'I'm here to get results, not to treat people with kid gloves.'

What they expect is confrontation, denials and counter-accusations *unless they make their criticisms first*. Consequently, their behaviour is characterized by certain features:

- exaggerations
- generalizations
- degeneration into petty fault finding
- personalization
- excessive prescriptions and orders full of 'should', 'ought' and 'must'.

Example one

Situation

A new member of staff who joined a section six weeks ago in a clerical capacity is having difficulty mastering the detail of the job. Due to extreme work pressure the other team members cannot spare the time for prolonged on-the-job coaching which had been available in the past. The staff member has a natural arrogance which makes her feel she has now mastered the job, despite your having recently pointed out several errors.

Another, significant error has occurred. Although it was caused by another department, any other member of your staff would have noticed it. Even an inexperienced staff member should have recognized the inconsistency and raised it as a query:

Manager: (in front of everyone) 'Who the hell's responsible for this document?'
Staff member: 'It's one of mine. Is anything wrong?'
Manager: 'Wrong? Of course it's bloody wrong. A child of three could have noticed it's wrong. It's got the wrong ruddy clause in it.'

Staff member: 'Well, it's not my fault. That's how it came from Sales Department.'

Manager: 'Haven't you learned anything in the last six weeks? That clause only goes into contracts with a purchase option. You're supposed to notice these things.'

Staff member: 'If we didn't work to such stupid deadlines I'd be able to wouldn't I?'

Manager: 'That I doubt! You're so damned sure of yourself, advice goes in one ear and out of the other. What you ought to do is listen more and stop thinking you're so damned clever. If there's not a marked improvement from you, it's back to Personnel. For crying out loud; if you're not sure – ask!'

The outcome of this confrontation is a staff member who is more concerned about how she has just been treated than about the behaviour she needs to change.

The potential for reprimands and criticism to sour relationships makes some managers go to the opposite extreme to that described above. Some minimize the problem in their minds, hoping that it will be overtaken by events. Others attempt to address it, but to minimize the 'confrontation' they 'sugar-coat' or dilute the message.

They ignore their own rights while exaggerating those of the staff member. Their self-talk gives the staff member too great a benefit of the doubt, or minimizes their own ability to handle the situation:

'This department is too busy for an inexperienced person.'
'Why do I always get the people no one else wants. It's not fair.'
'I'm useless at handling these situations. They always go wrong for me.'

The consequent expectation, therefore, is of reluctance to raise the issue, an uncomfortable experience or a conversation that gets out of control.

Example two

Manager: 'Look, I . . . er . . . hope you don't mind my mentioning this, but that document you sent to Despatch had a slight problem with it. We seem to be getting . . . er . . . one or two such problems lately and I was wondering if there was . . . er . . . anything you weren't quite sure of.'

Staff member: 'Oh, I wondered why it had that clause in, but as it came from Sales I assumed it was OK.'

Manager: 'Ah . . . Sales . . . yes . . . they're always getting it wrong. Can't trust them at all. Always have to watch what they send out. But I was wondering . . . didn't you think that perhaps something was just a tiny bit wrong?'

Staff member: 'Well, I did wonder, but everyone was so busy I didn't like
                to disturb them.'
Manager: 'It's just that it's caused a bit of a stir upstairs, you see,
                and the boss is . . . er . . . screaming for blood, if you know
                what I mean.'
Staff member: 'Well if the Department wasn't so understaffed maybe I
                could have a *proper* training programme.'
Manager: 'Of course . . . yes . . . No, I'm not suggesting you're to
                blame, goodness gracious, no. It's just that . . . well . . .
                if you could watch those clauses in future it could be . . .
                er . . . better.'

The outcome of this situation is that the staff member resents the implied
accusation, and feels vindicated in laying the problem at the manager's
door for not arranging a prolonged training programme. The manager has
confirmed in his/her data banks the discomfort and ineffectiveness of such
confrontations.

So, reprimanding staff or criticizing them can be a great way of causing
resentment, reducing productivity, undermining people's confidence, and
showing that you are basically unfair – unless it is done correctly. But how
do you reconcile your rights and those of your staff. You have a right to
acceptable standards of performance, to point out when those standards
are not being met, to attempt to change people's behaviour, to be listened
to, and to honesty from your staff. They have a right to be treated with
respect, not to feel threatened, to fair treatment, to make reasonable mistakes, to defend themselves from unjust criticism, to be listened to, and to
a good working relationship with their boss.

These rights can be acknowledged in positive self-talk: 'I have a responsibility to maintain standards, so the matter must be addressed but with care,
sensitivity and by concentrating on my intended outcome.' The expectation
then becomes one of an open, honest and objective discussion, focusing on
behaviour not on personalities; a discussion which not only results in
improved performance, but in a strengthened working relationship.

Before examining how to reprimand or criticize assertively, it will be
useful to bear in mind certain points about effective reprimanding and
criticizing.

You *focus on the behaviour* that is behind the problem and not on the
person. Of which of the following two criticisms would you rather be on
the receiving end?

'Your trouble is, you just don't give a damn about detail.'
'Errors like this aren't usually made by people of your experience.'
'You're just plain lazy.'
'Your output is only three quarters that of everyone else.'

In short, factual/descriptive words are preferable to evaluative or emotional ones. Words that have a 'red rag' effect on people are weakness, stupid, fault, should, must, never, ought, persistently, and so on. They are often used by critical managers to bolster their case and, as such, are best avoided.

Staff have a right to fair treatment. That means proving you are fair, not just thinking it. The easiest way of doing that is, after having described the problem, to ask if the details you have described are correct.

As you have been factual/descriptive, a denial is unlikely unless, of course, you have genuinely misunderstood – in which case you need to know now before you make a fool of yourself and alienate a potentially productive member of staff.

Explain what you would like to happen in future, but do so in factual/descriptive terms. After all, you want the staff member to be in no doubt about the behaviour you want. Vague terminology like, 'You've got to do better', or '. . . a vast improvement', or '. . . so just shape up and fly right, OK?' is woolly management of the worst sort and favoured, typically, by managers suffering delusions of adequacy.

Body language also needs attention. The staff member has to feel you are open to their response but that, if fair, you will be persistent. This feeling is best achieved if you sit or stand at the same level to avoid any intimidating dominance. Your manner has to be relaxed but serious, and your voice tone neutral and pace of speech steady. Statements need to be brief and factual. Eye contact needs to be steady.

An assertive reprimand/criticism may, therefore, go like Example three.

Example three

Manager:	'Sarah, could you come in for a moment, please?'
Staff member:	'Yes, Val?'
Manager:	'The boss had just handed me this contract from Despatch. Is it one that you sent?'
Staff member:	'Yes, that's my signature. Is something wrong with it?'
Manager:	'The contract is for rental. However, it contains the clause used in contracts with a purchase option. Did you notice it?'
Staff member:	'Yes, I thought it was a bit odd, but as it came that way from Sales Department I assumed it was OK.'
Manager:	'Sales Department aren't qualified to do that sort of work which is why we act as the final arbiters on contracts. Last week you noticed three errors on documents they sent us. How come this one slipped through?' (pointing out a discrepancy, broken record)
Staff member:	(Beginning to look agitated) 'It's not my fault. Everyone's so busy. I feel as if I'm disturbing them if I keep asking

them things. And now you're blaming me for getting it wrong. It's not fair.'

Manager: 'I'm neither finding fault nor allocating blame. An error has been made and I'm finding out what we need to do to ensure it doesn't recur. Busy or not, you've noticed errors like this one before, so why did this one slip through?' (signposting, pointing out a discrepancy, broken record)

Staff member: (No longer agitated but looking ashamed) 'I'm sorry Val. It was my fault. I saw the clause and thought it was a bit odd but I had to leave early. My boyfriend is going abroad for a month and I wanted to see him off. Had I double checked the clause I'd have missed his flight. So I gave Sales the benefit of the doubt. I'm sorry.'

Manager: 'Let me check that. You thought the clause might be wrong but because you had to be away early you hoped that Sales had got it right and took a gamble?' (probing)

Staff member: 'Yes, I'm sorry.'

Manager: 'Are you aware of the problem that's been caused?' (probing)

Staff member: 'No. How bad is it?'

Manager: 'The delivery had to be held up and everyone from the Sales Director to the customer is after my blood.'

Staff member: 'Oh no. I'm really very sorry.'

Manager: 'I'll handle it. What concerns me more is the decision you took. You decided to take a gamble rather than seek assistance. Why?' (self-disclosure, basic assertion, probing)

Staff member: 'Everyone is *so* busy. I was afraid they'd just tell me what to do to put the contract right and then I'd have missed my boyfriend's flight.'

Manager: 'Were they aware of why you had to leave early?' (probing)

Staff member: 'No. I thought they might think I was shirking so I kept it to myself.'

Manager: 'I'm glad you've felt free enough to be open with me. How can we prevent this kind of thing happening again – without you missing an important personal occasion?' (self-disclosure, probing)

Staff member: 'I'll just have to ask for help and if I explain the reason fully people will probably help me.'

Manager: 'Yes, and if they don't – ask me. A bit of forward planning might help too. Like letting everyone know when your boyfriend is due back?'

Staff member: 'Yes – and Val – thank you.'

I ended this example with a 'thank you' because when reprimanding or criticizing this way, people are usually grateful – both for your having pointed out the problem, and for pointing it out in such a positive manner – firm but fair.

In summary, the purpose of reprimanding and criticizing is to change someone's behaviour, not to wreak vengeance on them. The ideal situation is where you both feel 'up' at the end of it. I am reminded, at this point, of a quote from Field Marshal Montgomery, famous for his North African campaign in World War II:

'The final test of a leader is the feeling you have when you leave his presence. You have a feeling of uplift and confidence.'

This 'acid test' is true in situations like reprimanding and criticizing.

A summary on reprimanding or criticizing a staff member is given in Figure 6.

Rights

Yours	Theirs
Agreed standards of performance Attempt to change others' behaviour Constructively criticize Be listened to Honesty	Respect/dignity Fair treatment Not to feel threatened Make reasonable mistakes Defend themselves from unjust criticism Be listened to Good working relationship with boss

Self-talk

I have a responsibility to maintain standards, so the matter must be addressed but with care, sensitivity and by concentrating on my intended outcome.

Expectation

An open, honest and objective discussion dealing with behaviour, not personalities, which improves performance and strengthens our working relationship.

Behaviour

Appropriate timing and environment. Plenty of signposting. Point out discrepancy, probing, basic assertion, broken record and, as a last resort, pointing out a consequence. Listening. Neutral tone of voice, calm pace, good eye contact.

Outcome

Achieved	Avoided
Permanently improved performance Strengthened relationship Staff member feels alright You feel alright Your personal credibility up	Temporarily improved performance Weakened relationship Staff member does not feel alright about you, and possibly self You do not feel alright about staff member, and possibly yourself

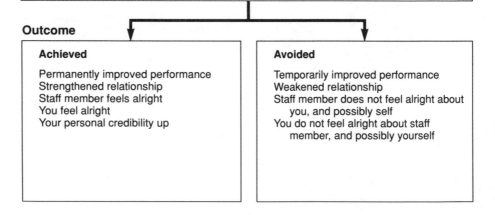

Figure 6 *Reprimanding or criticizing a member of staff: summary.*

Chapter 10

BEING REPRIMANDED
OR CRITICIZED

Much what was said about reprimanding or criti-
cizing in the previous chapter also applies to this chapter. An effective
interaction tends to benefit both performance and relationships, while an
ineffective interaction has a detrimental effect. The differences, however,
are that the previous section looked at how to deliver criticism effectively,
and this chapter examines how to receive criticism effectively. The issue of
being in charge of you, therefore, is different – you have more intense
feelings to control. As criticism is in the same category as personal attack,
the usual feelings relate directly to the fight or flight response. We can feel
victimized, and so counter-attack or defend ourselves, or we can see it as
further proof that we are not alright. This response is primarily due to the
replay of data bank tapes recorded in childhood, and in short, we find it
easy to take criticism personally – particularly when most people deliver it
so badly (see previous chapter), and it is tempting for us. Similarly, it is
sometimes easy for us to shut out the message and, in the case of unjust
criticism, fail to alter the other person's opinion of us.

Before we look at some examples, I should like to point out that in this
chapter we largely concentrate on how to handle three types of reprimand/
criticism being aimed at you – *just, unjust*, and the persistant but aggravating
teasing that is for many people what the last straw is to a camel's back.
These categories are worth examining.

Just criticism

Here is an analogy – from whom do shopkeepers, restaurateurs and manufacturer's learn how to improve their products – satisfied customers or
customers with complaints? The answer, of course, unpalatable though it
may be, is from customers with complaints.

So too with just criticism. It is free advice on how to improve as a friend,
spouse, colleague, boss or subordinate. Unfortunately, because we tend to
react against criticism, and because criticism is often badly delivered, it is
so easy to ignore or react against the way it is delivered rather than the
content of what is delivered – a bit like refusing to accept a Christmas
present because you dislike the paper in which it is wrapped.

Example one

Senior manager:	'Val this isn't the first contract your people have sent out with the wrong clause in it. If you don't start to get it right fast there'll be trouble.'
Junior manager:	'Me? That's a laugh. If that excuse for a manager in Sales could get it right I wouldn't inherit his problems.'
Senior manager:	'You leave Sales to me and worry about your own department.'
Junior manager:	'I'd worry a lot less about my department if I could have a full complement of decent staff instead of the rejects Personnel send me.'
Senior manager:	'You get the same people as everyone else, but that's not good enough for you is it? Oh no, little Miss High and Mighty has to have the cream. Have you ever thought of training them? No, too bloody busy moaning.'

Well, that was an 'interesting' exchange! Relationships have been nicely
soured, and the issue of errors to contracts well and truly by-passed. The
real criticism of Val not organizing adequate training has been totally lost
because the Senior Manager threw it in as a by-the-way remark, and because
Val was so intent on counter-attack. It is worth pointing out that had Val
responded with 'flight' and gone down a submissive route, the key messages
would have been just as surely lost.

Example two

Senior manager:	'Val, this isn't the first contract your people have sent out with the wrong clause in it. If you don't start to get it right fast there'll be trouble.'

Junior manager:	'I know. I'm sorry . . . we try our best..but . . . well . . . there's just so much pressure at the moment.'
Senior manager:	'We're *all* under pressure, Val. That's no excuse. What I want to know is what you are going to do about it because if you don't get it sorted, I will.'
Junior manager:	'If only Sales wouldn't make so many errors. It's bad enough . . . well . . . you know . . . trying to get our own work done without . . . having additional problems.'
Senior manager:	'You just leave Sales to me, Val. Your errors aren't just Sales-related. I got you a new member of staff and you're still complaining!'
Junior manager:	'I know . . . I'm very grateful . . . it's just that . . . well, there's not really enough time to train her.'
Senior manager:	'Well, that's for *you* to manage. For crying out loud, Val, will you get sorted out?'
Junior manager:	'Yes, I'll try' (and to herself 'God, I just can't cope with this').

Val's half hearted attempts to shift the problem to Sales or to lack of time for training received no attention. Furthermore, as well as losing sight of the behaviour that needs altering, Val now feels very negative about herself, her job, and probably also her boss.

The difference between these examples and handling criticism assertively is twofold. The first thing you need to do is to put the brakes on your own emotions and avoid an immediate reaction (because there is a good chance it will be fight or flight). You need to drive a wedge between your behaviour and yourself. Criticism of your behaviour is not criticism of you. The second thing you need to do is to strip away the 'packaging' the other person has put around their message so that both of you can focus on real issues.

Example three

Senior manager:	'Val, this isn't the first contract your people have sent out with the wrong clause in it. If you don't start to get it right fast there'll be trouble.'
Junior manager:	'I see. I appreciate errors are never desirable but the situation sounds important.' (Empathy)
Senior manager:	'Of course it's important. It isn't just that we can fail to meet a deadline. It's hassle and aggravation all the way down the line, and this business is too competitive to risk losing even a single customer. It isn't just you. It reflects badly on me too, you know.'
Junior manager:	'Yes. I understand that. I'm aware of the problem, but

I'm concerned that my department is being singled out. Are you aware that many of the errors aren't originated by us but by Sales?' (empathy, self-disclosure, probing)

Senior manager: 'I am but we can't pass the buck on this one. Sales Department is under immense pressure to achieve high targets before the end of the financial year. If that means we have to cover for them, so be it.'

Junior manager: 'Yes, company performance is important with so many takeovers in our industry. I feel though that being below complement and having an inexperienced member of staff that I'm doing the best I can.' (empathy, basic assertion)

Senior manager: 'Yours isn't the only department that's understaffed nor with new staff. But we're talking about basic errors here, nothing complex.'

Junior manager: 'Have you any suggestions as to how I can put matters right?' (probing)

Senior manager: 'I'd have thought that as well as training up that new staff member, you need a simple visual checking system that makes it easy to get it right.'

Junior manager: 'That sounds good. I've seen Pete Madigan in Claims Department using them. I'll see him and get some ideas. I'll also get some suggestions from the team. Give me a couple of days and I should be in a position to let you know our solutions.'

Senior manager: 'Val, that would be great . . . You're good to work with. I can't talk straight like this to everyone.'

Junior manager: 'Yes. It's been a useful discussion.'

In this example, Val followed a sequence:

1. Listen and show empathy 2. Probe	Both these actions help you stay emotionally detached and, if the other person is emotive, helps them behave 'more openly and rationally'.
3. Decide whether you wish to accept the criticism or not	If it is just criticism you almost certainly should. If it is unjust, however, you may still decide to go along with it if circumstances make it sensible that you exercise your right *not* to be assertive (discretion sometimes being the better part of valour, and all that!).

4.   State what you will do, or ask the other person what they would like you to do

This shows that you have listened to their comments and decided to act on them.

5.   Agree action

6.   If appropriate, thank them for bringing it to your attention.

This approach has several benefits. It:

- helps you stay emotionally detached, and hence calm
- enables you to get to the bottom of the criticism and focus on that, rather than on the way it may have been delivered
- encourages the other person to be open, rational and assertive with you in future as they become aware that you are more easily influenced by that behaviour than by attempts at manipulation
- paves the way for a workable compromise if you have to meet in the middle.

It is also very similar to the approach adopted for handling unjust criticism. We will take the same example again, but this time let Val's boss exaggerate a bit!

Unjust criticism

Example four

Senior manager: 'I'm becoming sick and tired of the persistent errors coming out of your department, Val. I don't know what the hell's going on. At one time I could trust you to do a decent job, but now you've really gone down in my estimation.'

Junior manager: 'I'm very concerned to hear you say those things. May we talk about it?' (self-disclosure, probing)

Senior manager: 'We can talk about it as much as you want, but I want to see a big improvement and fast.'

Junior manager: 'Exactly what sort of errors are we talking about?' (probing)

Senior manager: 'Well there's the wrong clause in a contract that nearly went out yesterday for a start. The delay damn near cost us a customer.'

Junior manager: 'And any others? You mentioned the word "persistent" '. (probing)

Senior manager: 'There have been others. I can't recall them off-hand, but thankfully none as serious as that one yesterday.

	We're hanging on to that customer by the skin of our teeth, I can tell you.'
Junior manager:	'Just let me check to make sure I understand. You are concerned about errors in general coming out of my department, but the one causing real concern was the incorrect clause on a contract that went out yesterday?' (signposting, probing)
Senior manager:	'Yes, that's about it.'
Junior manager:	'I understand the problems that the incorrect clause has caused. I'm sorry about them, but I'd like to conduct my own investigation in the department to find out what happened before I can respond to you.' (empathy, basic assertion)
Senior manager:	'OK, I'll buy that but I'd like a verbal report from you this afternoon.'
Junior manager:	'No problem. However, that still leaves me concerned that you feel my department is persistently error-prone and getting worse. Why do you feel that?' (self-disclosure, probing)
Senior manager:	'With the pressure the company is under at the moment any errors costing time and money are problems we could do without.'
Junior manager:	'I understand the situation is the toughest for a long time, but do you really feel my department is getting worse or is it just that the business environment is becoming such that errors show up more?' (empathy, probing, pointing out a discrepancy)
Senior manager:	'You're probably right. I guess I'm just a bit jumpy at the moment and that incorrect clause made me lose my temper a bit. You are right though. Errors do show up more in the current environment.'
Junior manager:	'For a minute, you had me worried. I thought I'd fallen from grace permanently. I've a team meeting tomorrow. I'll put *errors* on the agenda and see what we I come up with.' (self-disclosure, basic assertion)
Senior manager:	'That's good. Let me know how the meeting goes.'

In this example, Val has listened, showed empathy and probed. This has not only enabled her to stay emotionally detached and so avoid a fight or flight response, but has enabled her to consider the information provided by her boss and decide not to go along with it. Rather than openly disagree, however, she uses probing and pointing out a discrepancy to encourage her boss to re-think his opinion. The sequence she follows is:

1. Listen.
2. Probe.
3. Decide whether you wish to go along with the criticism.
4. Probe/point out a discrepancy.
5. State your position.

The approaches adopted for handling just and unjust criticism are identical until you decide into which category the reprimand or criticism falls. The approach to handling persistent teasing, however, is different.

Persistent teasing

I have included persistent teasing in this section because it is used by some managers as a means of relieving their conscience. They want to mention something to you, but feel that an oblique approach is easier: 'I don't want to make a mountain out of a molehill' is the usual way they retrospectively justify their behaviour.

The effect, however, is often counter-productive. Their own personal credibility is diminished because they cannot address the matter openly, and their remarks only serve to aggravate.

Persistent teasing, incidentally, also serves as humour in the minds of some people, but whether it is someone attempting to criticize you or simply have some fun at your expense, the method of handling it is the same – verbal judo! You use their own weight and momentum against them so that you either *set a limit* to the teasing or *draw into the open* the underlying reasons for it.

Here are two examples, the first showing a situation where the underlying reasons are brought out into the open, and the second showing a situation where the limit is set.

Example five

Situation

A recently promoted manager is significantly younger than his peers who, until the young manager's promotion, formed a cosy clique. The young manager's promotion appears to have ruffled the feathers of one of them, who lets it show by sarcastic comments – delivered in a jocular manner. The other managers in the clique maintain an embarrassed neutrality.

The young manager joins the clique for lunch one day in the staff restaurant:

Older manager: 'It's Boy Wonder! How's life on the greasy pole, then?'

Younger manager:	'So far so good.'
Older manager:	'That's what the optimist said who fell off the Empire State Building, ha ha. What's it like being the boss's blue eyed boy then?'
Younger manager:	'Why do you ask?' (probing)
Older manager:	'I just want to know what it's like permanently being in someone's good books.'
Younger manager:	'You believe the boss thinks well of me?' (fogging)
Older manager:	'He must do, promoting you at such a tender age.'
Younger manager:	'What is it about my age that makes my promotion so interesting to you?' (probing)
Older manager:	'When we were your age no one ever got promotion. People had to have a few grey hairs before they were eligible, not like now.'
Younger manager:	'Promotion criteria have changed.' (fogging)
Older manager:	'I'll they say have. You had to *work* your way up when I was young. Nowadays they take people straight out of college.'
Younger manager:	'Yes, more people go on to higher education these days, but why does that cause you a problem?' (fogging, probing)
Older manager::	'It doesn't cause me a problem.'
Younger manager:	'Oh, for a minute I thought you were concerned that I'd had some sort of unfair advantage.' (self-disclosure)
Older manager:	'What is this? All I did was make a comment.'
Younger manager:	'Your comments concerned me so I thought I'd find out if we have a problem.' (self-disclosure, basic assertion)
Older manager:	'Well, we didn't.'
Younger manager:	'You're quite sure now? It's just that with the remarks you keep making it seems that there might be.' (probing)
Older manager:	'No. There isn't a problem.'
Younger manager:	'Good, if we're going to work together, I need to be sure that we feel alright about each other. If ever a problem does arise will you be sure to let me know?' (basic assertion, probing)
Older manager:	'Yeah, sure.'
Younger manager:	'Good.'

In this example the younger manager obeyed the cardinal rule of being on the receiving end of criticism – stay emotionally detached. He also let the older manager know that such comments were unwelcome, not by an outburst which could have permanently soured the relationship and subsequently made the younger manager feel embarrassed, but by carefully placing the ball back into the older manager's side of the court. The older manager was clearly bothered about the way promotion criteria had changed, and was given an opportunity to discuss it openly (although he chose not to, perhaps recognizing that his feelings were mainly jealousy). It is to be hoped that the older manager also learned that if he wanted to communicate anything to the younger in the future, a direct and open approach would produce better results.

The next example concerns setting a limit.

Example six

Situation

A female manager is taking evening classes in a variety of topics. Some are of general interest, such as medieval history, and others are business related, such as economics. A male colleague thinks it only worthwhile taking business-related topics, and persistently teases the female manager to encourage her to take only the 'right' courses:

Male manager:	'Is that next year's enrolement form?'
Female manager:	'Yes.'
Male manager:	'I suppose you're going to be wasting time doing more of that history rubbish.'
Female manager:	'I suppose I am.' (negative assertion)
Male manager:	'You must be crazy, that stuff is going to get you nowhere.'
Female manager:	'You're probably right.' (negative assertion)
Male manager:	'History's bunk. If I were you I'd concentrate solely on business-related topics.'
Female manager:	'Yes, if you were me you would.' (fogging)
Male manager:	'What's the matter? All I'm trying to do is stop you wasting your time.'
Female manager:	'Nothing's the matter, but why is studying history a waste of time?' (basic assertion, probing)
Male manager:	'Because it's rubbish.'
Female manager:	'You don't like history?' (fogging)
Male manager:	'No, I don't.'
Female manager:	'Is there any reason why I have to dislike what you dislike?' (probing)
Male manager:	'No.'
Female manager:	'I'm studying history because I like it in the same way that you're not studying it because you don't like it. Is there a problem with that?' (basic assertion, probing)

Male manager:	'No.'
Female manager:	'Good. It's just that if there was a problem with each of us liking and disliking different things I'd like to discuss it, but if there's not, I'll get on with my enrolement form.'
Male manager:	'Oh. . . . er. . . . OK.'

In this example, the female manager failed to rise to the male manager's bait. Had she succumbed and failed to enrol, she would have felt bad about both herself and the other manager. Had she fought back with one or two biting comments she would have detrimentally affected a working relationship – not of her initiation but, if the other person is not being sensible, maybe you have to be sensible enough for two.

Instead she let the other manager know that such 'games' do not work with her. If he wished to express his views he could do so – but openly. If he wished to prescribe how she 'should' behave, his prescription would have no effect. At this stage, it is worth making a point: people behave out of habit a great deal. It may take quite a few such 'lessons' to help someone break a habit of persistent teasing – but it is worth it in the long run.

In summary, being reprimanded or criticized is likely to hit the playback button on many childhood tapes and bring out much of the old feelings of guilt, shame, inadequacy, resentment, anger, frustration, and so on. Accordingly, you will fight or flee as an automatic and learned response. You therefore need to drive a wedge between the 'attack' and your emotions.

The best way of staying emotionally detached is to remember that criticism is only someone else's opinion of you. Whether you agree or disagree with their observations, accept or reject their opinion, is up to you. If you decide that the criticism (the message not the packaging) is just, you might as well see what you can learn from it. If you decide that the criticism is unjust, you might as well see if you can alter the other person's opinion. If the reprimand or criticism comes in the shape of a persistent tease, either draw out the real problem so that it is in the open where you can both discuss it, or alternatively, show the other person where you are drawing the line. Even at the extreme, no-one can insult you without your permission.

Into whichever category the reprimand or criticism falls, the ideal solution is to resolve the issue and end up with a better working relationship than that which the interaction began.

A summary of being reprimanded or criticized is given in Figure 7.

Rights

Yours	Theirs
Respect, dignity Fair treatment Not to feel threatened Make reasonable mistakes Bring criticism out into the open Defend myself from unjust criticism Be listened to Good working relationships	Agreed standards of performance Attempt to change others' behaviour where it affects them Constructively criticize Be listened to Honesty

Self-talk

Criticism is only someone else's opinion of me or my behaviour. I can accept it, reject it, or attempt to modify it. My behaviour is not me; even if I have made a mistake, I am still alright.

Expectation

An open, honest and objective discussion concentrating on behaviour, not personalities. Possibly having to persevere to achieve that. Keeping emotions in check. A clear understanding of one another.

Behaviour

Plenty of listening, probing, self-disclosure and basic assertion. Showing empathy. Verbal judo to handle the teasers. Neutral/concerned tone of voice. Relaxed posture. Steady eye contact.

Outcome

Achieved	Avoided

Learning from a mistake
Strengthened, more open relationship
You feel alright
Other person feels alright
Personal credibility up
	No change in behaviour where a change
	    was necessary
	Weakened relationship
	You and possibly other person not
	    feeling alright

Figure 7 *Being reprimanded or criticized: summary.*

Chapter 11

HANDLING
AGGRESSIVE
PEOPLE

Aggression comes in many shapes and sizes, from physical attacks through verbally abusive onslaughts, to seemingly benign remarks that nevertheless touch a nerve. Common to all of them, however, is the desire to 'win' at someone else's expense, to undervalue them, or to put them down. In this chapter we look at verbal aggression and how to handle it.

To help you, this chapter is split into two parts. The first deals with 'heavy' verbal aggression, and the second with the 'lighter' form of verbal aggression often referred to as a 'put-down'.

'Heavy' verbal aggression

The first reaction of most people when confronted by heavy verbal aggression is shock. It is frequently unexpected, and takes us by surprise. This aspect of heavy verbal aggression tends to numb the response we would like to make – using our verbal problem solving skills – and trigger our fight or flight response.

Another feature of heavy verbal aggression also makes it difficult for us to respond rationally – the accompanying body language. Aggressive people tend to adopt an expansive posture; they tend to lower their eyebrows, set their jaw and stare hard; they wag or jab a pointed finger at us. In other words, they exhibit the same non-verbal signals with which impatient parents coerce their children. Recalling your data banks, therefore, the stimulus is perfect to replay some of those childhood tapes.

Remember, those tapes replay feelings and emotions. So what sort of feelings and emotions will well up inside someone on the receiving end of heavy verbal aggression? Fear, dislike, inferiority, injustice, anger and retaliation would be typical. Whether you then adopt fight or flight behaviour will probably depend on several factors, such as your self-image, what passes for acceptable behaviour within the culture of your organization, and probably also the hierarchical or status differences between you and the other person.

The most fundamental influence on whether you adopt a fight or flight response to heavy verbal aggression, however, will be your self-image. Is it your role in life to be spoken down to or to fight back, to always be 'unlucky' enough to be on the receiving end, or to be a rebel kicking against injustice? The surprise element of heavy verbal aggression makes it easy to react in your pre-programmed way.

In most circumstances, heavy verbal aggression will come from people senior to you because they have the immunity of status to feel safe in displaying such behaviour. While it could also come from people junior to you, it is less likely to do so, as being a martyr does not pay the household bills. So the examples used here concentrate on handling aggression from people senior to you.

If their behaviour triggers your fight response, after your initial shock, you will fight back with just as much aggression, not let them succeed in talking to you like that, or however you prefer to describe it. In our terminology you will respond aggressively.

Your response may include reciprocal gestures and tactics – confrontational posture, raised volume, finger pointing, exaggerations, generalizations, sarcasm, etc. Perhaps you can visualize these mannerisms accompanying the following dialogue.

Example one

Situation

A senior manager reacts negatively to a report written by a junior manager. He bursts out of his office clutching the report as the junior manager is walking past in the corridor:

Senior manager:	'Smith! What the bloody hell's this?'
Junior manager:	'What's what . . . I don't know . . .'
Senior manager:	'This report. It's useless. Where did you write it, cloud bloody cuckoo land? We'll be the laughing stock of the entire company if this goes out.'

Junior manager:	'Now hang on a minute. I only followed the terms of reference you gave me.'
Senior manager:	'Terms of reference? I said it had to be practical.'
Junior manager:	'And creative. Correct me if I'm wrong but did you or did you not say you wanted something creative?'
Senior manager:	'Creative? This is so far out of court Walt Disney couldn't even use it.'
Junior manager:	'Look, don't criticize me just because you haven't got the guts to do anything radical.'

Well, there's another fine mess! Two managers who should be working in concert are now poles apart, and the relationship discordant in the extreme. The senior manager will probably do the report him or herself, thus losing any of the junior manager's ideas and alienating the junior manager to an even greater extent. Furthermore, I would not want to be the junior manager at annual appraisal time.

If, instead of fight, the other person's behaviour triggers your flight response, you will probably do your utmost to avoid the conflict, whatever the cost to yourself. Your response will probably include typically submissive gestures like avoidance of eye contact, uncomfortable fidgeting, excessive agreeing, and self-flagellation. Again, perhaps you can visualize these mannerisms accompanying the following dialogue.

Example two

Situation

As for Example one:

Senior manager:	'Smith! What the bloody hell's this?'
Junior manager:	'What's what . . . I don't . . .'
Senior manager:	'This report. It's useless. Where did you write it, cloud bloody cuckoo land? We'll be the laughing stock of the entire company if this goes out.'
Junior manager:	'Oh . . . I . . . er . . .
Senior manager:	'Don't you ever read terms of reference? I said I wanted something practical not something that belongs in a ruddy fairy tale.'
Junior manager:	'I'm sorry . . . I . . . er . . . thought you wanted something . . . er . . . creative.'
Senior manager:	'A few good ideas – *practical* ones. Not this codswallop. You don't think, that's your trouble.'
Junior manager:	'No . . . I . . .'
Senior manager:	'Well . . . you'll just have to do it all again. Have it on my desk by noon tomorrow.'

Junior manager: 'But . . .'
Senior manager: 'And no buts. Noon tomorrow. And don't mess it
                       up this time.'

Once again, the two managers are poles apart. The senior manager's opinion of the junior manager has not changed, and the junior manager is probably going through all sorts of mental turmoil.

So if the suddenness of heavy verbal aggression tends to trigger a fight or flight response, and if neither response does anything to make the other person behave any better, it seems that you can only handle the situation effectively if you do two things:

- control your reaction so that you respond assertively
- behave in a way that encourages the other person to behave assertively as well.

If you can achieve these aims there is a good chance that you will also resolve the problem in a mutually satisfactory manner, end up feeling alright about yourself, and having effectively 'educated' the other person in that the best way to try and influence you is to do so assertively.

The sequence of actions most likely to achieve this outcome is:

1.	Fogging	This will help you stay calm by buying you time. Furthermore, as you restate their concerns you can do so in a more rational way. Even if you repeat what they have said word for word, they may continue in a way that throws more light on their concerns.
2.	Probing	Their continued talking may act as a pressure release valve on their emotions. It also helps you remain 'detached' and, if you ask the right questions, it may also encourage them to behave more rationally/assertively by stripping away some of the exaggerations, generalizations and sarcasm so beloved by aggressive people.
3.	Basic assertion	Once you know what problem you are dealing with you can state how you see it/feel about it/what you would like to happen, as appropriate.
4.	Broken record	You can stand your ground on it . . .
5.	Workable compromise or point out the consequence	. . . until a satisfactory compromise can be agreed. Alternatively, if the other person refuses to budge you can explain the consequences of a stalemate.

Example three

Situation

As for Examples one and two:

Senior manager:	'Smith What the bloody hell's this?'
Junior manager:	'What's what . . . I don't . . .'
Senior manager:	'This report. It's useless. Where did you write it, cloud bloody cuckoo land? We'll be the laughing stock of the entire company if this goes out.'
Junior manager:	'There's a problem with the report?' (fogging).
Senior manager:	'I'll say there's a ruddy problem with it. How can I take suggestions like these to the Board. They'll think I've gone bonkers.'
Junior manager:	'The ideas are a little unusual for their purpose.' (fogging)
Senior manager:	'Unusual? I'll say they're unusual.'
Junior manager:	'You expected something less radical.' (fogging).
Senior manager:	'Of course I did. These are conservative people we're dealing with. If we're going to change them we've got to do it one step at a time.'
Junior manager:	'Are all the ideas too radical or could any of them be satisfactorily modified?' (probing)
Senior manager:	'The new logo and reorganization of Customer Services may have some potential, but putting *everyone* through the same training programme and toll-free telephone calls from customers will just be thrown out.'
Junior manager:	'So some of the ideas are worthy of discussion. It may be that I misunderstood what you meant by being creative. If we run through the report together perhaps we could look at how to re-present it.' (self-disclosure, basic assertion)
Senior manager:	'You should know! You've been around long enough.'
Junior manager:	'Perhaps I should. However, I would still feel more confident of producing what you feel the Board will accept if we could work together on it.' (negative assertion, broken record).
Senior manager:	'But I shouldn't have to spoon-feed my managers.'
Junior manager:	'No, you shouldn't. That's why I'm not asking for that. I just see the benefit of us ensuring that we're on the same wavelength. If not, my next draft of the report may still not hit the nail on the head, as you see it.' (fogging, broken record, pointing out a consequence)
Senior manager:	'OK, but I need it by noon tomorrow.'
Junior manager:	'So if we can get together before lunch, I can re-write it this afternoon, have it typed in the morning and it'll be ready by noon.'

Senior manager: 'OK, let's meet at eleven.'

As a result of this dialogue, the two managers are going to work together to produce a report the Board will accept. Their mutual understanding will improve. The junior manager's self-esteem remains intact, and he or she can even have the satisfaction of having been the architect of a solution which both of them will find worthwhile.

As for the tactics in handling aggressive people, did you notice how the fogging helped the junior manager resist the temptation to join in? And how it also encouraged the senior manager to be more explicit about the problem – a trend which the probing continued? All of which enabled the junior manager to state how he or she felt about the situation and guide the senior manager towards a solution.

It is probably worth pointing out that, being a concocted example, it had a happy ending. Real life will not always be like that. There are two points, however, which I believe are worth making. First, while adopting this approach does not guarantee a successful outcome, it at least gives you a sporting chance. Allowing your fight or flight responses unlimited freedom guarantees failure. Second, in handling aggression, you have two aims – to respond assertively yourself, and to encourage the other person to also behave assertively. If you cannot achieve the latter aim, you can at least be 100% successful in the former. You can be in total control of yourself and, as a result, feel alright about yourself. This comment is not intended to induce feelings of self-satisfaction. There is a practical reason for it. The more you feel alright about yourself, the more your self-talk, expectations and behaviour will be positive.

Put-downs

Just as 'heavy' verbal aggression is a problem because it is sudden, put-downs are a problem because they are usually mild. We *want* to respond to them, however, because while the put-down might appear small, the underlying attitudes are still robbing us of our rights. So, while a put-down is apparently very small, it is nonetheless aggressive. It is still someone trying to win at your expense, to undervalue you.

Put-downs are usually short and indirect, and they occur much more frequently than the heavy verbal aggression described above. They can take many forms.

Type of put-down	*Example*
Nagging	'Don't tell me you're *still* working on that report?!'
Making decisions on your behalf	'If I were you I'd face up to it and find a new job.'

Patronizing	'That'll probably be too difficult for you. You'd better let me help.'
Stereotyping you	'Well, that's just typical of someone in your position.'
Raising doubts about your judgment	'You don't honestly think anyone's going to take you seriously do you?'
Describing you or your actions in exaggerated and/or emotional terms	'You're talking absolute and undiluted rubbish!'

If heavy verbal aggression is a blunt instrument, a put-down is a sharp knife. Volume and surprise are not material to its success. Its cutting edge lies in its sarcastic, belittling or dismissive tone. As a result, they are tricky rather than difficult to handle.

Most recipients see them for what they are – a thinly veiled verbal attack. We know, however, that if we respond as our emotions prompt us to, we are in danger of being accused of over-reacting or being emotional.

Example four

Situation

A manager is discussing with a colleague a forthcoming meeting which will be difficult. The colleague would really like to be given all the glory for himself:

Manager:	'It's going to be a difficult meeting. There's bound to be a lot of flak flying. Apparently, they're fielding their top negotiator.'
Colleague:	'That'll probably be too difficult for you. You'd better let *me* handle it.'
Manager:	'I'm quite *capable* of handling it *myself*. THANK YOU!'
Colleague:	'OK, OK, keep your hair on! I'm only trying to help. Just don't ask me for any help when it all goes wrong, that's all.'

The manager's reaction is understandable but not very productive. For all we know, the colleague has some good advice tucked away which will now remain unavailable to the manager.

An alternative response is to allow the put down to confirm a negative self-image, as in Example Five.

Example five

Situation

As for Example four:

Manager:	'It's going to be a difficult meeting. There's bound to be a lot of flak flying. Apparently they're fielding their top negotiator.'
Colleague:	'That'll probably be too difficult for you. You'd better let *me* handle it.'
Manager:	'Oh . . . I was . . . sort of thinking . . . I'd do it myself . . . er . . .'
Colleague:	'Take my advice. Whoever asked you to take it on wasn't doing you any favours. With all due respect, I've seen people like you get eaten alive in these meetings.'
Manager:	'Er . . . well . . . if you could help a bit, I . . .'
Colleague:	'If I were you, I'd back down on this one. You leave it to me.'
Manager:	'Oh . . . er . . . OK.'

Our manager was well and truly put-down there because the put-down confirmed a self-image and expectation that the meeting would be too difficult. No amount of adequate preparation will overcome that hurdle, so the colleague's attempted manipulation succeeded.

The aim of handling a put-down is the same as when handling heavy verbal aggression – to respond assertively, and to encourage the other person to also behave assertively. The approach, however, is slightly different. It requires the use of probing and basic assertion, or a combination of the two.

Example six

Situation

As for Examples four and five:

Manager:	'It's going to be a difficult meeting. There's bound to be a lot of flak flying. Apparently they're fielding their top negotiator.'
Colleague:	'That'll probably be too difficult for you. You'd better let *me* handle it.'

Manager: 'What makes you think it'll be too difficult for me?'
                (probing)
Colleague: 'I've seen these meetings before. People like you get eaten
                alive in them.'
Manager: 'How do you mean – people like me?' (probing)
Colleague: 'You've got no real negotiating experience. Their top
                negotiator will use all sorts of ploys and gambits to put
                you on the defensive.'
Manager: 'Like what?' (probing)
Colleague: 'What is this, a lesson or something?'
Manager: 'It could be. I intend handling the meeting myself but I'll
                welcome any advice you may have.' (basic assertion)

In this example I deliberately employed probing to demonstrate how a put-down situation can be turned into a beneficial one – for both parties. The manager should learn to handle the meeting successfully, and the colleague should have learned that to achieve his or her way in a future situation, a direct (assertive) approach may be better. For example:

'Meetings like that can be very difficult for inexperienced negotiators. They'll employ all sorts of ploys and gambits to get the upper hand. How would you feel if I volunteered to handle it on your behalf?'

Some attempted put-downs are less manipulative and purely dismissive, and are often dealt with sufficiently by using basic assertion to signal that the put down has not worked. For example:

Put-down	*Response*
'Don't tell me you're *still* working on that report?'	'Yes, I am'
'If I were you I'd face up to it and find a new job.'	'I like my job so I'd rather achieve a solution where I am.'
'That'll probably be too difficult for you. You'd better let me help.'	'Thank you, but I believe I can handle it.'
'Well that's just typical of someone in your position.'	'It's the way I'm acting now. Whether it's typical or not is irrelevant.'
'You don't think anyone's going to take you seriously do you?'	'Yes. That's why I suggested it.'
'You're talking absolute and undiluted rubbish.'	'I believe I'm not.

Whether you employ probing or basic assertion usually depends on whether to achieve your aims you simply need to signal that the attempted put-down has not worked, or whether you need to discover the reasons for it. In the former case, basic assertion will probably be sufficient. In the latter case, probing is essential.

Whichever approach you adopt, please pay special attention to the tone of your voice. You will soon see what I am driving at if you say the following sentence in three ways – to rebuke the other person, to sound hurt, and to gently enquire:

'How do you mean – people like me?'

One final point – bear in mind that we are all learning beings. The significance of this point is, first, that where you have encountered aggressive people in the past, you may have 'learned' how to react to them. Perhaps you avoid them as much as possible, or avoid standing up for yourself in case they are aggressive towards you, or maybe you misconstrue even innocent remarks from them and retaliate without thinking?

Second, this point also suggests that people who frequently behave aggressively towards you can learn not to – but you may have to persevere. In the interim, you may have to be content with achieving your first aim of responding assertively yourself.

A summary of handling aggressive people is given in Figure 8.

Rights

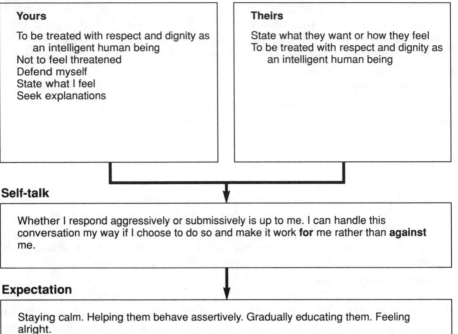

Yours

To be treated with respect and dignity as
    an intelligent human being
Not to feel threatened
Defend myself
State what I feel
Seek explanations

Theirs

State what they want or how they feel
To be treated with respect and dignity as
    an intelligent human being

Self-talk

Whether I respond aggressively or submissively is up to me. I can handle this
conversation my way if I choose to do so and make it work **for** me rather than **against**
me.

Expectation

Staying calm. Helping them behave assertively. Gradually educating them. Feeling
alright.

Behaviour

Fogging, probing and listening, basic assertion; and, if necessary, broken record and
pointing out a consequence. Neutral posture. Neutral tone of voice. Neutral facial
expression. Steady eye contact.

Outcome

Achieved

You feel alright
Purpose of aggression failed
Probable positive outcome
Possible 'education' of other person

Avoided

Soured relationship
Diminished self-esteem
Negative repercussions

Figure 8 *Handling aggressive people: summary.*

Chapter 12

HANDLING SUBMISSIVE PEOPLE

It is a common fallacy that submissive people do not need 'handling'. 'Surely, as they tend to do as they're told', the argument goes, 'all you have to do is treat them assertively and everything will be alright?' Not so – as you will discover as you read on.

First, consider what you already know. Submissive people tend to avoid conflict even at the expense of themselves; they acknowledge other people's rights but not their own; they undervalue their own contribution and exaggerate other people's. Submissive behaviour has a persistent pay-off; submissive people absolve themselves from taking action on the basis that, as they will fail anyway they might as well do so before they begin and save all the effort of trying! They can adopt cynicism as a line of least resistance, and feel justified in doing so. They can avoid responsibility and 'enjoy' the easier life of a 'loser'. *WARNING* – if any of this sounds attractive, beware of the price submissive people pay. They perpetually under-achieve, and they rarely feel alright about themselves.

This sort of inferiority and insecurity manifests itself in recognizable behaviour. Submissive people tend to be quietly spoken. They take a long time to get to the point. Their speech is hesitant and rambling. They are quick to agree (whether they really agree or not). They belittle themselves and their contribution, both actual and potential. They will easily side with the majority or a more dominant personality (not hard to find). As far as team effort is concerned, they can be well-meaning passengers or skilful manipulators – so let us look at handling both categories.

The well meaning sort tend to be low contributors because they stay well within the safe zone. They are also low in initiative for the same reason.

Hence, with all but safely predictable tasks they seek guidance, sometimes delegating upwards, and need constant emotional support to indicate that what they are doing is acceptable.

Situation

A member of staff has delayed a report until perilously close to the deadline. One section of the report requires information from the sales department. The staff member defers potential conflict with Sales, despite the near certainty that to do so will result in more conflict with both his/her manager *and* Sales. That, however, is the way submissive people operate. They defer potentially uncomfortable confrontations even though the problems will only snowball, resulting in an even bigger confrontation and more discomfort later on.

Most managers, understandably, would be annoyed and let it show. Consequently, the staff member may find it even more difficult to own up to problems or deliver bad news in future. The manager's opinion of the staff member will probably deteriorate, with the result that the staff member is 'not trusted' with challenging or important assignments and so retracts into the safe haven of mediocrity. The staff member's contribution is therefore well below its potential. Such situations need careful handling.

An alternative way of handling this situation is as follows:

Example one

Manager:	'How's that report coming along? You were going to let me see a draft before it goes out.'
Staff member:	'Well, . . . I'm afraid I . . . er . . . haven't quite got to that stage yet.'
Manager:	'This is later than we agreed. What's the problem?' (pointing out a discrepancy, probing)
Staff member:	'I'm sorry. I'm just having a bit of difficulty getting the information from Sales. They promised the information by Wednesday at the latest . . . I have chased them but they . . . er . . . said they were a bit pushed at the moment . . . I did try.'
Manager:	'The information hasn't arrived by the agreed time and your attempts at reminding them have been ignored.' (fogging)
Staff member:	'Yes.'
Manager:	'It's not easy communicating deadlines to a department as busy as Sales.' (empathy)
Staff member:	'I did try.'

Manager:	'I'm sure you did. What do you propose doing about it?' (empathy, probing)
Staff member:	'Well, . . . I'll just have to try again. . . . I suppose.'
Manager:	'Yes. We need to move fast because the deadline is so close. When will you contact them?' (basic assertion, probing)
Staff member:	'Now . . . er . . . yes, now.'
Manager:	'Good. How will you get them to move on it?' (probing)
Staff member:	'Er . . . I'll speak to the Sales Manager . . . let him know that the information is for a report to the Chief Executive, and that the information from his department is ridiculously late.'
Manager:	'Good. A suggestion, though . . . instead of telling him it's "ridiculously late", try "hasn't arrived when your staff said it would" . . . it's less emotive.' (supporting)
Staff member:	'Yes . . . right . . . I'll do that now.'
Manager:	'If you have any problems, I'll need to know straight away.'

In this example the manager did several things: he avoided 'attacking' the staff member; that would only exacerbate the problem in the staff member's eyes, and further reduce his or her self-esteem. The manager did this by using fogging and probing to stay emotionally 'detached'.

A further benefit of fogging and probing is that these two tactics combine to help the staff member re-state the problem from 'Sales Department won't send me the information to finish the report' to 'I haven't convinced Sales Department of the urgency of the situation.'

This not only helps the staff member 'own the problem', but also generates a solution. A final benefit of fogging and probing is that it reduces what for many managers is a natural 'parental' tendency to take over the problem. They thereby avoid adding to their own workload, stealing learning opportunities from their staff, and educating staff to delegate upwards. *In other words, the problem was turned into a coaching opportunity.* This is worth emphasizing.

So far, we have looked at fogging and probing as a kind of verbal judo whereby you turn the tables on the other person. The eminent psychologist Carl Rogers, however, sees them as tools for coaching and counselling. He describes five behaviours displayed by people in coaching/counselling situations.

Behaviour	*Description*	*Example*
Evaluative	You pass judgement on the other person	'You're just too soft with these people'
Interpretive	You identify a cause of the problem without checking your facts	'Your trouble is you can't tell when people are leading you on.'

Supportive	You provide empathetic comments but little else	'I know . . . Sales are always difficult to handle.'
Probing	You seek more information	'Who did you speak to in Sales and what did you say to them?'
Reflective (ie fogging)	You repeat back or paraphrase what they have just said to you	'Your attempts to remind them have been ignored.'

The five behaviours are listed in descending order of frequency but in *ascending* order of effectiveness. In this type of situation, most people would display evaluative behaviour passing judgement on the staff member, even though it would not achieve what they want. Few people would probe or fog even though they are the best ways of getting the staff member to own the problem and generate a practical solution. Add a measured amount of support and empathy and you have a staff member whose self-talk is shifting from 'I always get the rotten jobs' to 'I think I can crack this one.'

The second category of a submissive person is the skilful manipulator. Like the well-meaning passenger, they too suffer low self-esteem, but it tends to manifest itself in them trying to avoid what they see as uncomfortable situations by using their manipulative skills to wriggle out of them, leaving someone else with the problem.

Example two

Situation

It's Wednesday and a manager is about to leave the office for a business trip, returning Friday afternoon. She needs some data analyzed ready for her return and, everyone in her department being exceptionally busy, she decides to delegate it to the least pressured subordinate:

Manager:	'John, as you know, I'm out of the office until Friday afternoon. I need this data analyzed by my return. I'd like you to handle it please.'
Staff member:	'Oh . . . well . . . er . . .'
Manager:	'You seem unsure. What's wrong?'
Staff member:	'Well . . . that . . . er . . . may leave me with a bit of a problem.'
Manager:	'What sort of problem?'
Staff member:	'Well, I'm not exactly sure I've . . . er . . . got time.'
Manager:	'John, we're all busy. It's an exceptionally busy time of year but I need this data analyzed.'
Staff member:	'Well . . . leave it with me . . . I'll do my best.'

Manager:	'John, the timescale on it is critical. I need to know. If it isn't ready by Friday afternoon, I can't write my part of the company's annual report. I need to know.'
Staff member:	'Well . . . as I said . . . I'll do my best . . . I usually muddle through somehow.'
Manager:	'Forget it. I'll take it with me. That way I'll *know* it'll be done.'

One up to the skilled manipulator! He knew that the manager could not risk the analysis not being ready, and combined that with generating sympathy for the willing workhorse so that the manager would retrieve the problem.

The manager could, however, have handled the situation like this:

Example three

Manager:	'John, as you know, I'm out of the office until Friday afternoon. I need this data analyzed by my return. I'd like you to handle it please.'
Staff member:	'Oh . . . well . . . er.'
Manager:	'You seem unsure. What's wrong?' (empathy, probing)
Staff member:	'Well . . . that . . . er . . . may leave me with a bit of a problem.'
Manager:	'What sort of problem?' (probing)
Staff member:	'Well I'm not exactly sure I've . . . er . . . got time.'
Manager:	'I appreciate we're all very busy at the moment but I need to know. Are you saying it won't be done?' (empathy, basic assertion, probing)
Staff member:	'Oh no . . . no . . . I just can't guarantee it.'
Manager:	'I know it isn't easy but I need to know one way or the other.' (empathy, broken record)
Staff member:	'Well, . . . I'll do my best.'
Manager:	'John if it isn't ready by Friday afternoon I can't write my part of the company's annual report. I need to know one way or the other.' (pointing out a consequence, broken record)
Staff member:	'Yes . . . OK . . . It'll be done.'
Manager:	'Would you like me to run through your in-tray with you to mark priorities because, as I say, I need this analysis by Friday?' (probing, broken record)
Staff member:	'No . . . that's fine. It'll be ready Friday lunchtime.'
Manager:	'Thanks.'

Examples two and three begin the same way. The main difference is in the manager's use of broken record. This lets the staff member know that the issue will not go away. He has to address it, not sidestep it.

In summary, then, submissive people need handling too, some to bring out the best in them and others to stop them wriggling out of their duties. Assertive managers exercise their rights to good performance from their staff, to staff who own the problem, and to open and honest communication. They also help staff members stand up for their rights such as not feeling threatened, being listened to, treated fairly, and support from their boss.

A summary of handling submissive people is given in Figure 9.

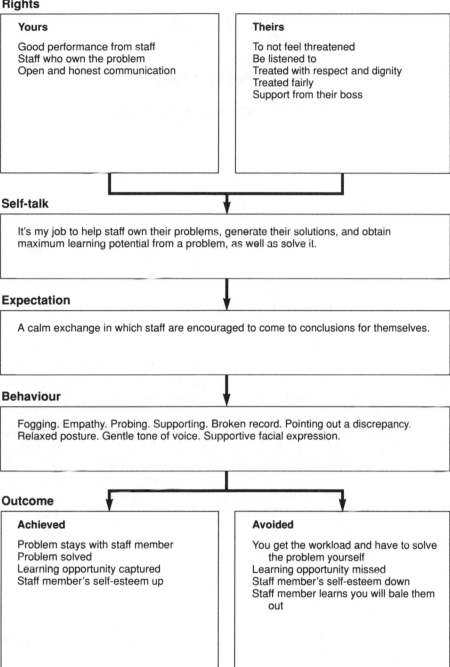

Figure 9 *Handling submissive people: summary.*

Chapter 13

HANDLING RESENTMENT

On courses, when I ask people to write their own role-play exercises, there is one topic that comes up with surprising regularity – handling people who resent your promotion! It comes in two main categories.

First, having to work with a managerial colleague with whom you competed for your current post, or who regarded themselves as the natural successor to the post's previous incumbent. In other words, you got 'their' job and they don't like it. Second, being promoted *in situ* so that you are now in charge of former work colleagues and have to make the progression from team member to team leader. This latter category seems to be increasingly common amongst executives as companies cut back on the cost of relocation. It has long been common at junior levels and in small companies. Both categories give rise to a dilemma in the minds of the promoted managers. How do they establish their authority without alienating their former colleague(s)?

The aggressive response is thankfully rare. Most people know instinctively that to adopt a 'Right you lot, I'm in charge now!' approach is hardly the best way to win friends and influence people. The submissive response is by far the most common.

When dealing with former colleagues or colleagues who wanted the same job, promoted managers experience the following sorts of self-talk:

'Jean was equally suited to this post. I was lucky to get it.'

'If Bill had got this job instead of me I'd feel hurt and resentful. I'd better treat him very gently.'

'I'm going to feel awkward giving these people instructions.'

'How *can* I exert my authority; they know me too well. They know all my weaknesses.'

The consequence of these thoughts is that in real life as well as in role-play exercises, recently promoted managers:

- apologize for having been promoted
- suggest it was due to the luck of the draw
- admit they cannot think why the assessment panel selected them
- display self-conscious and submissive behaviour when delegating, giving instructions, resolving conflict and/or handling aggression/put-downs,

all of which is designed to minimize their own discomfort when addressing their former colleague(s). Conversations typically go like this:

Example one

Situation

Bill and Joyce were colleagues who both applied for the vacant position of manager of the department in which they work. Bill has been there five years to Joyce's two, was once regarded as the previous manager's natural successor, and was surprised and hurt when Joyce got the job. Joyce was selected because of her previous experience with another employer, and her more creative approach was regarded by the assessment panel as important to the department's future. Joyce and Bill are having their first meeting since Joyce's promotion:

Joyce:	'Well . . . here we are then.'
Bill:	'Yes . . . here we are.'
Joyce:	'I must say . . . I never thought I'd be sitting here.'
Bill:	'No, neither did I.'
Joyce:	'I don't really understand why they chose me.'
Bill:	'. . . .'
Joyce:	'I mean . . . with your experience and all . . . I really thought you'd get it.'
Bill:	'I was certainly hoping to.'
Joyce:	'I guess I was just lucky.'
Bill:	'Yes.'

Bearing in mind what was said in Part One about behaving by default rather than by design, I ask course participants what behaviour they consider will actually make the unsuccessful candidate feel worse about not getting the job? You guessed it, the successful candidate apologizing for having been promoted, suggesting it was luck, and so on.

So what should the successful manager do in such a situation? First, think positively:

> 'The assessment panel are experienced at selecting candidates. I must have the qualities they are looking for.'

> 'If Bill had got this job instead of me I'd feel hurt and resentful. I'd better prove to him, therefore, that I have the qualities to be his boss.'

> 'Giving my former colleagues instructions may make me feel uncomfortable – but everyone has a learning curve in a new job and I'm no exception.'

> 'I *can* exert my authority because I know their strengths and weaknesses *and* how to get through to them.'

Positive thoughts lead to positive expectations and positive behaviour.

Example two

Joyce:	'Thank you for coming in, Bill. We need to discuss budgets but before we do, there's another matter I'd like to raise.' (signposting)
Bill:	'Yes, what's that?'
Joyce:	'As you know, we both applied for this job. I was selected. I feel that if the situation had been reversed, I might feel a bit uncomfortable about reporting to a former colleague. So I wanted to ask how you felt about it.' (self-disclosure, probing)
Bill:	(Abruptly) 'Fine.'
Joyce:	'It's important to me personally and to the successful functioning of the Department that we get on OK, so I believe it's important that we continue the good relationship we've always enjoyed. So are you sure?' (self-disclosure, broken record)
Bill:	'Well, since you mention it, I don't feel too good about it.'
Joyce:	'In what way?' (probing)
Bill:	'I'm bloody disappointed! I wanted the job didn't I?'
Joyce:	'I'm sure you are disappointed, but how do you feel about

me? Can we still work well together?' (fogging, probing, broken record)

Bill: 'I could have done a damn good job. I've been in the department for five years.'

Joyce: 'You could. However, the appointment's been made so I need to know if we can work together.' (fogging, basic assertion, broken record)

Bill: '. . . . It won't be easy, Joyce. I'll be honest with you, I really wanted the job. I feel hurt that I didn't get it. I'm not saying you won't do a good job. I'm sure you will. I think it'll just take time for me not to feel disappointed. . . . In answer to your question, yes. We've got on well together for two years now, I certainly won't do anything to spoil it.'

Joyce: 'Bill, that's good news. Thank you. If ever you feel any different will you let me know?' (basic assertion, probing)

Bill: 'Sure . . . and thanks for raising the matter. I'm glad we've cleared the air.'

Let us examine Joyce's approach. She used signposting to keep the communication clear. She used self-disclosure to show that she was being open and honest, and to encourage Bill to reciprocate. She used basic assertion to state what she wanted or how she felt. She was economic with her words getting to the point quickly. Fogging acknowledged what Bill had said, but did not dwell on it. Probing involved Bill and got him talking, and broken record let him know that the issue would not go away until it was resolved. Finally, Joyce never apologized for having been promoted.

The result is that her personal credibility is probably up in Bill's eyes. Bill's resentment has probably diminished. Joyce has tackled a difficult issue and succeeded with obvious benefits for her own self-image.

A summary of handling resentment is given in Figure 10.

Rights

Yours		Theirs
Open and honest communication Support from staff		Speak freely without fear of recrimination To be listened to To be counselled

Self-talk

Resentment does not go away of its own accord. It needs to be brought out into the open and addressed. I may hear some things which make me uncomfortable – but they are just someone else's opinion.

Expectation

To persevere for an open and honest conversation; to be emotionally detached but also understanding; to resolve the issue.

Behaviour

Signposting. Self-disclosure. Basic assertion. Fogging. Probing. Broken record. Brevity. Non-emotional responses and facial expressions. Moderate eye contact.

Outcome

Achieved		Avoided
Resentment tackled Personal credibility up Self-image up Better relationships		Cause of resentment justified Resentment festers Personal credibility dented Poor relationships

Figure 10 *Handling resentment: summary.*

Chapter 14

DELEGATING AN UNPLEASANT TASK

Delegating is one of the most frequent reasons for contact between managers and staff. How you approach it reveals the beliefs you have about yourself and about them.

Managers who believe they are the 'top dog' and their staff are simply order fodder delegate in one way, while managers who believe they have to 'buy' the goodwill of their staff, delegate in another. Delegation is a 'shop window' of your management style. It says a lot about *you*.

Nowhere is this more true than where a recently appointed manager is delegating an unpleasant task. (The same could be true for an experienced manager. I have chosen an inexperienced manager as an illustration because the feelings are intensified.) The main feeling is fear of rejection.

Rejection is something that makes people feel uncomfortable. We know how we felt as a child when parents withdrew their affection (however temporarily), or when playmates ostracized us. This feeling is intensified for a recently appointed manager because they are still establishing their personal credibility. Their authority is on the line. Asking someone to do something unpleasant raises all their doubts because it is a situation where there could be potential conflict. Aggressive and submissive managers have different responses to conflict.

Aggressive managers adopt a 'no prisoners' or a 'shoot first and ask questions later' approach. They know they have to establish their credibility, and see delegating an unpleasant task as a trial of strength from which they must emerge victorious. Their approach is therefore abrupt and one-sided.

Example one

Situation

A manager has a task to perform which, although important is mundane, time consuming and unpleasant. A thankless task if ever there was one. He decides to delegate it:

Manager:	'Fred, here's the file on the European Market. I want you to put the analysis together – I need it by Friday, OK?'
Staff member:	'But shouldn't Sally be doing that? She's got more experience of that sort of situation.'
Manager:	'I'm asking you to do it, OK?'
Staff member:	'It's a bit mundane though, are you sure there's . . .'
Manager:	'Look! Someone's got to do it and you're the one I've decided on. Now get a move on.'

There is no doubt that managers adopting this approach normally win the trial of strength. But what do they actually achieve? The task is delegated to the person they selected, and it may well be done satisfactorily. Their personal credibility is minimal, and staff motivation will be aimed at avoidance rather than participation. Such managers are helping alienate staff from their work, with the consequent impact on productivity discussed in Part One.

Submissive managers do not see the situation as a trial of strength but as an opportunity to buy co-operation. They use flattery, try to generate sympathy, or make the other person feel responsible for the consequences of not accepting the task.

Example two

Manager:	'Fred, thanks for popping in. Everything alright?'
Staff member:	'Yes, fine. And you? Everything alright with you?'
Manager:	'Oh . . . OK, yes . . . just fine. . . .'
Staff member:	'Good.'
Manager:	'I was wondering if you could possibly do a small job for me.'
Staff member:	'Well I'm a bit pushed at the moment actually.'
Manager:	'Oh yes . . . of course . . . I know . . . we're all very busy at the moment. . . . But it's this analysis of the European Market. It's a trifle late, you see.'

Staff member:	'But shouldn't Sally be doing that? Europe's her responsibility.'
Manager:	'Yes, I know but she's off on a course next week and must finish what she's currently doing before she goes.'
Staff member:	'It's just so ruddy boring. . . . When do you need it done by?'
Manager:	'Well . . . I was rather hoping to have it done by Friday actually.'
Staff member:	'Friday? That means I'll *really* have to burn the midnight oil on it!'
Manager:	'I'd do it myself, Fred, honest. But I've got this other deadline as well, you see.'
Staff member:	'Can't anyone else do it?'
Manager:	'But you're brilliant at these analyses, Fred. Everyone says how good you are at them. The boss himself said so.'
Staff member:	(Flicking through file) 'There's mountains of the stuff. It'll take ages.'
Manager:	'Please don't let me down on this Fred. I'm really counting on you. My neck'll be on the block if it isn't finished on time. I've always been able to rely on you in the past.'
Staff member:	'OK, OK.'
Manager:	'Oh thanks, Fred. I really appreciate it.'

On this occasion the manager has successfully bought the co-operation, but not much else. No personal credibility has been established, if anything it has been diminished. The staff member probably thinks of the manager as having little authority, and next time there is a potential confrontation the staff member may well be less accommodating.

So how would staff prefer to see it done? Well, they probably accept that managers have a right to delegate tasks, and that some of those tasks will be less pleasant than others. However, they want to be treated with respect and dignity as intelligent human beings. That means discussing with them why the task has to be done, why within that timescale, and why by them. That way they feel they are treated fairly. They also maybe want a chance to air their feelings about it, and to feel they have an element of control in what is happening to them. All these desires are evident in how an assertive manager would approach delegating an unpleasant task.

Example three

Manager:	'Thanks for coming in, Fred.'
Staff member:	'That's OK.'
Manager:	'Fred, we're all very busy at the moment. You no less than anyone else. However, I'm going to ask you to take on one more job which needs to be completed by Friday.' (empathy, signposting, basic assertion)
Staff member:	'Well, I *am* a bit pushed at moment. What job *is* it?'
Manager:	'The analysis of the European Market.'
Staff member:	'But that's Sally's responsibility!'
Manager:	'Ordinarily, it is. However, Sally's on a course next week, and I've agreed with her that I want all her outstanding jobs completed before she goes.' (negative assertion, basic assertion)
Staff member:	'But I'm up to my ears already!'
Manager:	'You're very busy but not all your jobs have such tight deadlines as this analysis. Also as you were in charge of the European Desk before Sally joined, you're experienced at doing it.' (fogging, basic assertion)
Staff member:	'But it's so ruddy boring. Page after page of statistics.'
Manager:	'There is a lot of it but you're experienced at doing the analysis. I want you to do it, Fred.' (fogging, broken record)
Staff member:	(Reluctantly) 'Alright. I'll do it.'
Manager:	'Thank you. But you're not happy about it, are you?' (probing)
Staff member:	'No.'
Manager:	'Is it just that it is a monotonous job or is there something else?' (probing)
Staff member:	'I just thought I'd left this sort of clerical work behind. It's like a step backwards.'
Manager:	'I feel the same myself on occasions. Are you worried that I'm going to make a habit of it?' (self-disclosure, probing)
Staff member:	'Frankly, yes. I don't want this to be the thin end of the wedge.'
Manager:	'I see how that would concern you. Jobs like this will come along from time to time. I'll do my best to ensure they are allocated in such a way that people accept them *and* that the jobs are done well; I *won't* compromise in quality. When there is a problem we'll sit down and discuss it openly, as we're doing now. How do you feel about that?' (empathy, basic assertion, probing)

Staff member: 'It sounds fair to me . . . and reassuring. I'll get started on this now. If I run into any problems can I come and see you?'

Manager: 'Yes please.'

Staff member: 'OK. Bye.'

This manager successfully delegated the task just like the other two managers but in a different way. Consider the following characteristics:

- *to the point quickly* without being abrupt. An oblique approach encourages people to 'smell a rat'. The suddenness of an abrupt approach could easily trigger the staff member's fight or flight response. Getting to the point quickly and calmly reduces the likelihood of contradictory signals coming from your body language.
- *being firm without being apologetic.* Standing firm on key issues without apologizing for doing so. Apologies in this situation will either look submissive or patronizing.
- *being empathetic.* Being aware of what it must look and feel like from their viewpoint, and showing that you are so aware.
- *seeking and acknowledging* their opinions and feelings and, where appropriate, addressing their concerns.

It is my belief that such an approach to delegating an unpleasant task would successfully establish a manager's authority and credibility as someone who is firm, considerate and, of great importance, a good listener.

A summary of delegating an unpleasant task is given in Figure 11.

Rights

Yours	**Theirs**
To decide who does what by when To be the final arbiter To be listened to	To be treated with respect and dignity To be treated as an intelligent human being To be treated fairly To say how they feel/state their opinions To be listened to To have at least some control over what is happening to them

Self-talk

Delegating an unpleasant task is an opportunity to establish myself as the sort of manager for whom staff feel respect and loyalty. It is also an opportunity to get to know someone better.

Expectation

A to-the-point discussion in which I remain firm but also encourage the member of staff to be open so that we can resolve jointly any problems.

Behaviour

Empathy. Signposting. Negative assertion. Fogging. Basic assertion. Probing. Broken record. Good eye contact. Neutral tone of voice. Relaxed, attentive posture. No unnecessary apologising.

Outcome

Achieved	**Avoided**
Successful delegation Staff member feels valued Personal credibility of manager enhanced Open and trusting relationship established	Task not delegated or only accepted begrudgingly Manager's personal credibility and possibly authority diminished Loyalty and motivation diminished

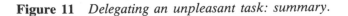

Figure 11 *Delegating an unpleasant task: summary.*

Chapter 15

RESOLVING CONFLICT

The traditional view of management, and hence much traditional management training, is one of managing down the line. Planning, organizing, directing and controlling staff; the style in which staff are managed; the skills with which they are led.

While this is all very well, it is only one view of what management is about. While considering the trends discussed in Part One (flatter, leaner organizations, devolved authority, matrix structures and rapid response to customer requirements), another view of management appears alongside the traditional one, i.e. that management is about *influencing* up, down and across organizational reporting lines. *Peer teamwork*, therefore, takes on as much significance as *staff motivation* in the repertoire of skills essential to modern management.

Interacting with staff is one thing. Even in democratic organizations their different position in the structure makes them susceptible to agreeing with the boss because of the difference in grade and the direct reporting relationship. Interacting with peers is another thing altogether.

Peers do not do as they are told. Frequently, not even as they are asked. Sometimes they are not even open to persuasion. Yet in the areas of cost reduction, productivity improvement and quality control, peer teamwork, synchronization between departments and mutual support are essential to organizational effectiveness. It is almost as if the propensity for conflict rises in direct proportion to the damage it can cause and, therefore, so does the need to resolve it.

That is why this chapter examines conflict between peers and not conflict between manager and staff. (Having said that, however, if you are experiencing conflict with your staff, this chapter will still be relevant if you hope to achieve a win/win outcome.)

Opportunities for conflict between management peers are rife. One department's attack on costs is another's quality problem; a quality drive in one area is an extra procedure in another; Marketing's sales push is Customer Relations' headache; Audit's desire for security provides problems from a customer for the sales staff. A Martian eavesdropping on many a management meeting would probably ask 'Who's winning?' (Sadly, but not surprisingly, the answer would be, 'the competition'.) Differences of opinion are inevitable, but conflict is not. The problem for many managers is that conflict is seen less like an area for discussion and more like a trial of strength, a tug-of-war where one side's gain is automatically another's loss.

We know that good managers are determined and will stick to their guns, even against overwhelming odds, if their belief in their principles and in the efficacy of their position is strong enough. Such people are usually admired.

Unfortunately, behaviour which is right in one situation is not necessarily appropriate to another. A simple distinction conveniently overlooked by macho managers who are out to win at all costs. Sadly, what they 'win' is their own way, which may not necessarily be what the organization needs to achieve its main objectives. Such managers are usually promoted. There builds up, therefore, an organizational culture of toughness, confrontation and tenacity, but with a belly-button focus that makes life easier for more broad-minded competitors.

But what is the alternative? In some organizations, peace and harmony are courted to such an extent that productivity is stifled. No decisions are taken unless consensus is assured and, because nobody wants to create problems, every attempt to design the proverbial racehorse is not only well behind schedule, it also results in the proverbial camel. Once again, the competition has an open goal.

But now a word of caution. I have highlighted two extremes. I have painted a picture using only black and white – no shades of grey – to make the points that:

- an adversarial/aggressive approach to conflict will detrimentally affect teamwork and commitment
- a submissive/consensus approach to conflict may only result in bland compromise
- neither approach achieves worthwhile results
- an assertive approach is what is required, because assertive people know how to stand their ground but they are also good listeners.

Example

Situation

ABC Systems is a computer company. Bob, the manager in charge of the Despatch Department, intends to cut costs by subcontracting deliveries to an independent trucking company. The contract would account for a substantial part of the trucking company's revenue, and they hope to secure the contract by submitting an exceptionally competitive tender. John, Sales Manager (North) has severely criticized Bob for the decision on the grounds that contract drivers will not take care of the product, nor treat customers respectfully; neither will they be reliable – all of which will have obvious repercussions for complaints and lost customers. John has demanded that Bob reverse his decision before the contract is signed. Bob has refused on the grounds that he cannot meet his budget targets unless he subcontracts. Their meeting collapsed when John stormed out. Sarah, Sales Manager (South), shares John's concerns, and has gone to discuss the matter with Bob.

Bob:	'Hi, Sarah, come in . . . but if John's asked you to use your feminine charms to get me to change my mind on subcontracting, you're wasting your time.'
Sarah:	'Thanks for the compliment. No he hasn't, however, I would like to discuss subcontracting with you.' (negative assertion, signposting)
Bob:	'I'm not changing my mind, Sarah. Subcontracting is the only way I can achieve my budget targets.'
Sarah:	'The decision is primarily financial.' (fogging)
Bob:	'Primarily. I'll be signing up a young company that is trying hard to do it right. We'll account for 30% of their turnover so I can strike a hard bargain. They won't risk losing that by upsetting us so I think that John's fears are unfounded.'
Sarah:	'They could be. I wasn't aware that you were under so much budget pressure.' (negative assertion, self-disclosure)
Bob:	'I'll say. The problem is that with our own drivers they spend a substantial amount of time doing nothing, waiting for deliveries to be made up. So I've been paying them for nothing a lot of the time. With subcontractors, I'll only pay when they're making deliveries.'
Sarah:	'I see. The reasons for the decision are much clearer now.' (empathy)
Bob:	'I tried explaining it to John but he just wouldn't listen.'
Sarah:	'I suppose not . . . How do you think customers will react?' (negative assertion, probing)

Bob:	'How do you mean? Surely as long as their computers get delivered on time, that's all they care about.'
Sarah:	'Punctuality is important but so are many other things.' (basic assertion)
Bob:	'Like what?'
Sarah:	'Computers are fragile things. Part of our promise to customers is that we'll take care of them from initial systems analysis to systems installation. We design quality systems, build quality computers and check that the quality is perfect, but if the truck driver manhandles the box . . . well!' (basic assertion)
Bob:	'I never thought of it from that point of view.'
Sarah:	'Our own drivers know the scene but a contractor's driver may not. Similarly, many of our clients are small businesses where the delivery driver speaks directly to the decision maker. Our own drivers are trained in customer care. Are the contractors?' (basic assertion, probing)
Bob:	'I don't know. I never thought of that either.'
Sarah:	'Bob, let me summarize the situation as I see it and perhaps you'll let me know if I've misunderstood anything.' (signposting)
Bob:	'Sure.'
Sarah:	'You're under pressure to cut costs and have decided to subcontract deliveries for that reason. I would rather you retained our own employed drivers for reasons of quality and customer care. In those respects, we're far apart.'
Bob:	'Yes . . . that sounds accurate.'
Sarah:	'I can appreciate your need to cut costs. It's good for the company. How do you feel about my concern for quality and customer care?' (empathy, probing)
Bob:	'It's fully understandable . . . and it's good for the company.'
Sarah:	'So while we're far apart on some things, we're actually very close on others. Can we agree that whatever happens it will be a lot easier all round if it's good for Despatch, Sales, Customers, Contractor and ABC Systems?' (probing)
Bob:	'Yes, but I don't see how we can bring all those diverse needs together.'
Sarah:	'It won't be easy but I don't see how we can afford not to.' (fogging, basic assertion)
Bob:	'Any thoughts?'
Sarah:	'Well, how about asking the haulage contractor to allocate regular drivers to us? If we're going to account for 30% of their revenue, that shouldn't be too difficult. If we have

regular drivers we can train them in the ABC culture, even put them through our customer care programme. As long as my customers are happy, I'll be happy.' (probing, self-disclosure)

Bob: 'Yes . . . yes . . . that might even keep John happy too. Hey, we currently survey our own drivers' performance with customers. Maybe we could get survey performance part of the contract with the haulage company. After all, the better they perform, the more likely we are to stick with them.'

Sarah: 'That's a great idea.' (basic assertion)

Bob: 'I'm meeting them tomorrow afternoon. Could you come along?'

Sarah: 'Sure, and John too?' (probing)

Bob: 'No, just you. I want the haulage company to agree to all this willingly, not get dragged into it kicking and screaming.'

It looks then that Sarah has succeeded where John failed. Bob concentrated on what he wanted (contractors), and John focused on what he wanted (no contractors). They had a tug-of-war and John, seeing that he wasn't going to win, dropped the rope and stormed out.

Sarah has adopted both a broader view and an assertive approach that has encouraged Bob to examine the same view. Her field of vision includes not only what she wants, but also what Bob wants and what the company needs (see Figure 12).

Neither of them would accept each other's demands, but could appreciate each other's position and they both readily agree on what the company needs.

John's tug-of-war approach was aggressive. He would not listen to Bob's views, nor accept that any approach other than his own was correct. As Bob could be equally aggressive, their conversation foundered. In contrast, Sarah's approach was to:

- use *verbal judo* to sidestep any attempted aggression from Bob
- carefully *signpost* the discussion and show *empathy* for Bob's position so that he would not misinterpret her approach
- *probe* carefully to uncover the motives for Bob's decision and how he felt about her proposals
- determine the characteristics of a successful outcome
- use *basic assertion* to state her position, but only after she had created a climate of mutual understanding
- concentrate on areas where *agreement* was natural

It is my belief that whether you are resolving conflict with a trade union,

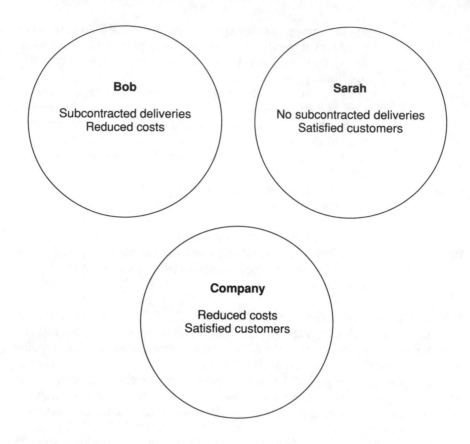

Figure 12   *Broader field of vision.*

a customer, a supplier, a colleague or a member of staff, your relationship will suffer if both of you do not feel comfortable with the outcome. Assert-ive people are more likely to achieve such outcomes than their aggressive or submissive counterparts because they are better at:

- resisting attempts to make them respond emotionally
- discovering the motives and priorities of the other person
- rethinking what a 'win' looks like to them
- encouraging the other person to rethink what their 'win' looks like
- standing their ground when they need to

It is in this way that their personal credibility amongst their staff, colleagues and superiors is enhanced.

A summary on resolving conflict is given in Figure 13.

Rights

> **Yours and Theirs**
>
> To do what is beneficial to you, your department and your company
> To do what is necessary to achieve objectives
> To expect co-operation from other members of the management for the good of the
>   company
> To question decisions
> To receive honest answers to sincere questions
> To make proposals and have them properly considered

Self-talk

> Conflict is only a solution waiting to be discovered. By listening, finding out and
> considering we'll probably discover a solution superior to one that we could invent
> individually.

Expectation

> To be patient, because conflict can trigger people's fight or flight response; to involve
> people and encourage them to be open; to be persistent in what I know to be right; to
> think laterally for a win/win solution.

Behaviour

> Empathy. Signposting. Negative assertion. Fogging. Probing. Basic assertion. Broken
> record. Proposing. Neutral tone of voice. Good eye contact.

Outcome

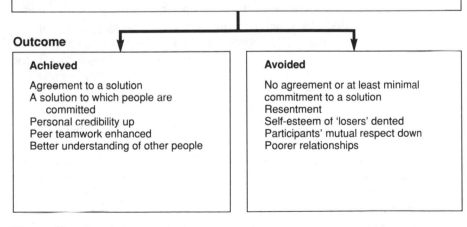

Achieved	**Avoided**
Agreement to a solution	No agreement or at least minimal
A solution to which people are	commitment to a solution
committed	Resentment
Personal credibility up	Self-esteem of 'losers' dented
Peer teamwork enhanced	Participants' mutual respect down
Better understanding of other people	Poorer relationships

Figure 13   *Resolving conflict: summary.*

Chapter 16

SAYING 'NO' TO A REQUEST

If you are one of these people who has no difficulty in saying 'No' to someone else, you will probably wonder what all the fuss is about. Yet refusing a request is something many people find intensely difficult. As a result, they often bring problems on themselves by accepting more than they can realistically accomplish; they agree to things, and subsequently regret doing so; they become known as a 'soft touch'.

The reasons for their reluctance to say how they really feel are many. They are worried that the other person may become angry and respond aggressively; they feel hurt or let down and blame them or regard them as selfish. They believe that to say 'No' will jeopardize their right to ask for anything in the future. They automatically assume that their needs are subordinate to other people's, and they therefore have no right to refuse. They accept unquestioningly other people's view of the 'rules' and assume that, even though they do not want to, co-operating must be the 'right' thing to do, otherwise the other person would not have asked them!

Another category of people who have difficulty saying 'No' are those who initially refuse the request, but who subsequently capitulate under pressure, or find themselves *outmanoeuvred* and so have to agree.

Whatever the reason for saying 'Yes' instead of 'No', such people find themselves inconvenienced at the expense of others, agreeing to things they would prefer not to and taking on tasks which, for one reason or another, they cannot handle.

Aggressive people have no such difficulties. They find it easy to say 'No', but they do so in a way that appears arbitrary or hostile. Consequently, they upset and alienate people for no valid reason. Submissive managers trying to exert their authority sometimes switch to this approach, but the vast majority either say 'Yes' or say 'No' in such a way that by their tactics and body language they appear evasive and untrustworthy.

It appears, therefore, that by their reluctance to be open, people who cannot or who say 'No' to a request inappropriately not only cause practical problems for themselves, but they lose personal credibility, erode their self-esteem, or both. This chapter, therefore, is about saying 'No' properly. To illustrate the approach we will take a situation and gradually build up to the approach I recommend.

Situation

A staff member will be getting married shortly and wants a day off to go and look at household goods in a sale. Departmental workload is at a peak, and one of your six staff is off sick.

Example one

Manager:	'Yes, Gordon?'
Staff member:	'I was wondering if I could possibly have tomorrow off there's . . .'
Manager:	'Are you crazy? Have you see what the backlog is this month? With Peter away sick it'll be a miracle if we shift it . . . What's it for anyway?'
Staff member:	'Oh . . . nothing.'

The manager's reaction may not be forgivable, but it is understandable. The last thing a manager in that position would want is a 20% reduction in available staff but, having said 'No' and then thought about it, the true colours were displayed – 'The staff member has no right to ask for time off during the current situation. How dare he try and make life more difficult for me than it already is? People *should* subordinate all personal matters to work matters.' On a subsequent occasion, Gordon's fiancée may well encourage him to telephone in sick, such will be the likely feeling of injustice at the manager's arbitrary decision.

Example two

Manager:	'Yes Gordon?'
Staff member:	'I was wondering if I could possibly have tomorrow off. There's a sale on at a local furniture store and Sally

	and I would like to see if we can pick up any bargains.'
Manager:	'Gordon . . . I'm going to say "No". With the current backlog running at 200 letters and with Bruce being off sick I don't think we can manage. It's unfortunate and I'm sure that you and Sally will feel bad about it, but I hope you can see things from my position . . . Sorry.'
Staff member:	'Oh . . . OK.'

Although toned down dramatically from Example one, the effect on Gordon is still negative. This is primarily for two reasons. First, the manager's attempt at signposting was wholly misplaced. Instead of clarifying the communication process it confused it, because after the word 'No' Gordon was too busy wondering why/speculating on how Sally would take the news/ considering when else he could get there, and so on, to listen to the manager's perfectly reasonable and empathetic explanation. Second, Gordon, instead of being involved, was effectively on the receiving end of a small lecture.

Example three

Manager:	'Yes, Gordon?'
Staff member:	'I was wondering if I could possibly have tomorrow off. There's a sale on at a local furniture store and Sally and I would like to see if we can pick up any bargains.'
Manager:	'Oh . . . er . . . Gordon, it's a bit difficult at the moment, what with Bruce being off sick . . . and there's still quite a backlog at the moment, a bit over 200 letters actually, and well . . . what do you think senior management will say if they wander in, see piles of backlog and two empty desks, hey? And, to be honest, I know you're probably a special case getting married and all that, but what would happen if someone else then wanted a day off? Before we know where we are we're running on 50% efficiency. And between you and me, the boss has said he'll take a pretty dim view of anyone taking leave in the current situation so . . . you know . . .'
Staff member:	'You don't think I can then?'
Manager:	'Probably better if you don't actually.'

This manager has said 'No' after a fashion. It was long and rambling, and because so many reasons for the refusal were put forward it is difficult to tell, first, which is the main reason, and second, if he or she is being honest.

This latter point is a common mistake. People think that by stacking up a large number of reasons, their argument becomes more powerful. In fact, the reverse is true; a single compelling reason sounds like a single compelling reason; half a dozen compelling reasons for saying 'No' sound like a string of excuses.

Example four

Manager:	'Yes, Gordon?'
Staff member:	'I was wondering if I could possibly have tomorrow off. There's a sale on at a local furniture store and Sally and I would like to see if we can pick up any bargains.'
Manager:	'Oh . . . er . . . Gordon, it's a bit difficult at the moment what with Bruce being off sick and . . .'
Staff member:	'I know. I wouldn't ask ordinarily, it's just that with the wedding coming up shortly we need to get some furniture.'
Manager:	'I'm not trying to be awkward, Gordon, it's just that we do have quite a backlog, you know.'
Staff member:	'As I said, I wouldn't ask if it wasn't for the wedding. With finances the way they are, we're having to hunt for bargains.'
Manager:	'I'm just bothered what other people will think if I start agreeing to days off with the backlog situation the way it is.'
Staff member:	'I don't get married every year . . . and Sally's set her heart on a three piece suite. If we leave it until the weekend we'll miss it.'
Manager:	'You're not leaving me much choice . . . OK.'

Gordon was *not* allowing the manager much choice. He used the broken record technique to good effect, and then finished off with a bit of manipulation. By the time the manager had 'used up' his/her third reason for not wanting to grant a day's leave, the ice was beginning to get thin. The way was then clear for Gordon to make the manager feel responsible for Sally's potential disappointment.

The manager could have handled Gordon quite well by refusing to accept responsibility for his and Sally's predicament, and by using the broken record technique to stand firm.

So, in the four examples we have seen so far, the main problems have been as follows:

- Example one – aggressive and apparently arbitrary refusal.
- Example two – a sudden refusal with reasons and empathy delivered

afterwards when they are bound to fall on stony ground. Gordon still feels hard done by.
- Example three – a typically submissive response – a long rambling refusal in which the 'No' was deferred and never actually arrived at.
- Example four – the manager was stumped by Gordon's persistence and guilt-inducing manipulation technique.

Each problem points to a way in which refusing a request can be made more efficient.

Here is a plan for saying 'No'. You will not need all of it on every occasion, but for reasons of explanation, here it is in detail:

- *Probe* – why have they made their request? What are the reasons for it? This will not only help you consider how you respond, but *proves* that your answer, when it comes, has been considered. Furthermore, it may help them appreciate the significance to you of their request. Finally, it 'signals' that you will not be 'bounced' into agreement.
- *Signposting – DON'T* – saying 'No' is the one time when signposting actually hinders the communication process, because your subsequent explanation usually falls on a preoccupied mind – the occupation having been triggered by your signposting.
- *K.I.S.S.* – Keep It Short and Simple. A long rambling justification may relieve your conscience, but it will look devious. The other person will feel they are being fobbed off. A concise response has much more credibility. So, if you feel you *should* justify your response, a single compelling reason carries significantly more weight than half a dozen reasons.
- *Workable compromise* – if appropriate, state what you *can* do. Very few requests require a 'Yes' or 'No' response. For example, 'I can't stay late that day; however, I could work through my lunch break, or 'I won't get all the report done today; however, if you could write the conclusion we can still finish it.'

    It is worth pointing out the significance of the word 'however' when suggesting a compromise or alternative. It carries none of the emotive undertones of the word 'but', as in 'Yes, but . . .'. As such it is more useful in this type of conversation.
- *Broken record* – if the other person is aggressive, persistent or manipulative, the broken record will help you stand your ground. Very few people will keep trying to get their own way after three or four broken record statements. It is particularly effective against 'manipulators' when combined with *negative assertion*. For example:

Gordon: 'Sally's going to be very upset.'
Manager: 'Yes, that's understandable; however . . .'

Example five

Manager:	'Yes, Gordon?'
Staff member:	'I was wondering if I could possibly have tomorrow off. There's a sale on at a local furniture store and Sally and I would like to see if we could pick up any bargains.'
Manager:	'I see. What made you want to go tomorrow rather than at the weekend?' (probing)
Staff member:	'Tomorrow, Wednesday, is the first day of the sale. All the good bargains will have gone by Saturday. I know it's awkward with Bruce being off, but we can only afford furniture if its heavily discounted.'
Manager:	'I know what it's like. Every bit counts when you're starting out. Tell me, though, are you aware that we are targeted to clear the backlog by the end of the week?' (empathy, probing)
Staff member:	'Yes, but I was hoping that as it's just one day it would be OK. You've always been so helpful in the past.'
Manager:	'Yes I have. How many backlog letters are you dealing with a day?' (negative assertion, probing)
Staff member:	'About 20.'
Manager:	'That's good, but it's too many to spread around the remaining team members. Gordon, I'm going to have to say "No".' (basic assertion)
Staff member:	'That's going to be a real disappointment to Sally. She's really got her heart set on a three-piece suite they have a great reduction on.'
Manager:	'I'm sure she will be disappointed; however, we're targeted to clear the backlog by Friday so I have to say "No".' (negative assertion, broken record)
Staff member:	'Is there no way I could have even some time off?'
Manager:	'What time does the store open?' (probing)
Staff member:	'At seven thirty in the morning as a kind of special promotion for the sale.'
Manager:	'If you and Sally got there for seven thirty, could you do what you want to do, but be back here for lunchtime and work through 'till about ten tonight?' (workable compromise)
Staff member:	'Yes . . . yes, I'm sure I could.'

Manager: 'OK, it's a deal.'

In this example, the manager adopted a credible approach. Probing was used to check the reason for Gordon's request and to guide Gordon to the conclusion that was coming. Empathy was used to demonstrate understanding of Gordon's position. Probing and empathy together made the refusal more just. Negative assertion and broken record were used to maintain detachment from Gordon's attempted manipulation, and to reinforce the decision. When Gordon showed some room for manoeuvre, however, the manager probed a little further to find a workable compromise.

In summary then, refusing a request is rarely easy. It is almost as if anyone who feels alright about it is likely to be aggressive, and anyone who feels uneasy about it will respond submissively and either say 'No' but cause bad feeling, or end up saying 'Yes'. An assertive approach, however, not only provides the tools with which to say 'No' effectively, but helps rid ourselves of the childhood programming that we 'should' co-operate or feel guilty if we do not.

A summary of saying 'No' to a request is given in Figure 14.

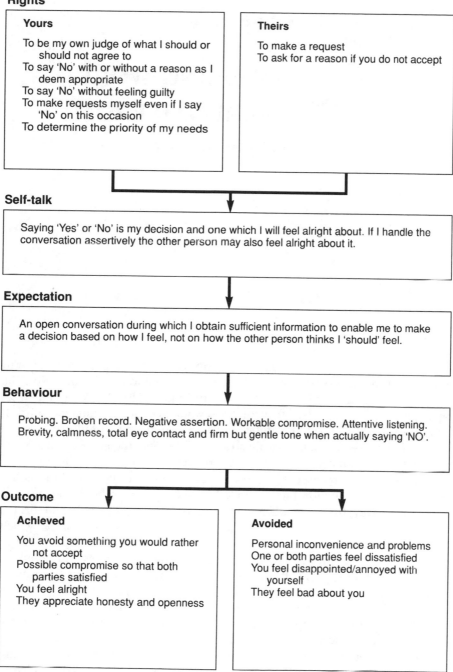

Rights

Yours

To be my own judge of what I should or
    should not agree to
To say 'No' with or without a reason as I
    deem appropriate
To say 'No' without feeling guilty
To make requests myself even if I say
    'No' on this occasion
To determine the priority of my needs

Theirs

To make a request
To ask for a reason if you do not accept

Self-talk

Saying 'Yes' or 'No' is my decision and one which I will feel alright about. If I handle the
conversation assertively the other person may also feel alright about it.

Expectation

An open conversation during which I obtain sufficient information to enable me to make
a decision based on how I feel, not on how the other person thinks I 'should' feel.

Behaviour

Probing. Broken record. Negative assertion. Workable compromise. Attentive listening.
Brevity, calmness, total eye contact and firm but gentle tone when actually saying 'NO'.

Outcome

Achieved

You avoid something you would rather
    not accept
Possible compromise so that both
    parties satisfied
You feel alright
They appreciate honesty and openness

Avoided

Personal inconvenience and problems
One or both parties feel dissatisfied
You feel disappointed/annoyed with
    yourself
They feel bad about you

Figure 14 *Saying 'No' to a request: summary.*

Chapter 17

HANDLING WORK OVERLOAD FROM YOUR BOSS

Many books on assertiveness are aimed at staff rather than managers and so, in the obligatory section on saying 'No', the subject of saying 'No' to the boss is included. This book is aimed at managers, and saying 'No' to your boss when you are a manager yourself requires slightly different handling. Let us examine this difference in more detail. I will use extremes to illustrate my points, recognizing that most situations will actually lie somewhere between the two.

Non-managers are used to taking orders. Whether they are blue collar workers on a production line or travelling sales people who spend most of their time away from the office they are on the receiving end of orders which they themselves must action. There is no additional stratum to which they can delegate the order. Sometimes their job allows virtually no discretion, as with the production line workers, and sometimes autonomy is encouraged and expected. In the final analysis, however, at this level in an organization you are on the receiving end of orders and, generally, do what is expected of you. A description that rings true for many people is that a manager/staff relationship is akin to a parent/child relationship. Authority is, on the whole, accepted without question.

Managers, on the other hand, are used to giving as well as receiving orders. Whether they are first line supervisors or middle ranking officers, they form a link in the chain of command translating corporate vision into reality on the 'shop floor'. The amount of discretion they are expected to exercise may vary, but managers are expected to be thinking beings, exercising their judgment in how they go about their tasks, and that judgment does not suddenly switch off when taking orders and switch on again when implementing them. They are more inclined, therefore, than their non-managerial colleagues to want to query or at least participate in receiving orders.

There are, however, certain complications to add at this stage. First, some managers do not know what their subordinate managers do, not in detail anyway. To begin with they tend to only hear about the problems and not the ordinary, everyday uneventful smooth running.

Second, many managers are under intense pressure to achieve. Not only is the business environment exceptionally competitive, globally as well as locally, but the work ethic is enjoying a marked resurgence after the flower power decades. They are often left with no apparent choice but to delegate more.

Work overload farther down the chain is becoming a serious issue – 'serious' because of volume and because of another slight twist. Once you are in the management chain certain factors are triggered. You probably have a career not just a job; you are expected to adhere to and uphold the corporate culture; you are assessed on achievement not on activity; you are probably salaried instead of paid hourly, and so are expected to work the hours necessary to achieve your objectives.

Put all these factors together and it is easy to see how the work can pile up. Rather than admit defeat, appear as if the job is too much for you, risk the reputation of someone who is anti-corporate culture, or risk the possibility of a poor annual appraisal with its repercussions for advancement, many managers soldier on working longer hours, seeing less of the family and becoming more autocratic and stressed. They probably also wonder 'What's wrong with me?', and become suitable breeding ground for a mid-life crisis.

As I said, these are extremes. But how many times have you felt like the overloaded manager? Are those occasions becoming more frequent? Are you beginning to think there's more to life than 12 hours a day at work? Is the overload a temporary occurrence that will pass, or is it because you allowed in the thin edge of the wedge from your boss and you've now got to the thick end? If so, *you do not just need courage, you need diplomacy as well.* But let's start with the courage.

Courage is internally generated not externally applied, so you have to look to your own self-image, life plan, rights and self-talk. Most overloaded managers I encounter believe, first, that they are the ones at fault for not being able to handle the pressure. It is a real blow to their self-image to feel that the job 'is too much' for them. Second, they believe that to suggest that it is not they but the company which is out of step is corporate blasphemy, and will result in personal excommunication or immediate exile to the company equivalent of Siberia. In other words, people who feel this way are ignoring a fundamental right – to be their own judge.

The courage that is required, therefore, is to make a decision. Do you want to live your life this way? If you do, fine. If you do not, why should it be because there is something wrong with you? Why cannot it be because the way you want to be managed is different from the way you are managed? Below are some common types of negative self-talk associated with work overload from the boss, together with some positive alternatives:

- *I just can't handle this persistent pressure*
  I can handle reasonable pressure for necessary reasons, but whether I handle unreasonable pressure for unnecessary reasons is my decision.
- *If I complain they'll think I'm not as good as they are*
  I am my own person. If I think that something is not right I am free to say so. Other's opinions of me are just that – opinions.
- *The culture here is to work hard and to be seen to work hard. I can't defy that*
  It's achievement not image that gets results. The current workload is hindering my effectiveness.
- *My boss works all hours and expects his managers to do the same*
  My boss is entitled to set his priorities in life just as I am entitled to set mine.

Thinking this way, you can at least approach the problem constructively. All you have to do now is act – but do so diplomatically. Diplomatic action is easier if you can first appreciate the issue from your boss's prospective. He or she probably wants from you the same sorts of things you want from your staff – results, honesty, trust, loyalty, and so on. It will help your case and your presentation, therefore, if you approach the discussion from this angle!

Notice I said 'Your case and your presentation'. The way you put over your argument will have as much, if not more, effect than the argument itself. Part of your presentation will be the words you use – 'I want to be more effective' will have a greater impact than 'I want less pressure from you.' The other part of your presentation will be your verbal and non-verbal communication skills.

It is probably also as well to consider beforehand how your boss may react – aggressively, submissively, manipulatively, and so on. That way you can have a mental dress rehearsal, and so be prepared.

Here is an example of how a discussion on work overload could go.

Example

Situation

Roger is manager of an Employee Relations Section within a Personnel Department. He has three Personnel Officers and two clerk/typists in his section. He reports to the Personnel Director. The company is undergoing significant organizational change which is creating additional work for most functions, including Personnel. Roger, however, feels that his Director, Charles, is creating more work than is actually necessary, and is delegating work to Roger as if he was a personal assistant rather than a manager with a section to run and objectives to achieve. Roger's working hours are building up dramatically, and he is suffering more stress than he has done before. He decides to discuss the matter with Charles at the beginning of their regular morning meeting:

Roger:	'Charles, there's something I'd like to discuss with you. Something I need your help on.' (signposting)
Charles:	'OK, fire away.'
Roger:	'It's a sensitive issue and I'm not really sure how to broach it.' (signposting, self-disclosure)
Charles:	'Just go straight for it, that's usually the best way.'
Roger:	'OK. As you know, we're all very busy at the moment. We haven't been running this long and this hard for a long time.' (empathy)
Charles:	'Yes . . . ?'
Roger:	'I believe that my current volume of work is not only bad for me personally, but is making it difficult to achieve my key objectives. That concerns me so I'd like to discuss it with you.' (basic assertion, self-disclosure)
Charles:	'Are you saying you can't handle the job any more?'
Roger:	'No. I can handle my job and I can achieve my objectives; however, the additional miscellaneous tasks are taking up more time than I can afford to allocate if I am to achieve my key job objectives.' (basic assertion, broken record)
Charles:	'Roger, we're all under pressure. That's a fact of life at the moment. Perhaps its too much for you?'
Roger:	'I don't believe so. As you know I've worked these hours before. What I haven't had are so many miscellaneous tasks diverting my attention from my key job objectives.' (basic assertion, pointing out a discrepancy, broken record)
Charles:	'Maybe it's just a question of prioritizing. Perhaps you need to manage your time better.'
Roger:	'I've checked that. All the work is urgent or important or both. I believe it's the *volume* of miscellaneous tasks that is causing the problem.' (basic assertion, broken record)
Charles:	'Well, delegate more.'
Roger:	'I've worked on my delegation for the last six weeks. I'm confident now that my staff are working on activities contributing to my section's objectives. I'd prefer not to pull them off such work.' (basic assertion)

Charles: 'Then maybe you'll just have to work longer hours.'
Roger: 'That is a solution. However, I'd prefer not to because
              the stress of longer hours builds up and makes me less
              efficient in achieving my key objectives.' (negative
              assertion, self-disclosure, broken record)
Charles: 'No one else has complained.'
Roger: 'Probably not, and I'm not complaining now, just
              discussing a concern about the volume of miscellaneous
              tasks.' (negative assertion, self-disclosure, broken record)
Charles: 'So what do you think ought to happen?'
Roger: 'Well . . . I've thought about this and I'd like us to be
              more critical about the volume of miscellaneous tasks
              and the deadlines they're given.' (self-disclosure, basic
              assertion)
Charles: 'Why us?'
Roger: 'As a dedicated manager, I'll always try and do what you
              ask of me. So I can't cut back on miscellaneous tasks
              unless you cut back on delegating them to me.' (self-
              disclosure, basic assertion)
Charles: 'OK . . . let's go into this in a bit more detail.'

Roger has achieved the first two of his three aims – to broach the subject
without feeling guilty or inadequate, and to engage his boss in meaningful
discussion about it. Whether he achieves his third aim of getting his boss
to throttle back on the miscellaneous tasks will depend on the rest of their
conversation. That the conversation has moved on positively to discuss the
details of delegated tasks is an encouraging sign.

So how was Roger able to take the conversation that far?

1.   He kept his *thoughts positive*. He did not blame himself for his feelings
     nor his boss for doing what the boss thought was right. He accepted
     there was a difference and decided to address it.
2.   He used *signposting* to warn his boss that something delicate was
     coming up.
3.   He used *empathy* to show he was on the same wavelength as his boss.
4.   He used *self-disclosure* to show that he was being open and honest.
5.   His *basic assertion* was not only concise; it presented the problem in
     terms of organizational effectiveness rather than 'I want'.
6.   He did not respond emotionally to his boss's taunts about not being
     able to handle the job any more, or about being the odd one out.
     Instead he remained detached from them by using *negative assertion*,
     and stuck to his point using the *broken record*. Eventually his boss
     decided that more could be achieved by discussing the matter ration-
     ally.

Even if, at the end of the discussion, his boss refuses to relent, it is unlikely that his opinion of Roger will go down. There had been no aggressive outburst nor submissive whining, just a mature adult to adult discussion. Also, Roger will be confident in his own mind that his feelings about himself and his workload can still leave his self-esteem intact.

A summary on handling work overload from your boss is given in Figure 15.

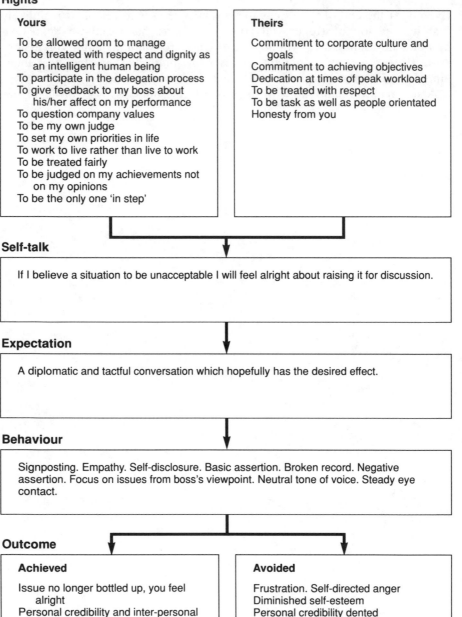

Rights

Yours

To be allowed room to manage
To be treated with respect and dignity as an intelligent human being
To participate in the delegation process
To give feedback to my boss about his/her affect on my performance
To question company values
To be my own judge
To set my own priorities in life
To work to live rather than live to work
To be treated fairly
To be judged on my achievements not on my opinions
To be the only one 'in step'

Theirs

Commitment to corporate culture and goals
Commitment to achieving objectives
Dedication at times of peak workload
To be treated with respect
To be task as well as people orientated
Honesty from you

Self-talk

If I believe a situation to be unacceptable I will feel alright about raising it for discussion.

Expectation

A diplomatic and tactful conversation which hopefully has the desired effect.

Behaviour

Signposting. Empathy. Self-disclosure. Basic assertion. Broken record. Negative assertion. Focus on issues from boss's viewpoint. Neutral tone of voice. Steady eye contact.

Outcome

Achieved

Issue no longer bottled up, you feel alright
Personal credibility and inter-personal skills respected
Overload reduced

Avoided

Frustration. Self-directed anger
Diminished self-esteem
Personal credibility dented
Interpersonal skills brought into question
Overload maintained

Figure 15 *Handling work overload from your boss: summary.*

Chapter 18

TELLING YOUR TEAM ABOUT TOUGH TARGETS

If the following occurrence has never happened to you perhaps you can imagine it:

Rumours have been around for several days about the strict new budget regime. Activity amongst senior managers is frantic. Then directors commence individual meetings with their senior managers and they with their middle managers, and so on. Your manager emerges from his or her boss's office with an ashen face and deeply etched frown, and calls a team meeting in 20 minutes. You guess it is to be given the news about the increased productivity targets and draconian budget cuts.

There are two ways in which managers tend to deliver such news. The first is to allow their feelings of injustice and pessimism to cloud their entire presentation.

Example one

Manager:	'Look, I . . . er . . . don't quite know how to say this,' (shifts from foot to foot and glances nervously at the audience and then back to the table at which he is standing) 'But these are our new targets.' (Turns over flipchart to reveal figures)
Staff (as one):	'Bloody hell/crumbs/ouch.'

Manager:	(still nervous, now wringing hands) 'Now . . . I . . . er . . . know they're a little bit stiff but . . .'
Staff member 1:	'Stiff? They're ruddy rigid.'
Staff member 2:	'Bloody impossible.'
Staff member 3:	'No way.'
Manager:	'Yes . . . I know . . . but it's no use getting at me. I'm as upset as the rest of you . . .'
Staff member 1:	'Didn't you tell them that those figures are impossible?'
Manager:	'Well, I did try but . . . they . . . er, weren't exactly in a listening mood.'
Staff member 2:	'Not in a listening mood? Well I don't mind telling them a thing or two.'
Staff member 3:	'Those figures can't be achieved with our current headcount levels.'
Manager:	'Ah yes . . . headcount. The . . . er . . . new headcount levels are on the next page.'

Why has the manager gone about the presentation this way? Well he had probably thought to himself, while still in a state of shock, 'This is impossible. We'll never do it. Why is it happening to me? It's not fair!'

And what are the staff probably thinking? 'The company's gone crazy, it can't be done, why didn't this wimp of a manager tell them that?' They feel very bad about the new targets, bad about the manager, and generally bad about the whole situation.

The second way in which managers elect to deliver such news is most intriguing. They work on the basis that if their staff detect any lack of confidence in their manager, any doubt about the new targets in his presentation, then they will feel demotivated. If, on the other hand, they see that he feels confident about the new targets, then they will accept them with open arms.

Example two

Manager:	'OK team. As you know, there have been rumours around for some days now about the company's new targets we're all going to get. Well we've got them now, and I'm delighted to say they're not as bad as I thought they would be.' (Big grin, hands on hips, swaggering style) 'Here they are.' (Turns over flipchart to reveal figures).
Staff (as one):	(Gasps!)
Manager:	'There, I told you they weren't too bad.'
Staff member 1:	'Not too bad . . . Boss, they're . . . impossible.'
Manager:	'Nothing's impossible to us. We're the A-Team.'

| Staff member 1: | 'But everybody's working flat out as it is.' |
| Manager: | 'Now come on! We've had stiff targets before. We're the best. We'll crack this with room to spare. You watch my lips, room to spare. It looks difficult from here, but wait until you start working on it, you'll be surprised how easy it is. Come on, say after me,' (thumping palm with fist, big grin) 'room . . . to . . . spare.' |

Where the first manager chose to wallow in self-pity, the second manager has tried to turn himself into a cheer leader. He has probably thought to himself, 'These are crazy targets, but if the team sees that I'm confident and enthusiastic they'll accept it and we just might stand a chance.'

And what are the staff probably thinking? 'Who's kidding whom? Does the boss think we're children? What's next on the agenda, Snow White and the Seven Dwarves?' They feel bad about the new targets, bad about the manager for trying to hoodwink them, and generally bad about the whole situation. The difference between the second situation and the first is that the staff of the second manager may agree to humour him for a while, while the staff of the first manager will 'prove' that the new targets are unachievable.

An alternative to the self-pity and fairy tale approaches is for the managers to treat their staff as intelligent human beings who know frighteningly tough targets when they see them and to be totally honest with them.

Example three

Manager:	(sitting at table along with everyone else) 'Thank you for coming in. I promised that as soon as I had news of our new targets I'd share it with you. The new targets are now available. Does anyone have any questions before I begin? . . . OK, here goes.' (Rises to turn over flipchart, then rejoins the group.)
Staff (as one):	'Phew/Crazy/Impossible.'
Manager:	'Anybody want to say anything specific?'
Staff member 1:	'Boss, is this serious?'
Manager:	'Yes, these are our new targets.' (basic assertion)
Staff member 1:	'But they're crazy. There's no way we can increase productivity 15%.'
Manager:	'Very probably, but they're still our new targets.' (negative assertion, broken record)
Staff member 2:	'Did you tell them that 15% is impossible?'
Manager:	'Yes.'
Staff member 2:	'So what did they say?'

Manager:	'They said these are our new targets, so what I'd like to discuss are our plans for achieving them.' (broken record, basic assertion)
Staff member 3:	'What's the point in discussing plans if the targets are impossible?'
Manager:	'Probably none, but if 15% is impossible maybe 14% is slightly less impossible so we'll discuss the best plans we can.' (negative assertion, broken record)
Staff member 1:	'Well I don't like it.'
Manager:	'Don't like what, Jean?' (probing)
Staff member 1:	'These new targets.'
Manager:	'What don't you like about them?' (probing)
Staff member 1:	'We gave them another 7% last year, how can we possibly turn it up again and this time by 15%.'
Manager:	'I don't know. How did we do it last time?' (self-disclosure, probing)
Staff member 1:	'We examined everything that went into the percentage calculation and identified what aspects of production we could tweak a percent or two. In the end we got 7%.'
Manager:	'OK let's start there again. It's unlikely to deliver the full 15% but at least it'll be a start. After that we'll have to be more creative.'
Staff member 2:	'You're not going to let up on this are you?'
Manager:	'Is there any point? None of us wants these new targets but we've got them. If we can achieve them it'll be good for the company and for us. Now I suggest we do what we normally do when there's a problem and work out together what we do about it.' (probing, self-disclosure, empathy, basic assertion)

What were the key elements of this manager's approach?

- *Openers*: at no time did he attempt to hide facts or his feelings from his staff.
- *Persistence*: his use of the broken record technique let everyone know what was real – the targets were there to stay, so the only option was to discuss plans that at least went some way to meeting them.
- *Avoidance of manipulators*: there were several attempts to shift the focus of the meeting away from the new targets to the sanity of the target makers, the manager's ability to defend his staff and to the logic of not discussing something that cannot be achieved anyway. On each occasion the manager used *negative assertion* to avoid the manipulators, but to show that he had heard.
- *Involving*: the manager probed to discover the reasons behind an

objection, and to treat it not as an obstacle but as a stepping stone. He also let it be known that he wanted team discussion on the new targets because he would not be providing answers.

- *Respect*: above all, he gave his staff respect. First, by not treating them to the spectacle of a manager indulging in self-pity; second, by treating them as adults; and finally, by acting like a leader and focusing on results.

Of all these elements, it is probably the openness, involvement and respect that will harness the commitment of the tcam – and as it is they who will be producing the 15%; that's an important ingredient to success.

A summary of telling your team about tough targets is given in Figure 16.

Rights

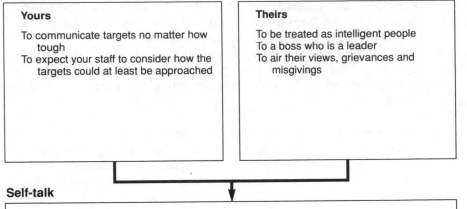

Yours

To communicate targets no matter how
   tough
To expect your staff to consider how the
   targets could at least be approached

Theirs

To be treated as intelligent people
To a boss who is a leader
To air their views, grievances and
   misgivings

Self-talk

Passing on tough targets is not pleasant, but any flak will be aimed at the targets, not me. I may just be a messenger of them, but I have to own them first if I want my staff to own them as well.

Expectation

An initial rough-ride which becomes smoother as staff move from the 'Ouch' response to 'How to' thinking.

Behaviour

Self-disclosure. Basic assertion. Broken record. Negative assertion. Probing. Openness and honesty. Neutral voice tone, moderate eye contact, relatively formal posture.

Outcome

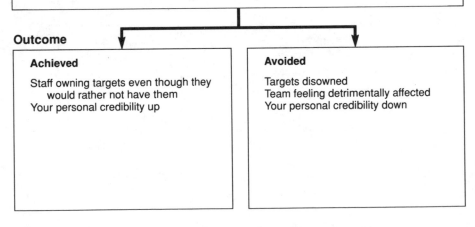

Achieved

Staff owning targets even though they
   would rather not have them
Your personal credibility up

Avoided

Targets disowned
Team feeling detrimentally affected
Your personal credibility down

Figure 16 *Telling your team about tough targets: summary.*

Chapter 19

GIVING PRAISE

When Messrs Peters and Waterman were researching information for their hugely successful book *In Search of Excellence*, their conclusions were not what they had anticipated. They found that success, instead of coming from sophisticated management and control systems, came from *people*, pure and simple. The prime factor distinguishing successful companies from the rest was positive employee attitudes.

Whether or not someone feels good about their work usually depends on what they get out of it. People who perform well receive four main benefits from their work: (1) money; (2) a feeling of belonging; (3) a sense of achievement; and (4) a belief in their own self-worth.

Of these benefits, money is the most variable. Most people know someone who is paid a pittance but who still performs well, and someone who is paid exceptionally well considering their pitiful performance! But how many people do you know who can feel as if they do not belong, believe they are achieving nothing, and feel bad about themselves and still perform well? The last three benefits are imperative for good performance. They make the difference between those people who work to their full potential and those who do just enough to keep their jobs. They tend to exist where people are actively involved in their work and their workplace, achieve challenging goals and, finally, receive recognition for their achievements. Accordingly, this chapter concerns giving praise.

Praise is something that managers tend not to give enough of. It was Robert Townsend, former Chief Executive of the Avis Corporation, who referred to the word 'Thankyou' as the most underused form of remuneration in most companies. The reason for praise being so underused is twofold – managers do not appreciate its value, and they do not know *how* to praise effectively. So, I will begin this section by looking at the value of effective praising. Praising is a *behaviour shaper* and a far more powerful one than criticism.

Being incapable of telepathy, most of us learned how to interact with others because of the reaction our behaviour induced in other people. We knew that a negative response (scolding, criticizing, or worse) was unpleasant, so we tried to avoid it. Conversely, we knew that a positive response (smiling, praise) was pleasant, so we tried to ensure we received more of it.

A general rule therefore emerges: criticism shows people what to avoid and makes them feel bad; praise shows people what to do and makes them feel good. That good feeling embraces a great deal. Praising makes us feel more secure, more valued; it strengthens relationships; it makes us feel more worthwhile as a person. We like these feelings so we do more of the behaviour that earns the praise, even after the praise is withdrawn. Conversely, a critical environment creates a downward spiral of low self-esteem, poor morale and deteriorating motivation; it creates resentment because people feel they cannot win and their efforts are never recognized. Resentment increases and people use their initiative to avoid criticism. Yet many managers feel more comfortable managing (ensuring people do what they want, in the way they want it done, i.e. *shaping behaviour*) by criticizing rather than praising – which must be about as sensible as trying to cram rush hour traffic down a narrow country lane while an adjacent six lane highway is empty! The data banks they filled in childhood must have included some very odd 'rules' about praise.

So praise is an effective behaviour shaper, motivator and productivity enhancer. It can be widely applied and costs nothing. Yet many managers fail to capitalize on it, and others try but fail because they do not know *how* to praise.

There are four main types of ineffective praise. They either diminish or negate any potential benefit from the praise. They are illustrated below in the following situation: a staff member has handled a customer complaint so effectively that the customer has faxed a complimentary letter to the Chief Executive.

1. Plastic praise

This is the sort of praise that is as genuine as plastic flowers or plastic leather. Only occasionally does it look good initially, and it never withstands close scrutiny. It is usually delivered in one or more of the following ways:

- with minimal or no eye contact
- while the manager is concentrating on something else
- fleetingly before the subject is changed abruptly to something else.

Example one

Manager: (sorting through papers allocating some to his briefcase and some to his filing tray. Attention throughout is on the papers) '. . . the meeting starts at ten so I'll not be in tomorrow. By the way, the Chief Executive was very complimentary about the way you handled that customer . . . So when I get back on Friday I'd like you to have the staff meeting agenda ready. I don't understand . . . one of my files is missing.'

The basic message is 'What I'm doing is far more important than what you could be feeling.'

2. Critical praise

This is the sort of praise that leaves people feeling raw. It has a negative effect on them, negating any possible benefit.

Example two

Manager: (with direct eye contact) 'Well done. You handled that customer very effectively . . . What a pity you can't do that more often.'

or:

Manager: 'That was very impressive . . . for someone like you.'

or:

Manager: 'You handled that customer really well. Your written work leaves a lot to be desired, but you're good face to face.'

The underlying message is 'A nice try but it was just a flash in the pan so don't get carried away. In my book you still have a lot to improve on.'

3. Conditional praise

Conditional praise is used as a 'bribery' to 'buy' a favour, or as a 'sweetener' to make it easier for the manager to subsequently deliver criticism.

Example three

Manager: (Overtly relaxed and casual) 'That was really good the way you handled that customer. I and the Chief Executive were most impressed . . . Tell me how do you feel about working late tonight?'

or:

Manager: (Anxiously) 'That was really good the way you handled that customer . . . I was most impressed . . . so was the . . . er . . . Chief Executive . . . er . . . I was wondering though, you . . . er . . . seem to be going home slightly earlier than everyone else. I was just . . . er . . . wondering if there was a . . . problem.'

Conditional praise used either as bribery or as a sweetener is manipulative in the extreme.

4. Confusing praise

There are two extremes of confusing praise; that which exaggerates and glorifies the staff member's performance, and that which, while praising it, reduces it to the ranks of mediocrity.

Example four

Manager: (with uncontrollable enthusiasm) 'That was really great. I really am very impressed. Well done. Absolutely super.'

and:

Manager: (with guarded sincerity) 'That was *quite* good. I also understand the Chief Executive made a small mention of it. Not *too* bad at all.'

The underlying message is 'I'm not really sure how to do this so let's go over the top on it or, alternatively, because I feel a bit exposed saying this I prefer to stick to the safe ground of general platitudes.'

Of these four types of ineffective praise, the first two are beloved by managers who tend towards aggressive behaviour. Plastic praise, for example, is dismissive of other people, and is indicative of someone who believes they are more important than anyone else. Critical praise is used by people who feel far more comfortable wielding the big stick of criticism, and so it creeps in even when they are praising. As a result their true disposition completely eclipses the praise.

Conditional and confusing praise are usually the domain of submissive managers, because asking direct or exposing their true feelings makes them feel vulnerable. It is much safer, therefore, to overwhelm the other person with superlatives, to 'sweeten' them, or to avoid extremes altogether and dilute the praise accordingly.

In reviewing this chapter so far, it is possible to put together the what, where, when and how of effective praising:

- *What:* whatever you want to encourage – effort, dedication, loyalty, accuracy, quality, timeliness, tidiness, appearance, productivity, initiative, mutual support, openness, and so on. If it relates to involvement or achievement, it is worth praising. One final point on 'What'. Praise against their standards not yours. People tend to improve by small incremental steps, not by leaps and bounds. Praising a 'good try' which fell short of the mark will encourage a better try next time.
- *Where*: the general rule praise in public and reprimand in private has some validity, but it is not universal. Ceremonial praisings, for example, have to be done in public. Awarding the quarterly prize to the top sales person loses its impact if it is done privately. Short 'Thankyous' can be done virtually anywhere, in public or in private. A sincere person to person praising may carry more impact if it is done privately without the potential distraction of onlookers.
- *When:* as close in time to the behaviour you wish to encourage as possible. The closer the praise to the behaviour the more automatic the connection, and hence the greater the impact of praise as a behaviour shaper.
- *How:* describe the behaviour you are praising. Spell out the behaviour so that they will be clear in their minds what it is you are praising them for.

  State how you feel about it. This step may sound odd to many managers, especially because I am also recommending that you then pause for a couple of seconds and, while your message is sinking in, you make direct eye contact with them. These actions combine to add gravity to the praising. (If you are in any doubt about this step, please re-read Example one.)

Finally, encourage them to keep up the good work.

Note: there is an added and worthwhile addition where the behaviour you are praising is substantial (say, part of a large project) and that is to use probing to help them identify why they performed well and where else they can apply that behaviour. In this way, you not only give them a great psychological stroking, you also turn the praising session into a coaching session.

Example five

Manager:	'Thanks for popping in. I just wanted to congratulate you on the way you handled Mr Brown this morning. As you know, I've been in meetings all day so I've only just heard about it.' (signposting, self-disclosure)
Staff member:	'Thank you.'
Manager:	'As I understand it, Mr Brown had a complaint about faulty merchandise we had supplied him and he really lost his temper at you over the 'phone?'
Staff member:	'That's right. He gave me a real earful.'
Manager:	'You stayed calm, got him to tell you exactly what the problem was, pulled a few strings with Despatch and had a replacement with him by lunchtime.'
Staff member:	'Yes, Despatch didn't want to know to begin with, but I persevered. They soon came round.'
Manager:	'I know it went down well with the Chief Executive when Mr Brown faxed him a complimentary letter. I think what I admire most is the way you persevered with Despatch. It would have been easy to leave Mr Brown with faulty merchandise for a couple of days until Despatch were going that way, but you hung in there. And now we have a loyal Mr Brown and a Chief Executive who is pleased with us. It makes me feel very proud. So, once again thanks.' (self-disclosure, basic assertion)

It is a sad state of affairs that, to many managers, what the staff member did would not have warranted praise because 'It's what they're paid to do'. Resentment, due to lack of recognition, would increase, and the commitment gap would widen.

With increasing competition, you would think that managers would want to capitalize on any and every opportunity to encourage good performance. And with change being the normal, instead of a temporary state of affairs, you would have thought that managers would also want to capitalize on any and every opportunity to shape the behaviour of their staff.

Effective praising seems an ideal way of doing that.

A summary on giving praise is given in Figure 17.

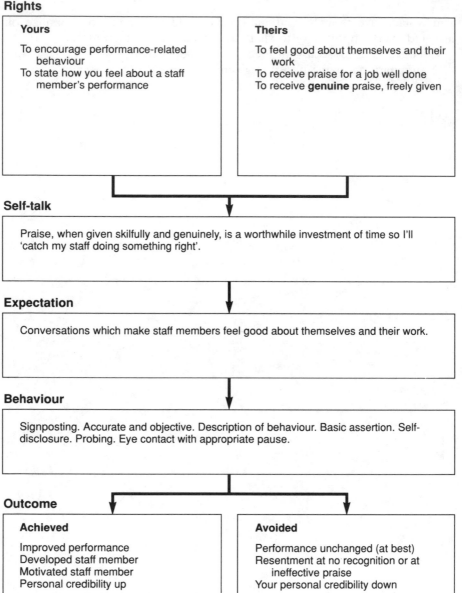

Rights

Yours

To encourage performance-related
  behaviour
To state how you feel about a staff
  member's performance

Theirs

To feel good about themselves and their
  work
To receive praise for a job well done
To receive **genuine** praise, freely given

Self-talk

Praise, when given skilfully and genuinely, is a worthwhile investment of time so I'll
'catch my staff doing something right'.

Expectation

Conversations which make staff members feel good about themselves and their work.

Behaviour

Signposting. Accurate and objective. Description of behaviour. Basic assertion. Self-
disclosure. Probing. Eye contact with appropriate pause.

Outcome

Achieved

Improved performance
Developed staff member
Motivated staff member
Personal credibility up

Avoided

Performance unchanged (at best)
Resentment at no recognition or at
  ineffective praise
Your personal credibility down

Figure 17   *Giving praise: summary.*

Chapter 20

BEING PRAISED

You mean, you have to be assertive to be praised?

No. However, in the last chapter we saw four types of ineffective praise, most of which were either dismissive or manipulative – exactly the sort of things which assertive behaviour is capable of countering. So in this chapter we see how an assertive person could handle the examples of ineffective praising described in the last chapter. (So if you have not yet read it, I suggest you do so now.)

Example one (plastic praise)

Manager:	'. . . the meeting starts at ten so I'll not be in tomorrow. By the way, the Chief Executive was complimentary about the way you handled that customer . . . So when I get back on Friday I'd like you to have the staff meeting agenda ready. I don't understand . . . one of my files is missing.'
Assertive person:	'The Chief Executive said some complimentary things. (fogging)
Manager:	'What? . . . Oh, yes. Said that he wished more people would use their initiative to turn dissatisfied customers into satisfied ones.'
Assertive person:	'That's nice. And did you say anything to him?' (probing)

Manager:	'I told him you were one of my best people and a good example to quite a few other departments in this company.'
Assertive person:	'That was very thoughtful of you. Comments like that are very motivating.' (basic assertion, self-disclosure)
Manager:	'You deserved them. You did well.'

Example two (critical praise)

Manager:	'Well done. You handled that customer very effectively . . . what a pity you can't do that more often.'
Assertive person:	'I don't do it often enough?' (fogging)
Manager:	'Well, it would be pleasant to turn every dissatisfied customer into a satisfied one, wouldn't it?'
Assertive person:	'Very pleasant. But is there a problem in the way I normally handle customers?' (fogging, probing)
Manager:	'No . . . I didn't mean to imply that.'
Assertive person:	'And you're pleased with the way I handled this one?' (probing)
Manager:	'Oh yes – and so was the Chief Executive.'
Assertive person:	'That's good. What exactly did he say?' (probing)

Example three (critical praise – continued)

Manager:	'That was very impressive . . . for someone like you.'
Assertive person:	'For someone like me?' (fogging)
Manager:	'Well you can be a bit straight with people, you know. You don't suffer fools gladly.'
Assertive person:	'But this time I was impressive? (fogging)
Manager:	'Yes, you were.'
Assertive person:	'In what way?' (probing)
Manager:	'It isn't easy to calm an angry customer nor to galvanize Despatch into action. That was good.'
Assertive person:	'Thank you.'

Example four (critical praise – continued)

Manager:	'You handled that customer really well. Your written work leaves a bit to be desired, but you're good face-to-face.'

Assertive person:	'I'm better face-to-face than I am in writing.' (fogging)
Manager:	'Yes, your written work lacks precision and clarity.'
Assertive person:	'And face-to-face?' (probing)
Manager:	'Face-to-face you're a different person. People warm to you. But you can be persistent as well, like you were with Despatch. That was good.'

Example five (conditional praise)

Manager:	'That was really good the way you handled that customer. I and the Chief Executive were most impressed . . . Tell me, how do you feel about working late tonight?'
Assertive person:	'That's good to hear. What exactly did the Chief Executive say?' (self-disclosure, probing)
Manager:	'He said he wished more people would use their initiative to turn dissatisfied customers into satisfied ones. I told him you were one of my best people and a good example to quite a few other departments in this company.'
Assertive person:	'That's made me feel very good. Feedback like that is important when you're under pressure, which is why I feel bad about not being able to work late tonight.' (self-disclosure)

Example six (conditional praise – continued)

| Manager: | 'That was really good the way you handled that customer . . . I was most impressed . . . so was the . . . er . . . Chief Executive . . . er . . . I was wondering though, you . . . er . . . seem to be going home slightly earlier than everyone else. I was just . . . er . . . wondering if there was a . . . problem.' |
| Assertive person: | 'Only two nights a week. I'm doing an evening class in assertiveness. What exactly was it about the way I handled the customer that impressed you?' (basic assertion, self-disclosure, probing) |

Example seven (confusing praise)

Manager:	'That was really great. I really am very impressed. Well done. Absolutely super.'
Assertive person:	'Thank you. That's good to hear. What is it about the situation that has made you so pleased?' (probing)
Manager:	'The way you persevered with Despatch . . .' and so on.

Example eight (confusing praise – continued)

Manager:	'That was *quite* good. I also understand the Chief Executive made a small mention of it. Not *too* bad at all.'
Assertive person:	'Thank you. It's always good to get positive feedback. I'd like to ask you, though, what was it that I did that has attracted so much attention?' (self-disclosure, signposting, probing)
Manager:	'Oh, without doubt, getting Despatch to deliver a replacement before lunchtime the same day. Your initiative and persistence – definitely.'
Assertive person:	'But, I still don't understand. Why is it so noteworthy?' (self-disclosure, probing)
Manager:	'Not many people would have done it. Most people would have taken Despatch's word that it couldn't be done and left it at that, but you hung in there.'
Assertive person:	'I hope you don't mind me asking, but how do you feel about that?' (signposting, probing)
Manager:	'Actually rather proud that through your good work the Chief Executive regards this department in a favourable light.'
Assertive person:	'Thank you. It feels good to hear you say that.' (self-disclosure)

From these examples, you can see how a few simple assertive techniques and tools can secure the attention of a dismissive manager, draw out any potential problem areas of a critical manager and return attention to the praise, sidestep bribery without having to forfeit the praise and, finally, sharpen focus on why you are being praised. The main tools and techniques used were signposting, fogging, self-disclosure and, above all, probing.

It should also shape your boss's behaviour so that in future your praisings will be useful and genuine.

A summary on being praised is given in Figure 18.

Rights

Yours	Theirs
To feel good about yourself and your work To receive praise for a job well done To receive genuine praise, freely given To encourage your boss to behave assertively	To be listened to To make mistakes

Self-talk

If I'm going to be praised, I'd like it to be genuine and sincere.

Expectation

To use my assertive skills to clarify, in their mind as well as mine, what I am being praised for.

Behaviour

Signposting. Fogging. Self-disclosure. Probing.

Outcome

Achieved	Avoided
You know what behaviour is valued and so you can repeat it If your boss was not clear as to the value of your praiseworthy behaviour, he/she is now More honest relationship with your boss	Being aggravated by ineffective criticism Being discouraged from high performance behaviour

Figure 18 *Being praised: summary.*

Chapter 21

PERFORMING WELL IN MEETINGS

Although some forward thinking organisations are slashing the number of working parties and committees to remove corporate log jams, the number of meetings is increasing. People, quite rightly, are coming together more often to consult, share information and take decisions jointly. There are not only more departmental meetings involving a permanent working unit, there are also more team meetings consisting of members brought together matrix fashion to tackle particular issues.

Meetings are important: first, because decisions are taken in them (it is to be hoped); second, because in bringing people together, they act as a 'shop window' – you are on display, as it were, to the other meeting participants – your behaviour will affect, therefore, their perception of you; and third, because of this 'display' aspect, they involve risk – you could show yourself up, or be shown up by someone else in front of staff, colleagues or, perhaps most damaging to career prospects, senior management. Add to these three factors the general observation that meetings are frequently badly managed with insufficient preparation, a poor agenda, inappropriate attendees and inadequate process control, and you have a breeding ground for dysfunctional behaviour.

Dysfunctional behaviour falls broadly into the aggressive and submissive categories. Aggressive people tend to overstate the case with exaggerations and generalizations. They attempt to score points off some attendees to shine in front of others. They will use patronizing and sarcastic remarks to ensure they obtain their own way. They will be stubborn to avoid being seen as weak.

Submissive people find it easy to agree with the majority, or with more dominant attendees, even where it is against their interests. They will be reluctant to disagree or put forward their views if they contradict someone else. When it is their turn to speak up they may ramble, water down what they have to say if it is at all contentious, or be reluctant to lay their cards on the table. When they do not understand something they will be reluctant to seek clarification.

So people with aggressive tendencies want to act as bulldozers to get their own way, while people with submissive tendencies want to be passengers, anonymously flowing with the tide. Hardly a recipe for organizational efficiency! But how can assertiveness help your performance in meetings?

To begin with, what are your rights? You probably have a right to state your opinions openly, understand what is being discussed, disagree with what is being said, stand your ground if you believe you are right, compromise and encourage others to do so, propose suggestions, make a contribution and, generally, ensure that your scarcest of resources, time, is being used to good effect. And what of the rights of other attendees? Presumably the same as you. They have just as much right to fight their corner, disagree with you, not change their minds unless you convince them to do so, and so on.

Let us 'eavesdrop' on a meeting so that we can see how these rights manifest themselves in practice to the benefit of all concerned. The meeting is attended by:

- Janice, Customer Care Manager
- George, Sales Manager
- Alan, Production Manager
- Linda, Technical Adviser

and concerns the effect on the Customer Care Department of a spate of faults on the domestic products manufactured by the company. The faults were traced to poor quality components and have now been rectified, but the complaints have left a significant backlog of telephone calls and correspondence with the Customer Care Department:

Janice:	'. . . so, to shift the backlog quickly and . . . er . . . to regain customer confidence, I was going to ask . . . if . . . anyone could possibly spare any staff, only temporarily you understand.'
George:	'Not a prayer. I've got all my people running hard at the moment trying to patch up relations with distributors.'
Janice:	'Yes, well that's what I was thinking, you see . . .'
George:	'Try Alan, Production's not exactly inundated with orders at the moment.'

Alan:	'Oh no, absolutely definitely no. Production is down but I've also got a large number of people on repairs at the moment. Well with all these returned products someone's got to repair them, haven't they? And as my people assembled them in the first place they're the obvious choice. So all my people are hard pushed at the moment. They're all on overtime.'
George:	'There's your answer, Janice, go on to overtime. Do some real work for a change.'
Janice:	'Well it isn't really as simple as that . . . all my staff are mothers with young families . . . They . . . er . . . have to leave on time.'
George:	'Well that's your problem, you shouldn't have recruited them. Try Technical, they're the boffins who got us into this mess in the first place.'
Linda:	'We did misjudge a new supplier. Janice, what exactly do you need by way of additional resources?' (negative assertion, probing)
Janice:	'Well . . . er . . . three people . . . for a short while.'
Linda:	'How long is a short while?' (probing)
Janice:	'Two weeks maximum.'
Linda:	'And what sort of people would be ideal?' (probing)
Janice:	'People who are good with customers and distributors. They've got to know the product . . .'
George:	'You see, Production, I told you.'
Linda:	'Anything else?' (probing)
Janice:	'Above all, they've got to be good with customers and distributors. Know what makes them tick. How to persuade them and get them back on our side. That sort of thing.'
Linda:	'How do Production and Technical people fit that description?' (probing)
Janice:	'Not very well. They're more at home with machines than people and they tend to use too much jargon, so customers can't understand them.'
Linda:	'And Sales?' (probing)
George:	'Now just a minute. I've already explained that my people are already working every hour God sends. I can't spare anyone.'
Linda:	'Your people have a great deal on at the moment. And Sales, Janice?' (fogging, broken record)
Janice:	'Sales people would be ideal. They understand the product and they're good with customers and distributors.'
George:	'No way. All my people are trying to hang on to distributors.'

Linda:	'Distributors are very important to us. Janice, what proportion of your backlog relates to Distributors?' (fogging, probing)
Janice:	'about 60%.'
Linda:	'Let me summarize so far to make sure that we're all on the same wavelength. Due to misjudgment in my Department, we used inferior components. The number of complaints from customers and distributors has caused a significant backlog in Customer Care. Production is down because demand is down, but Alan's people are also fitting replacement components to returned machines. George's people are running hard patching up relationships with Distributors.'
Alan:	'Yes, that's a fair description.'
Janice:	'Yes.'
George:	'So where does that bloody well get us?'
Linda:	'The only people qualified to help shift the Customer Care backlog are Salespeople.' (basic assertion)
George:	'You caused the ruddy problem, you fix it.'
Linda:	'If I could I would. However, the only people qualified to help in Customer Care are Sales people.' (broken record)
George:	'And what about my Distributors?'
Linda:	'Janice, could you organize work in such a way that your people deal with domestic customers and George's deal with Distributors?' (probing)
Janice:	'Oh yes, quite easy.'
Linda:	'George, I'll lend you two of my technical people, if that will help while three of yours are with Customer Care.' (workable compromise)
George:	'I haven't said I'll help yet.'
Linda:	'Your people are the only ones qualified to help. The boss will be pretty upset if we don't reach a decision on this. Janice, how do you feel about it?' (broken record, pointing out a consequence, probing)
Janice:	'I'd feel very happy about it.'
Linda:	'George, if three of your people are with Customer Care for two weeks liaising with Distributors as well as shifting the backlog, is there any other impact on Sales you would like to raise?' (probing)
George:	'No, it's only liaising with Distributors that was my concern.'
Linda:	'Good, so can we say we cracked it?' (consensus seeking)

Janice clearly began the meeting feeling nervous. She was easily dominated by George's aggressive style of interrupting, sarcasm and turning suggestions into orders. Alan's contribution was minimal and neutral. Linda began with a lot of listening which continued as she became involved through her use of probing. Her use of probing also included people so that all the attendees were involved. She refused to be goaded by George using negative assertion and fogging to sidestep his attempts to trigger her emotions. She stayed on track using broken record and her summary helped pull together the various strands of argument that had been raised.

The main assertive tools and techniques of value in meetings are:

- Signposting – to clarify and lubricate the communication process
- Basic assertion – particularly if it is concise
- Probing – to seek information, involve the more quiet attendees, and to encourage others to rethink their positions.
- Summarizing, pointing out discrepancies and consequences – to control the pace and direction of the meeting
- Broken record – to stand firm where necessary, and to encourage the more stubborn attendees to come to a workable compromise
- Negative assertion and fogging – to acknowledge that you have heard someone but to avoid becoming emotionally triggered by what they have said.

In summary, then, if meetings are on the increase for good reasons, it makes sense to capitalize on them to achieve something worthwhile. By using your assertive techniques, you can not only make meetings more productive, you enhance your own performance in them. In view of their 'shop window' characteristics, that can only be of benefit.

A summary on performing well in meetings is given in Figure 19.

Rights

Yours	Theirs
To state my opinions openly To understand what is being discussed To disagree with what is being said To stand my ground if I believe I am right To compromise and to encourage others to do so To propose suggestions To be listened to To make a contribution To ensure that my time is being used to good effect	To fight their corner To disagree To not change their minds unless convinced to do so (i.e. the 'mirror image' of yours)

Self-talk

By using my assertive tools and techniques to good effect I can perform well in this meeting helping it achieve worthwhile conclusions.

Expectation

To encourage those who are not focused on a positive outcome to do so; to sidestep the point scorers and aggressors; to encourage the passengers.

Behaviour

Signposting. Basic assertion. Negative assertion. Fogging. Probing. Broken record. Summarizing. Pointing out discrepancies and consequences. Eye contact, 'newsreader' posture, good breathing and voice projection.

Outcome

Achieved	Avoided
Worthwhile meeting Personal credibility up Incremental education process for others on how meetings can work Better out of meeting relationships	Little of value achieved Personal credibility unchanged or worse Out of meeting relationships unchanged or worse

Figure 19 *Performing well in meetings: summary.*

Chapter 22

TALKING TO A POOR LISTENER

According to some researchers, we spend up to 75% of our working lives communicating – 10% writing, 15% reading, 30% talking, and 45% listening. Throughout our schooling and often our professional development, it is the reading and writing that receive most attention. Talking receives some attention, particularly where presentations are concerned. Listening, however, rarely receives any attention at all.

It is probably because we do so much listening, but do it badly, that the comment is sometimes made about assertiveness that 'It's all very well but my boss/staff/colleagues/suppliers/customers just don't listen.' Such people realize that much assertiveness is aimed at 'conflict' situations where the other person is listening, just not responding the way you would like them to. They have difficulty relating assertiveness to everyday situations where either someone is doing them the discourtesy of not listening or someone is generally bereft of listening skills. So, can assertiveness help you communicate with a poor listener? Let us begin by looking at what it is that poor listeners do.

First, such people *do not pay attention* to you and your message. They are more preoccupied with what they are thinking rather than with what you are saying.

Example one

Manager 1:	'. . . so I started thinking. Even though the decision is being made on the 12th, if I rewrote that section tonight, had it typed in the morning, we'd have the afternoon for any amendments and still be able to submit it before 5 o'clock. We'd get the same benefits from the reorganization at about half the cost. What do you say?'
Manager 2:	'There's no time to rewrite the plans, the decision's being made on the 12th.'

Manager 1 no doubt got the impression that Manager 2 was not listening.

Another version of the 'What I'm thinking is more important than what you're saying' attitude is the 'Yes . . . but' response.

Example two

Manager 1:	'. . . so, if I rewrote that section tonight we can still get it in by the deadline.'
Manager 2:	'Yes, but we'll never get it typed in time.'
Manager 1:	'We could if you primed the typing pool now and asked the supervisor to have a typist on standby.'
Manager 2:	'Yes, but they're bound to be amendments.'
Manager 1:	'So proof each page as it comes off the printer.'
Manager 2:	'Yes, but then I couldn't tell if there were linking problems between pages.'

The 'Yes . . . but' response effectively says 'If I listen to you there's a chance you'll be right and then I'll have to do something, so I'd rather close my ears thank you.'

Second, people who don't listen *misunderstand the type of communication* you are sending. This often results when a listener's attention wanders and they 'rejoin' the conversation but are now out of date in it. Alternatively, they may only hear selected words and ignore body language, tone of voice, overall context, and so on, and so misunderstand you.

Example three

Manager 1:	*means* 'The Board is very cost conscious at the moment. They'll expect to see big cost savings.'
Manager 1:	*says* 'How do you think the Board will react to the report?'
Manager 2:	*hears* 'The Board won't like your report.'

Manager 2:   *responds* 'What the hell's wrong with it?'

Third, *they interrupt*. This is another characteristic of the 'What I'm thinking is more important than what you're saying' mentality, and is one of the most discourteous traits of an aggressively bad listener.

Example four

Manager 1:   'So, I was thinking, if I took the report home to . . .'
Manager 2:   'We're not re-writing the whole report there's just not time.'
Manager 1:   'Only the section on . . .'
Manager 2:   'And then there's typing. You know how busy the typing pool is.'
Manager 1.   'Well, I thought that if I . . .'
Manager 2:   'And amendments. Don't forget the amendments.'
Manager 1:   'Yes, if I . . .'
Manager 2:   'No, best leave it. Sink or swim on the 12th.'

Fourth, those who don't listen *change the subject* when it is clearly inappropriate to do so.

Example five

Manager 1:   'So, I was thinking that if I took the report home tonight I could re-write that section, have a typist on standby for tomorrow morning. Proof read it as it comes off the printer and amend it before the deadline, no trouble. It's worth doing; the Board's very cost conscious at the moment. What do you think?'
Manager 2:   'Open plan.'
Manager 1:   'Pardon?'
Manager 2:   'Open plan. If there's enough money in the kitty next year I think we'll go for open plan.'

Finally, non-listeners *do not stop talking*, so they cannot possibly listen to you because you are not saying anything!

Example six

Manager 1:   'So, I was thinking, if I took the report home and rewrote that section . . .'
Manager 2:   'No point. Never get it typed.'

Manager 1:   'Yes but I . . .'
Manager 2:   'Backlog in the typing pool is dreadful. Very badly managed department, if you ask me.'
Manager 1:   'Well, what I . . .'
Manager 2:   'A dedicated typist. That's what we need for a project like this. Now if we had a typist dedicated to us for our sole use on this project there wouldn't be a problem.'

So, poor listeners do not pay attention, they misunderstand the type of communication you are sending, they interrupt, they change the subject, and they don't stop talking! There are several assertiveness tools and techniques that can affect these behaviours.

- Not paying attention – *probing or fogging* make the other person think and involve them. As the conscious mind will only handle one thought at a time, your probing and fogging substitutes their distracting thought for your intended one.

Example seven

Manager 1:   '. . . so I got to thinking. Even though the decision is being made on the 12th, if I rewrote that section tonight, had it typed in the morning, we'd have the afternoon for any amendments and still be able to submit it before 5 o'clock. We'd get the same benefits from the reorganization at about half the cost. What do you say?'
Manager 2:   'There's no time to re-write the plans, the decisions being made on the 12th.'
Manager 1:   'But is there time to re-write one section?' (probing)
Manager 2:   'No, it's got to be in by 5 o'clock tomorrow.'
Manager 1:   'If I rewrote about ten pages tonight and had a typist on standby for first thing in the morning, would there be time?' (probing)
Manager 2:   'Yes . . . there might be. We'd have to manage the proofing . . . and the amendments. Let's just run through the changes you want to make.'

Example eight

Manager 1:   '. . . so if I rewrote the section tonight we can still get it in by the deadline.'
Manager 2:   'Yes, but we'll never get it typed in time.'

Manager 1:	'You could if you primed the typing pool now and asked the supervisor to have a typist on standby.'
Manager 2:	'Yes, but there's bound to be amendments.'
Manager 1:	'Amendments bother you?' (fogging)
Manager 2:	'Yes, we'll get the re-written draft OK then we'll proof it, take it back to the typing pool supervisor and then there'll be a long queue. We can't guarantee it'll be ready by 5 o'clock.'
Manager 1:	'It's the lack of certainty of achieving the deadline that makes you unsure about my re-writing that section.' (fogging)
Manager 2:	'Yes, we'd have to persuade the typing pool supervisor to have someone else on standby for the amendments.'
Manager 1:	'That's a good idea. Let's talk to her straight away.'

- Misunderstanding the type of communication – this is a hazard of communication when people are listening. It is a double hazard when they are not. *Signposting* not only tells them what type of communication is on its way, it also grabs their attention.

Example nine

Manager 1:	*means* 'The Board is very cost conscious at the moment. They'll expect to see big cost savings.'
Manager 1:	*says* 'Let me just check something with you please. How do you think the Board will react to the report?' (signposting, probing)
Manager 2:	*hears* 'Have you thought about how the Board might react?'
Manager 2:	*responds* 'That's a good point. They're exceptionally cost conscious at the moment, aren't they?'

- Interrupting – interrupters do not listen. To encourage them to listen you have to first let them know you would prefer them not to interrupt (*basic assertion*), and second, let them know it does not pay off by continuing what you are saying (broken record).

Example ten

Manager 1:	'So, I was thinking, if I took the report home to . . .'
Manager 2:	'We're not re-writing the whole report there's just not time.'
Manager 1:	'Only the section on . . .'

Manager 2:	'And then there's typing. You know how busy the typing pool is.'
Manager 1:	'You're interrupting me. I'd prefer you not to.' (basic assertion)
Manager 2:	'Well, I just know we haven't got time to re-write the whole report and even if we did, we'd never get it typed.'
Manager 1:	'That's why I'm suggesting we re-write only one section and . . .' (broken record)
Manager 2:	'Yes but there's still typing.'
Manager 1:	'Please, you're not letting me finish my sentences. I'm suggesting we re-write only one section and with a typist on standby we can guarantee it being ready before five.' (broken record)
Manager 2:	'Oh . . . that's different.'

- Changing the subject – *pointing out the discrepancy* between what you are saying and how they are responding is usually enough to jolt them into listening. It has even more impact if you first gain their attention by *signposting* and then involve them by *probing*.

Example eleven

Manager 1:	'So, I was thinking that if I took the report home tonight I could re-write that section, have a typist on standby for tomorrow morning. Proof read it as it comes off the printer and amend it before the deadline, no trouble. It's worth doing; the Board's very cost conscious at the moment. What do you think?'
Manager 2:	'Open plan.'
Manager 1:	'Pardon?'
Manager 2:	'Open plan. If there's enough money in the kitty next year I think we'll go for open plan.'
Manager 1:	'Sorry, I'm not with you. I'm talking about cost savings this year and you appear to be talking about expenditure next year. Are we talking at cross purposes?' (signposting, pointing out a discrepancy, probing)
Manager 2:	'Oh . . . sorry . . . my mind was running on. Where did we get to?'

- Incessantly talking – there is only one way. You interrupt them. Not rudely or abruptly but with advance warning (*signposting*) and in such a way (*probing*) that they can carry on doing their favourite thing – talking – even if it is only to grant you 'permission' to have your say (*basic assertion*).

Example twelve

Manager 1:	'So, I was thinking, if I took the report home and rewrote that section . . .'
Manager 2:	'No point. Never get it typed.'
Manager 1:	'Yes but I . . .'
Manager 2:	'Backlog in the typing pool is dreadful. Very badly managed department, if you ask me.'
Manager 1:	'Well, what I . . .'
Manager 2:	'A dedicated typist. That's what we need for a project like this. Now if we had a typist dedicated to us for our sole use on this project there wouldn't be a problem.'
Manager 1:	'Pardon me for interrupting but I'd like to ask you a question.' (signposting)
Manager 2:	'Oh . . . OK then.'
Manager 1:	'I have an alternative to the dedicated typist. An alternative which will help us re-write a problem section of the report. Shall I tell you about it?' (basic assertion, probing)
Manager 2:	'Er . . . yes . . . alright then.'

Note: This approach is also useful when dealing with keen talkers to whom you would like to listen if only they could stay on the subject. For example:

Manager 2:	'. . . so, I then said, "Mr President, if . . ." '
Manager 1:	'Can I just check something?' (signposting)
Manager 2:	'Oh . . . er . . . yes.'
Manager 1:	'Fascinating though it is, is it relevant to how I should approach the typing pool supervisor?' (probing)
Manager 2:	'No . . . quite right . . . what I suggest you ask her is . . .'

This chapter should have given you insights into how to use assertive tools and techniques to make the most of your conversations with a poor listener. All the approaches I have illustrated correspond with what I believe your rights to be:

- To be attended to when you are talking to someone about an issue which concerns them.
- To think positively and avoid the 'Yes but' mentality.
- To believe that what you have to say is as important as what other people have to say.
- To state what you want or how you feel.
- To be listened to.

The chapter should also have encouraged you to ask a question of yourself while reading the illustrations of poor listeners – 'How many times do *I* do that?'

If you feel a bit embarrassed, please remember that listening is not only a key communication skill, it is also a key assertive skill. Truly assertive people are good listeners.

A summary on talking to a poor listener is given in Figure 20.

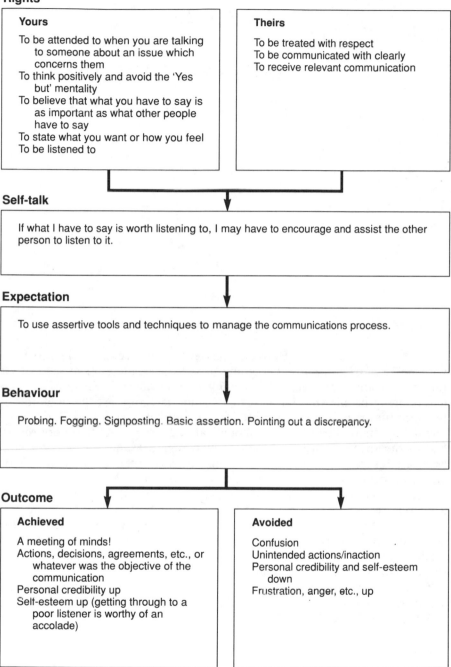

Rights

Yours

To be attended to when you are talking
  to someone about an issue which
  concerns them
To think positively and avoid the 'Yes
  but' mentality
To believe that what you have to say is
  as important as what other people
  have to say
To state what you want or how you feel
To be listened to

Theirs

To be treated with respect
To be communicated with clearly
To receive relevant communication

Self-talk

If what I have to say is worth listening to, I may have to encourage and assist the other
person to listen to it.

Expectation

To use assertive tools and techniques to manage the communications process.

Behaviour

Probing. Fogging. Signposting. Basic assertion. Pointing out a discrepancy.

Outcome

Achieved

A meeting of minds!
Actions, decisions, agreements, etc., or
  whatever was the objective of the
  communication
Personal credibility up
Self-esteem up (getting through to a
  poor listener is worthy of an
  accolade)

Avoided

Confusion
Unintended actions/inaction
Personal credibility and self-esteem
  down
Frustration, anger, etc., up

Figure 20 *Talking to a poor listener: summary.*

Chapter 23

SEEKING GUIDANCE FROM YOUR BOSS

How do *you* feel about seeking guidance from your boss? Anxious, guilty, like going to see the headmaster at school? Or relaxed, positive, and generally feeling comfortable? There are unfortunately many people who fall into the former category. At the mild end of the spectrum they simply feel a little inadequate at having to seek guidance about something they feel they 'should' already know. At the more severe end of the spectrum are those people who regard asking the boss for help as a last resort – the lesser of two evils, because their boss has a sink or swim, no prisoners attitude to 'stragglers' who cannot keep up.

Let us begin by considering why seeking guidance from your boss is not a pleasant experience. It could be because your boss is very busy and you feel guilty at having to bother him or her; you feel guilty or inadequate for not knowing what you feel you 'should' know; you didn't feel guilty or inadequate about seeking guidance until your boss made it plain that he/she thought you should feel that way.

As we know from Part One, thoughts give rise to expectations which affect our behaviour, so here are some examples of the kinds of behaviour to which these thoughts might give rise:

Example one

Situation

A manager has been asked to produce a manpower plan and skills inventory based on plans that his department will take responsibility for a new, up-market product. He received a brief explanation from his boss in a meeting last week, but now that he has sat down to do it he realizes he does not understand what is required, and so goes to see his boss:

Manager:	'Have you got a minute?'
Boss:	'I am a bit pushed at the moment.'
Manager:	'I'm awfully sorry to bother you. I'll keep it brief, if you're sure now is OK.'
Boss:	'Yes, yes, come on.'
Manager:	'Well . . . it's this manpower plan and skills inventory . . . I'm probably being very thick but I haven't quite grasped what it is that's required.'
Boss:	'Look, it's quite simple. Basic common sense really. Look at how the new product differs from the old one, see what new skills are required, consider how many of your current staff have those skills, estimate needs for training and recruitment, and construct a plan accordingly. Couldn't be simpler. OK?'
Manager:	'Er . . .'
Boss:	'If you're not sure check with Personnel – they know about these things. Anything else? I'm very busy right now.'
Manager:	'Er . . . no.'
Boss:	'Right, I'd better run then. And make sure that Manpower Plan is accurate. The Director has said he wants to see all of them.'

It is clear that this manager is not going to go very far with his planning. He still does not know what is required and, unless Personnel can bail him out, he will only have to 'bother' his boss again.

Managers who submissively ask for guidance have certain tell-tale signs. First, they usually defer the unpleasantness by putting off seeing their boss until the eleventh hour. They are over-apologetic and self-depreciating.

This behaviour has several consequences. The eleventh hour may not be convenient for the boss, and he or she may have conflicting priorities. The boss in Example one had to rush off to a meeting putting pressure on the manager not to persist. Excessive apology is poor signposting. It effectively says 'I feel very anxious about talking to you so please be nice.' It triggers impatience more than it triggers sympathy. Similarly with the self depreciating remarks. The speaker is 'fishing' for reassurance. What the speaker does not want to hear is 'No you're not thick and it isn't difficult, it just requires someone with a bit of self-confidence, you idiot!', which is probably what the manager's boss is thinking. So, far from encouraging help from the boss, the submissive manager's approach actually triggers disdain.

But do managers with aggressive tendencies fair any better? Well, what do we know about aggressive people when things aren't going well? They blame everybody but themselves: 'If only the boss had given me a proper briefing I'd be able to do it. We never bother with plans in this place anyway; they gather dust once written. What's all the fuss about anyway? We've had new products before and never bothered with all this. As if I didn't have enough to do.' Blame and exaggeration in their thoughts come through in what they say.

Example two

Manager:	'Have you got a minute?'
Boss:	'Well I am a bit pushed at the . . .'
Manager:	'It's this manpower plan and skills inventory.'
Boss:	'What about it?'
Manager:	'It just doesn't make sense. It's no good, I've got to have more direction on it.'
Boss:	'It's quite simple. Basic common sense really. Look . . .'
Manager:	'Well it doesn't make sense to me. It's not fair. I'm up to my ears at the moment and now this comes along. It's always the same. We never get enough time for these things.'
Boss:	'Everybody's under pressure at the moment. Now look, I'm very busy right now. You'll have to speak to my secretary. Try the end of the week.'

Managers who aggressively ask for guidance also have tell-tale signs. Because it is not their 'fault' that they need guidance they have to blame something or someone else. They have to belittle the task or the people who need it done.

Understandably, therefore, people do not feel predisposed to help them. In many cases of seeking guidance, the boss would recognize the significance of the task and so provide help anyway. The style of approach made by the manager, however, is bound to trigger a style of response. An undercurrent of resentment or hostility may well show through the boss's explanation.

So in seeking guidance from the boss there is a danger that feelings of vulnerability, guilt, inadequacy or resentment may show through in your approach. While I have used extremes to illustrate the point, ask yourself how *you* feel when seeking guidance from your boss. If you experience these or similar feelings to any degree there is the real possibility that they will show in your behaviour – however subtly. And remember, most people are adept at picking up non-verbal signals, even when they do not know they are receiving them.

But does approaching the boss assertively to seek guidance work, or do you have to be lucky enough to have an assertive boss? Let us revisit the examples with a different manager.

Example three

Manager:	'Can I speak to you a moment?' (probing)
Boss:	'Well I am a bit pushed right now.'
Manager:	'I see you're busy, so I'll keep it short. It's the manpower plan and skills inventory.' (empathy, signposting)
Boss:	'What about it?'
Manager:	'When you asked me to produce them I thought I understood what was required. Now I realize I don't. I want to get it right so I'd like to ask for some more guidance on it.'
Boss:	'It's quite simple. Basic common sense.'
Manager:	'I'm sure it is, but I still want to make sure I get it right.' (negative assertion, broken record)
Boss:	'Have you checked with Personnel? They know about these things.'
Manager:	'I'm sure they do. However, as I'm doing the work for you I want to make sure I get it right.' (negative assertion, broken record)
Boss:	'OK. Have you done a manpower plan before?'
Manager:	'Yes, it's the skills inventory I'm not sure about.' (basic assertion)
Boss:	'We're introducing a new product, right?'
Manager:	'Yes.'
Boss:	'So that will require new skills, right?'
Manager:	'I'm not clear. We've introduced new products before but haven't produced skills inventories for them.' (self-disclosure, basic assertion)
Boss:	'But this one isn't the same as all the previous ones.'
Manager:	'This one's different.' (fogging)
Boss:	'That's right. It's more up-market.'
Manager:	'We'll be selling it to different customers?' (fogging)
Boss:	'Exactly. Now what do you know about up-market customers?'
Manager:	'At a guess, I'd say that if they're paying more for the product they'd be more demanding, more critical, more discerning, expect more by way of service from us. That sort of thing.'
Boss:	'That sort of thing exactly. Now what sort of skills would your staff need to cope with such customers?'
Manager:	'Well . . . customer care skills, complaint handling skills,

	better telephone manner, oh . . . and probably better team working to ensure that the service levels stay high.'
Boss:	'And?'
Manager:	'And?'
Boss:	'And knowledge of the new, up-market products.'
Manager:	'Oh yes, fancy forgetting that. So what I do is list the skills we'll need and compare them against the skills we've got, and see where the gaps are. Is that all?' (probing)
Boss:	'Don't underestimate it. It's not easy.'
Manager:	'Do I compare the team against the new skills or each individual person?' (probing)
Boss:	'Each individual person.'
Manager:	'Why that way?'
Boss:	'Firstly, so that we can compile training plans, and secondly so that where you consider people untrainable, we can prepare a manpower plan that includes recruitment.'
Manager:	'Ah, now I see where it all fits in. This has been a really useful conversation. I feel much more confident that I'll be able to get it right now. Thankyou.' (self-disclosure, praise)
Boss:	'That's OK. Why not show me a draft before you submit the final plans?'
Manager:	'That would be helpful, thank you.' (praise)

Even though the busy boss tried to avoid spending time helping the manager, and even tried a little sarcasm, he still ended up providing the required assistance, and even volunteered more. How did the manager do it?

- by acknowledging that his boss was busy (empathy).
- steering his boss onto the same wavelength – very important when interrupting someone (signposting).
- sidestepping attempts (unwitting or otherwise) to trigger his emotions (negative assertion).
- stating accurately and concisely what the problem was and what he wanted (basic assertion).
- being open about how he felt (self-disclosure).
- reflecting back what the boss had said so that the boss would elaborate on it (fogging).
- seeking information and clarification (probing).
- encouraging his boss to provide further guidance (praising).

Notice that once the boss's initial attempts to avoid the interruption failed, he then started to provide information. It was at this stage that the manager's use of fogging and probing encouraged the boss to shift his style from simply giving information to getting the manager to think things through and work them out for himself – a process that turns problems into learning situations. So not only did the manager receive the help he needed, he received it in a way that proved effective and which helped the boss/subordinate relationship.

By thinking positively at the outset, you are more likely to approach your boss positively. By using appropriate assertive tools and techniques, you should also be able to overcome any reluctance on the part of your boss, and encourage him or her to turn a request for guidance into a coaching session.

A summary on seeking guidance from your boss is given in Figure 21.

Rights

Yours	**Theirs**
To full and comprehensible instructions	To honesty and openness from you
To guidance from my boss	To staff who own their problems
To support from my boss	To staff who use their initiative
To my boss's time	To staff who are keen to learn
To learn from my work	To choose how they manage their time
To feel alright about not knowing something	
To be treated with respect as an intelligent human being	

Self-talk

Learning at work is rewarding. It helps me improve my performance. Learning from my boss helps improve our working relationship.

Expectation

An honest but guilt-free admission of what I don't know, perseverance in seeking help, drawing out relevant information, feeling positive afterwards.

Behaviour

Empathy. Signposting. Negative assertion. Basic assertion. Self-disclosure. Fogging. Probing. Praising.

Outcome

Achieved	**Avoided**
Guidance obtained	Guidance not obtained
Knowledge improved	Relationship detrimentally affected
Relationship improved	Personal credibility down
Personal credibility up	Self-esteem down
Self-esteem up	

Figure 21 *Seeking guidance from your boss: summary.*

Chapter 24

REDUCING STRESS

If you cast your mind back to the story in Part One of the two business people stuck in the same traffic jam, you will recall that one of them suffered an acute increase in stress while the other remained calm. We saw that the problem was not the traffic jam but the reaction of the individuals to it.

That story sets the scene for this chapter. Its objective is to help you reduce the harmful effects of self-generated stress by considering the subject from an assertive viewpoint. But first a few general words about stress.

Most books and articles on the subject begin by making the point that not all stress is a problem. Many of us, for example, work better when we have a deadline, experience a feeling of accomplishment when we achieve something challenging – and maybe also slacken off if we feel that no-one cares about our work.

–Stress becomes a problem when it is excessive or prolonged. The release of adrenalin and other substances into the blood stream (as in the fight or flight response described in Part One) does more than make our hands clammy and our feet cold. It increases our blood pressure, increases the blood's clotting propensity, produces additional stomach acid, and depletes our stocks of vitamins B and C. When prolonged, these effects are not only harmful to our health, they also quickly drain us of energy, making us less able to cope with even reduced amounts of stress in the future.

It is also pretty uncomfortable to those around us. One reaction is to behave very submissively in an attempt to remove some of the stress of interacting with others. We try hard to be liked, being ultra-compliant, avoid unpopular decisions, and so on. A submissively manipulative reaction to stress is to 'forget' to do things, or to do them badly so that the task does not come our way next time. Or to do it with lots of sighs, moans and other signals of 'martyrdom'. An aggressive response is to try and prove that other people are as badly off as us by personally criticizing them, engaging in wildly derogatory generalizations about people, events, decisions, resurrecting past problems, comparing people against our ever-stricter 'rules', and by withdrawing co-operation. Stress does not just affect us, it affects people around us. It is a problem and requires action.

But where useful pressure ends and undesirable stress beings is impossible to answer because it all depends on individuals. What one person cannot cope with another may take in his or her stride, and a third may not even notice. Although the causes of stress may be external to us, our reaction is entirely self-generated. A significant amount of it is down to our *thinking*. So to examine how assertive thinking can help reduce stress, it will be useful, first to consider some typical causes; not the sudden shock causes such as bereavement or redundancy, but the ones found in everyday management.

First, there is human interaction. Work is an intricate network of relationships. It would be a miracle if they all went smoothly all of the time. In any society there will be conflicts. Include the additional factors of hierarchy, status, office politics, seemingly conflicting objectives, and so on, and you have a recipe for trouble. We know from Part One that more people react to conflict with their fight or flight response than with their verbal problem solving skills. Stress is the result and, for some people, even just trying to avoid conflict is stressful because of the impact it has on their levels of anxiety, guilt, and self-esteem.

Bionic role models are a second source of stress. Managers who work 12–14 hours a day and die or burn themselves out in their forties receive little publicity whereas those who feel fine after four hours sleep and get up ready for another hectic and lengthy day are often held out as examples to be emulated. Some people thrive on that sort of existence, while to others it is a death sentence. For some strange reason, those who can do it consider it normal and expect their underlings to keep up with them. The underlings see it as the behaviour to emulate and either wear themselves out trying or feel inferior if they cannot. Both states lead to stress.

Finally, there are those people who, perhaps because of their life plan, style of communicating with others, or because of their perception of rights, cannot cope with the accountability of management. Accountability for decisions, output, quality and deadlines causes them worry. Other factors such as the role conflict of perhaps managing people who are also friends, adds to the stress levels. It comes with the job, and is useful pressure to some people but undesirable stress to others.

You may well be able to add other causes of stress such as potential redundancy, retraining, restructuring or constantly shifting goal posts. The list is intended to be indicative rather than definitive. What is important is that by reading it you gain some appreciation of how, as with the traffic jam, stress is a result of how people respond to everyday situations rather than the situations themselves. The key, therefore, to reducing stress is in controlling your reaction to ordinary events.

The spring clean you gave your data banks in Part One is a significant step in controlling your reactions because we mostly respond according to our view of the world and our place in it. Much of that response is dictated by our data banks sufficiently frequently until it becomes habit. Table 2 demonstrates the links between events, the content of our data banks and our learned response.

Table 2   *Links between events, content of our data banks, and our learned response.*

Event	Data banks	Response
Conflict with a colleague	Other people are right	Capitulation. Poor self-esteem
A 'crisis' occurs	You can't hand difficult things	Panic
Criticism from your boss	You've got to be perfect	Exaggeration. Self-depreciation
Staff member asks too much of you	Don't refuse a request	Agreement. Self-reproach
Staff behaviour is rowdy	People 'should' behave with decorum	Verbal aggression

In other words, you *always* panic in a crisis, get disrespectful staff, are delegated rotten jobs, and so on. You may find it worthwhile asking yourself the following questions. Award yourself 3 points for often, 2 points for sometimes, 1 point for rarely, and 0 points for never:

1. Do you think of yourself as less worthy than others? ☐

2. Do you think pessimistically about yourself? ☐

3. Do you think pessimistically about life in general? ☐

4. Do you feel overwhelmed by events? ☐

5. Do you feel anxious at work? ☐

6. Do you see changes at work as problems? ☐

7. Do you do things for other people more often than you ☐
    want to?

8. Do you blame someone or something else for your circumstances?

9. Do you feel rushed?

10. Do you feel impatient with other people?

11. Do you hide your feelings?

12. Are you emphatic?

13. Do you tend to walk, eat and talk quickly?

Between 15 and 25 points should give you food for thought, and above 25 points should give you cause for concern because you could be suffering self-generated stress.

'Self-generated' means the cause is within your data banks and early programming, and will manifest itself in your self-talk. Think back to your last stressful occurrence. What were you saying to yourself? What self-image is that based on? What assumptions were you making about yourself and others involved? How rational or reasonable are these thoughts? What will be the natural consequences of such thoughts? What do those thoughts say about your rights and those of other people? Finally, how can you apply the rights discussed in Part One to turn negative self-talk into positive self-talk?

That last point is usually very difficult but of immense value to stress sufferers. It is difficult because a feature of stress (and, incidentally, also of clinical depression) is that sufferers build 'walls' around themselves. They become mentally insular and see things only from their own viewpoint – and that viewpoint is negative. The value of positive self-talk is twofold: first, it makes it easier to break the vicious circle of negative thoughts, negative behaviour and negative outcomes which stress sufferers experience; second, it addresses a real and problematic aspect of stress – that of *feeling out of control*; that you can do nothing to improve matters. As you restate negative self-talk in positive terms, you can put yourself back in the driving seat.

Negative self-talk	*Positive self-talk*
If these road hogs wouldn't drive so badly I'd still be in a good mood when I get home.	If I keep calm when these people drive badly I'll be in a good mood when I get home.
I just can't work these crazy hours any more	If I can organize myself better I can achieve my key priorities in less time.

I can't do everything I want to do within the deadline.	I can do what's essential within the deadline.
I don't like the loneliness of taking decisions alone.	I don't have to take decisions alone if I consult with my staff.
People don't behave the way I think they should.	If I let them behave the way they think they should maybe they'll perform better.
I feel that this job is too big for me.	I'm learning to fill the job.
I can't control two thirds of my day.	I can control one third of it.
I can't match their expectations.	My expectations are healthier/I can match some of their expectations.

With positive self-talk you are automatically tackling the main part of your stress – how you react to events and people. That frustrating delay before a meeting becomes useful last minute preparation time. A customer complaint becomes a good idea for product development. Scowls from the boss for going home 'early' become smiles from the family. Rejection of someone else's 'rules' becomes more confidence in your own. With that confidence you can set positive goals for yourself. Not to be less pessimistic, but to be more optimistic; not to criticize staff less, but to praise them more, and so on.

You can also use that confidence to tackle the situations with other people that cause you stress, resolve to address them and act assertively. When you do:

- be specific
- be open and honest especially about your feelings; present your side neutrally and factually
- *listen* to them
- decide what you will do next. Even if all you achieve is to have addressed the matter but the other person will still not co-operate, you will be surprised how elated and good you will feel.

A summary on reducing stress is given in Figure 22.

Rights

Yours and Everyone's

To be my own judge
To not respond to others' attempts to manipulate me
To have my own thoughts
To live my life by my rules
To think positively about myself, other people and events irrespective of what is in my data banks
To resist excessive or unremitting pressure
To control my own thoughts

Self-talk

The one thing in this world over which I have total control are my thoughts. I therefore choose to make them positive about me, other people and events, and will not allow others to turn them into negative ones.

Expectation

A happier, healthier existence. Being nicer to know and work with.

Behaviour

Address self-generated stress first, then the remaining 10%!!! caused by other people. Persevere. Small steps not giant leaps.

Outcome

Achieved

As in 'Expectation'

Avoided

Perpetuation of current stress levels

Figure 22   *Reducing stress: summary.*

Chapter 25

HANDLING PERSISTENT SALESPEOPLE

Some managers are accustomed to dealing with professional salespeople. They have had custody of their department's expenditure budget for some time, and are used to being in the role of 'buyer'. More managers are taking on this role, however, as companies and public utilities decentralize control, federalize their structures and practise competitive tendering with outside contractors. For the first time, therefore, many managers are taking responsibility for choosing how their department's money is spent. They are coming face-to-face with professional salespeople.

So far in this book we have looked at being in control of yourself and tackling other people's learned reactions to conflict. We have also looked at countering the learned manipulation techniques that people apply in an attempt to obtain their way. What we have not yet looked at is handling a *trained manipulator* – the professional salesperson!

At this stage in the chapter I feel I ought to do some signposting just in case any sales managers reading it are starting to worry!

Good salespeople work with buyers to reach an agreement with which they both feel comfortable. They help buyers make the right choice because that way their relationship develops into the future. As every salesperson knows, it is easier and more cost-effective to retain an existing customer than to seek out and convert a prospective customer. Many well trained salespeople will help you identify and specify a problem area, calculate its cost, and prove to you that investment in their offering will actually save you money. Many sales negotiators adopt the win/win philosophy of 'principled negotiation', seek and share information openly so that they and the buyer know that the correct decision has been reached.

Some salespeople, unfortunately, are more interested in achieving today's targets than in building a business base for the future. All they want is a signature on an order form, and they will use every known tactic to close the sale. This chapter is aimed at enabling you to stand firm against the tactics of unprincipled salespeople so that you achieve the maximum return on your budget expenditure. We do so by looking at the typical tactics of such salespeople, and see how the assertive tools and techniques we have learned can effectively counter them, leaving you to make your choices of expenditure in your own way and in your own time.

Tactic one – Pressure

Metaphorically speaking (and sometimes literally), salespeople have many doors shut in their faces and telephones slammed down on them. Therefore, to succeed against this persistent attack on their self-esteem, they have to have certain qualities – a thick skin, persistence and total deafness when they hear the word 'No'. These qualities come together in the first tactic they employ – pressure. Pressure will be used throughout the sales process but, as buyers rarely buy from salespeople they do not know, it is most obvious when they are trying to get that first appointment, usually via the telephone:

Salesperson:	'Good morning, Mr Smith. My name's Johnstone, William Johnstone from Ace Stationers. I'd like to come and see you to show you our latest range of stationery.'
Manager:	'Well actually I wasn't planning on buying any stationery just yet.'
Salesperson:	'That's OK Mr Smith, we're new in your area so I'd just like to show you our range so that when you do want to buy some we hope you'll come to us.'
Manager:	'Yes, but as I said. I wasn't planning on buying any just yet. Maybe not for six months. I'd hate to waste your time.'
Salesperson:	'No problem, Mr Smith, I have to be in your vicinity next week so it's no trouble to pop in.'
Manager:	'Well. . . . OK then.'

Think of this encounter from the point of view of salespeople. They have more to lose from not meeting you than you do. Lost commission, non-achievement of call rate, targets, and so on. They have more at stake than you have, so they are bound to push harder. The usual reaction is for the manager to give in and agree to a meeting to avoid the discomfort of refusing a perfectly reasonable and well argued request. All you have to do if you genuinely do not want to meet the salesperson is stand firm for longer than they are prepared to push:

Salesperson:	'Good morning, Mr Smith. My name's Johnstone, William Johnstone from Ace Stationers. I'd like to come and see you to show you our latest range of stationery.'
Manager:	'Thank you. However, I'm not buying stationery just yet so I'd prefer not to.' (basic assertion)
Salesperson:	'That's OK Mr Smith, we're new in your area so I'd just like to show you our range so that when you do want to buy some we hope you'll come to us.'
Manager:	'I understand. That's thoughtful of you. However, I'm not buying stationery at the moment so I'd prefer not to meet.' (empathy, broken record)
Salesperson:	'I have to be in your vicinity next week so I can easily pop in.'
Manager	'I'm sure you can. However, I'm not buying stationery at the moment so I'd prefer not to meet.' (fogging, broken record)
Salesperson:	'Would it be OK if I called again in, say, three months time?'
Manager:	'Yes. If I'm buying then we'll meet, but if I'm not we won't.' (basic assertion)
Salesperson:	'OK Mr Smith. Thankyou for your time.'

Broken record is an extremely useful technique to enable you to stand firm whilst remaining calm and, of course, polite. You have treated the salesperson courteously and also honestly. Both aspects are important. Discourtesy could make you and/or the salesperson feel bad. Dishonesty, however, is worse. To meet a salesperson just because you could not say 'No' in a telephone conversation will:

- make you feel uncomfortable
- waste your time
- waste the salesperson's time, which is unkind of you as some or all of their remuneration will be commission based. Hence, you are costing them money

Tactic two – Making assumptions on your behalf

The theory behind this tactic is that often people do not like making big decisions but are quite content to make small ones. All salespeople have to do, therefore, is ask you to make a small decision which assumes that the main decision *has already been made*.

Salesperson:	'Good morning, Mr Smith. My name's Johnstone, William Johnstone from Ace Stationers. I'd like to come and see you to show you our latest range of stationery.'
Manager:	'Well actually, I wasn't planning on buying any stationery just yet.'
Salesperson:	'That's OK Mr Smith. We're new in your area so I'd just like to show you our range for future reference. I'm in your vicinity next Tuesday. Do you prefer mornings or afternoons?'
Manager:	'Er . . . mornings usually but . . .'
Salesperson:	'Nine thirty or would you prefer ten thirty?'
Manager:	'I have a meeting at ten thirty.
Salesperson:	'OK, nine thirty it is.'

At this stage in a conversation with a salesperson this sort of tactic might be easy to notice, but farther into the sales process it is more difficult to recognize. Momentum will have built up, and a good salesperson will use this tactic when you are close to a decision but not quite decided:

Salesperson:	'So, you're satisfied as to our credentials and the quality of the stationery. Can I put you down for a trial order?'
Manager:	'Hmm . . .'
Salesperson:	'Would you like us to deliver monthly so that you qualify for bulk discount or would a weekly delivery put less pressure on storage?'
Manager:	'I'd prefer weekly – we're tight on space as you can see.'
Salesperson:	'OK, weekly it is. So, if you'll just sign here . . .'

After the salesperson has gone, or even while you are signing, you will probably have this nagging doubt that you are no longer in control. Your defence is firstly to recognize the tactic and secondly to do something about it:

Salesperson:	'So, you're satisfied as to our credentials and the quality of the stationery. Can I put you down for a trial order?'
Manager:	'Hmm . . .'
Salesperson:	'Would you like us to deliver monthly so that you can qualify for the bulk discount, or would a weekly delivery put less pressure on storage?'
Manager:	'That's a separate decision. I'd choose weekly because we're tight on space, but it's still a separate decision.' (basic assertion)

| Salesperson: | 'Oh . . . er . . .' |
| Manager: | 'We still need to agree a price within my budget.' (basic assertion) |

A straight statement to the salesperson (basic assertion) sends a clear signal that you will make your decision in your own way and in your own time and that tactics to by-pass that process will meet with no success.

Tactic three – Using logic against you

Western culture holds logic in high regard. We teach left brain thinking (comprehension, mathematics, sciences) in schools rather than right brain thinking (creativity, visualization). The terms 'irrational' and 'illogical' are derogatory when applied to people. When we were children, parents used logic to make us feel stupid, inferior and wrong.

Logic is what other people use to prove they are right and you are wrong. Early programming and our entire culture make it very difficult for us to come to terms with the fact that our feelings, intuition or gut reaction is either contradictory to someone else's logic, or that it is valid if it cannot be justified logically.

Salespeople are sometimes taught to use this inbuilt programming to their advantage by using logic to prove to us that we ought to sign the contract:

Manager:	'Come in Mr Johnstone, sit down.'
Salesperson:	'Thankyou, Mr Smith. Now then, as I gave you quite a few details over the 'phone and you have a meeting at ten thirty, perhaps I can come straight to the point.'
Manager:	'Good idea.'
Salesperson:	'We believe that today's marketplace is highly competitive. Do you agree?'
Manager:	'It is for many companies but we have a good reputation.'
Salesperson:	'But things can change very rapidly. New competitors, new technology. You wouldn't want to be left behind would you Mr Smith?'
Manager:	'Absolutely not.'
Salesperson:	'We believe that the image a company displays to its existing and prospective clients can have a significant effect on whether or not that company is invited to tender or can maintain a high price. Do you agree, Mr Smith?'
Manager:	'Oh yes. Image is very important.'
Salesperson:	'We further believe that while most companies spend countless sums of money on advertising, a significant image maker, their stationery, is often neglected. Do you agree with that?'

Manager:	'It sounds sensible.'
Salesperson:	'When did your company last review its stationery, Mr Smith?'
Manager:	'About three years ago.'
Salesperson:	'Oh dear, with competitors entering the market, that means it could be looking a little dated to your customers. Do you want that?'
Manager:	'Absolutely not.'
Salesperson:	'OK, let me explain how our unique service could prevent that happening.'

So even though Mr Smith does not want to buy new stationery he is being swept along by the conversation because it 'sounds logical'.

There are two tell-tale signs that salespeople are using the 'logic trap' to get you on the hook. The first is that they do most of the talking. They are more interested in what they have to sell than what you need to buy. The second is that they ask closed questions.

Closed questions, as we know from Part One, tend to generate a 'yes or no' answer. That is where the 'trap' comes in. They practice with an algorithm, such as that shown in Figure 23.

The algorithm is designed to 'paint you into a corner' so that your only way out is to accept their offer of help. This is known as the 'Gotcha Question' because whichever way you answer, the salesperson has gotcha!

Salesperson:	'Do you love your family, Mr Gillen?'
Me:	'Of course I do.'
Salesperson:	'Would you be upset to think of them living in poverty if anything happened to you?'
Me:	'Of course.'
Salesperson:	'Would you like to consider a low cost insurance policy to protect their financial security in the event of your untimely demise?'
Me:	'No.'
Salesperson:	(lead in to Gotcha question) 'But this policy will only cost a few pennies per member of your family per day.'
Me:	'I'm still not interested.'
Salesperson:	(Gotcha question) 'But how can your family's security not be worth a few pennies when you say you love them?'

The logic is irrefutable. How can I say I love my family and not be prepared to look after them? How can Mr Smith *not* want to consider new stationery when he has admitted how important it is to his company's future success? Doesn't he *care* about his company?

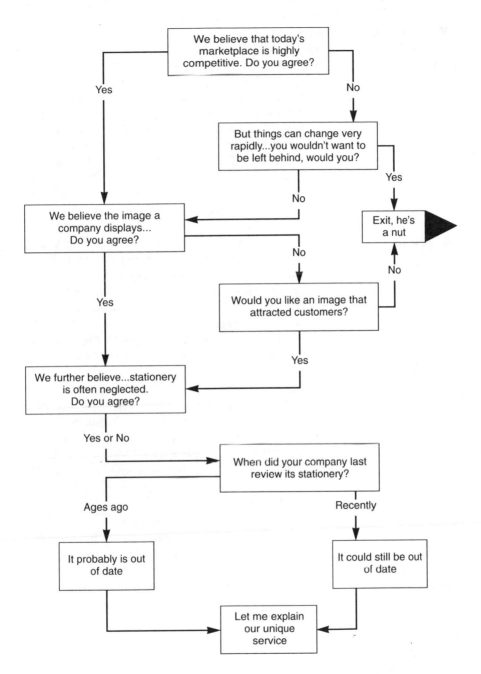

Figure 23 *Closed questions algorithm.*

You only have two ways out of the logic trap: first, to recognize that your intuition is as valid as their logic; and second to detach yourself emotionally from their arguments by using negative assertion:

Salesperson:	'OK, so I've explained how our unique service can safeguard your company's image. So can I put you down for a trial order? Weekly or monthly delivery?'
Manager:	'Neither, I'd like more time to think about it.' (basic assertion)
Salesperson:	'But you agree that your stationery is old hat.'
Manager:	'Yes but I'd still like more time to think about it.' (broken record)
Salesperson:	'But Mr Smith, how can you agree that your company's stationery is having a potentially damaging effect on its image and not want to do anything about it? That's not logical.'
Manager:	'It isn't. But I'd still like more time to think about it.' (negative assertion, broken record)
Salesperson:	'You're giving me the impression that you don't care about your company's image.'
Manager:	'I probably am.' (negative assertion)
Salesperson:	'But. . . . why can't you make a decision now?'
Manager:	'I don't know. I just know I want more time to think about it.' (self-disclosure, broken record)
Salesperson:	'But . . . what do you want to think about?'
Manager:	'I don't know. I just know I want more time.' (self-disclosure, broken record)
Salesperson:	'I've made a very generous offer on discount, Mr Smith.'
Manager:	'You have.' (negative assertion)
Salesperson:	'I've put a lot of effort in coming here today.'
Manager:	'You have. Thankyou.' (negative assertion)
Salesperson:	'Is that it then?'
Manager:	'No. I'll contact you when I've thought about it and I'll let you know my decision then.'
Salesperson:	'Oh . . . thank you.'
Manager:	'You're welcome and thank you for coming today.'

This approach will take practice. It is not easy sitting there knowing that the person opposite thinks you are crazy. To do otherwise, however, is to abdicate your right to be your own judge. Neither is it easy to avoid the logic trap of answering their questions:

Salesperson: 'What do you want to think about?'
Manager: 'Price.'
Salesperson: 'Oh let's talk about it.' (Where's my algorithm on price?)

Do that and you are back where you started.

No. Just remind yourself that it is your money, or your company's and you decide how, where and when it is spent – not the salesperson.

All salespeople are trying to do is sell their product or service. Some are very good at it. They are open and honest and build up long-lasting relationships with clients. Others are not so good and so use manipulative techniques to achieve a sale. Their motto appears to be that all is fair in love, war – and selling. Their manipulative techniques are sometimes crude and sometimes sophisticated, but they are all based on what sales gurus know about human nature – we respond to pressure, we prefer to avoid the 'exposure' of big decisions, we bow down to logic. So they apply subtle pressure, relieve us of the need to make big decisions, and use logic to lead us by the nose to the order form.

All *you* have to do is be assertive!

A summary on handling persistent salespeople is given in Figure 24.

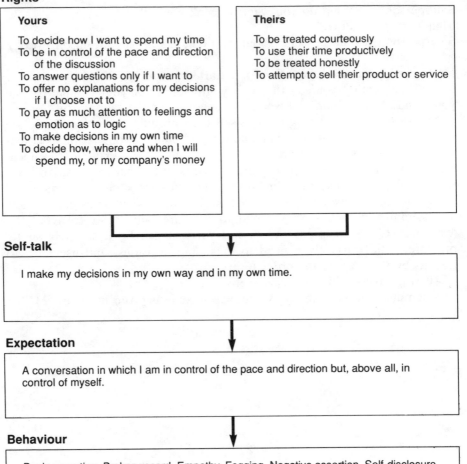

Rights

Yours

To decide how I want to spend my time
To be in control of the pace and direction
    of the discussion
To answer questions only if I want to
To offer no explanations for my decisions
    if I choose not to
To pay as much attention to feelings and
    emotion as to logic
To make decisions in my own time
To decide how, where and when I will
    spend my, or my company's money

Theirs

To be treated courteously
To use their time productively
To be treated honestly
To attempt to sell their product or service

Self-talk

I make my decisions in my own way and in my own time.

Expectation

A conversation in which I am in control of the pace and direction but, above all, in control of myself.

Behaviour

Basic assertion. Broken record. Empathy. Fogging. Negative assertion. Self-disclosure.

Outcome

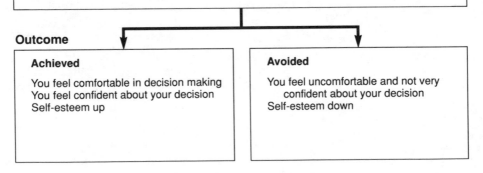

Achieved

You feel comfortable in decision making
You feel confident about your decision
Self-esteem up

Avoided

You feel uncomfortable and not very
    confident about your decision
Self-esteem down

Figure 24 *Handling persistent salespeople: summary.*

Chapter 26

CONCLUSION

You have now reached the end of this book but I trust not the end of your journey in assertiveness. The workout sheets and the individual sections in Part Two should have helped you identify what you want to do differently. To help further, though, I want to revisit certain central themes and suggest a way forward.

Perhaps the first point to make is that perception is individual. We each see the world differently. Often we group together with people who share similar views on marriage, work and leisure, but very rarely are people *totally* in tune with one another.

Our perceptions not only influence the way we see the world, they *are* our world. We each have our own way of viewing the way we, other people and events are and should be. We each have our own 'reality'. It was formed, primarily, during our early childhood. At that time we lived in a land of giants from whom we learned 'rules', formulated a self-image and developed a preferred way of communicating. Our perceptions, often based on a flight or fight response to conflict, are embedded deeply within us. They help govern our reactions to events by dictating our self-talk, expectations and behaviour.

When those perceptions are *restrictive*, they cause problems. We have a poor self-image, a negative life plan, and an unhelpful way of communicating and so on. When they are *empowering*, we have a good self-image, a positive life plan and an effective way of communicating. We also tend to be more tolerant of other people accepting that they have as much right to their perceptions as we have to ours, and that perceptions are just that – perceptions, not reality.

But does this mean we are locked into the vicious or virtuous circle prescribed during our formative years? The answer is a resounding 'No'! You and your perceptions exist separately. They are not you. The very fact that you can think about them separates you from them. They have been *learned*, and what has been learned can be unlearned and replaced with something else.

Assertiveness manifests itself through our *behaviour*, but that is only the third or tertiary level of assertiveness. People rarely behave assertively unless they have an *assertive mental attitude*.

An assertive mental attitude means having positive expectations about yourself, other people and situations. Having a 'half full' rather than a 'half empty' attitude. It means harnessing the self-fulfilling prophecy of expecting to do well. Not thinking rosy thoughts and hoping that everything will turn out fine but, like the weightlifter, giving yourself a sporting chance of success. In that way you can capitalize on your abilities rather than be held back by self-imposed limitations. Positive expectations and attitudes are the result of positive self-talk, the inner conversations forming a link between our data banks and our expectations. Together they constitute your assertive mental attitude – the secondary level of assertiveness.

Your self-talk springs directly from your data banks wherein are locked the self-image, life plan and preferred way of communicating that determine your basic perceptions. It is at this primary level of assertiveness that your rights are lodged (see Figure 25).

I have used a pyramid to represent this model to illustrate that

- your concept of rights forms the largest mass of your assertiveness;
- your attitudes, self-talk and expectations, if at all negative, can usually be traced back to your concept of rights on which they rest;
- assertive behaviour is the minor part of your assertiveness
- assertive behaviour cannot exist unless it rests upon the firm foundation of an assertive mental attitude which, in turn, cannot exist unless it rests on the broad and stable foundation of basic human rights.

The model should also provide you with an indication as to where you should commence your self-development programme in assertiveness.

Having completed the Assertiveness Profile questionnaire at the start of the book (and listened to the opinions of others using the second version of the questionnaire), you should have a view of where you fit in the aggressive/submissive/assertive model. If you also completed the Workout sheets you should have formulated an opinion as to what you need to do to become more assertive:

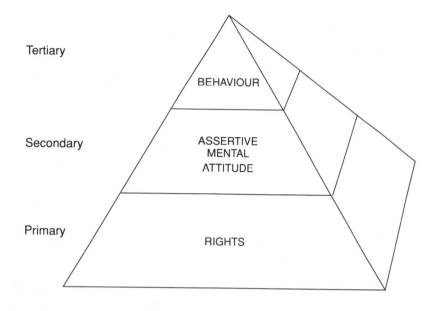

Figure 25 *Levels of assertiveness.*

- Can you become more assertive by simply addressing the tertiary level of behaviour, or will such attempts simply go the way of all superficial quick fix solutions and lack sustained durability?
- Can you simply address the secondary level of your assertive mental attitude to harness the power of positive self-talk and positive expectations? Athletes and business people the world over have discovered the performance advantages of a positive attitude. Is that enough for you? To succeed, is all you need a sporting chance to fulfil your natural potential?
- Alternatively, is the content of your data banks proving to be an unnecessary handicap? To live in the freedom of your future do you first need to break out of the straightjacket of your past? Can you achieve what you want in life without spring-cleaning your data banks?

If you only want to make minor changes, it may be sufficient to use the assertive tools and techniques to alter your behaviour. If you want to make moderate changes, you may also have to address your assertive mental attitude. *You*, however, are the only one who knows if you can achieve what you want in your job, your career and your life in general, without first reassessing your rights and those of others. *To change a situation, do you first need to change yourself?*

Examining rights is an effective way of reassessing your perceptions and maybe turning your own 'conventional wisdom' on its head. That may be a slow process; being 1% better at one little thing at a time. Slowly but surely and deliberately building up to a quantum leap of 1,000%. Alternatively, the 'quantum leap' may come in a rapid 180 degree shift in perceptions – just as it did in astronomy when Copernicus decided that it was the sun and not the earth that was at the centre of our solar system. Or just as it did when an overworked shopkeeper decided that life would be much easier if customers served themselves, thereby inventing the first supermarket!

Whether the reassessment of your perceptions is slow or sudden, one thing is certain. If the cause of your need to be more assertive lies in the primary level of assertiveness, *reassess them you must*. You cannot solve that type of fundamental problem by continuing the same level and type of thinking that created the problem in the first place. 'Private victories' in the primary and secondary levels will assist your success in the tertiary level. 'Public victories' in the tertiary level will assist your confidence in reassessing your perceptions, but will not render that reassessment redundant.

I believe that assertiveness is important to the healthy functioning of a human being. To constantly feel that you are either inferior or superior to other human beings is fundamentally unhealthy. Whether the ensuing frustration is with yourself or your 'underlings' is immaterial; persistent frustration trying to change the unchangeable is mentally and physically unhealthy. On the other hand, feeling fundamentally alright about yourself and about other people means that you can devote more of your energies to changing the changeable and extending the scope of your influence to include more of what is important to you. That may mean handling an aggressive colleague, resisting overload from the boss, resolving conflict, or consulting more with your staff.

The ability to influence is a crucial management quality (see the introductory Chapter on Reversing the domino effect). Organizational change is a permanent state and, for many people, one of its most frustrating aspects is the feeling of being out of control.

We know that much of today's organizational change involves such things as customer care, total quality, decentralization and cascading authority levels. Senior managers spend huge sums of money in incentives, massive off-the-job 'training' sessions, videos and so on in an attempt to win the motivation of the workforce. Such external interventions rarely deliver their promise, however, unless the basic rights relating to human interaction are such that people feel at least partially in control and alright about one another.

Effective organizations are simply a group of people working interdependently to achieve a commonly understood goal. To work interdependently, people *have* to feel alright about one another. There is no avoiding this fact. They do not necessarily have to like each other, spend their leisure time together or send one another Christmas cards, they just have to be straight and open with one another, and share relevant principles about the way they work together. Their perceptions relating to human interaction at work have to be 'in tune'.

It is my belief that if those principles stem from basic human rights, the task of motivating people to share organizational values and achieve corporate goals will be easier. Treating people with respect and dignity, listening to them, understanding their opinions, not trying to manipulate them, and so on, will address their motivational needs of security, belonging and self-esteem.

Effective organizational change rarely happens without such motivation at every level. Although change may be *led* by management, it is *actioned* by everyone. Their commitment to it cannot be ordered by hierarchical authority. Neither can it be summoned by technical authority. It can only be encouraged by authority based on personal credibility.

It is my experience that such credibility is never awarded to managers by their staff unless managers behave assertively, think with a positive assertive attitude and uphold assertive rights. Although behaviour is the manifestation of secondary and primary assertiveness, I have never known a manager/staff relationship where the manager's inner motivations were not completely transparent to the staff. A façade of democracy is received as patronizing and treated with the contempt it deserves. Genuine consultation, on the other hand, is received warmly and treated responsibly. Furthermore, the manager's 'right to manage' is strengthened in direct proportion to his or her growing personal credibility.

That is where 'the domino effect' begins. In human interaction, people detect insincerity, manipulation and attacks on their dignity. Individual incidents may be small, but their cumulative effect is to alienate from corporate values the very people essential to organizational effectiveness. It is also where 'the domino effect' can be reversed – in your everyday contact with other people using your personal credibility and assertive tools and techniques to unlock their motivation and direct their energies towards business objectives.

So, whether your reason for reading this book has been to improve your managerial effectiveness or simply to think and behave in a way that makes you feel better about yourself, I hope it has been worthwhile. If you have used the Workout sheets, you may have an excess of possibilities as to how you can put into effect the lessons you have learned. I should like to leave you, therefore, with five final questions to help concentrate your thoughts:

1. In one short sentence, what do you want to achieve at work?
2. What sort of staff, colleagues and boss do you need to help you achieve it?
3. What sort of behaviour do you need to encourage from your current staff, colleagues and boss to help them be like the people you described in (2) above?

4. What sort of behaviour do you need to exhibit to encourage that sort of behaviour?
5. To behave that way genuinely, what sort of perceptions do you need to share with them?

When I run courses I encourage feedback from the participants, and would like to extend the principle to readers of this book. So, if you wish to comment on what you have read or, even better, describe examples of how it may have helped you, I would love to hear from you.

> Terry Gillen Training
> P.O. Box 585
> Tring
> Hertfordshire HP23 5SX
> England

Suggested reading

Some of these books may further your understanding of yourself and of assertiveness.

Assertiveness at Work by Ken and Kate Back (McGraw-Hill, 1983).
   A thorough text on assertiveness as it applies in the workplace.

Beating Aggression by Diana Lamplugh (Weidenfeld & Nicolson, 1988).
   A remarkably comprehensive book on handling aggression. Although primarily aimed at women's personal security, it is a book of insights as well as useful advice, equally valid for men.

I'm OK – You're OK by Thomas A. Harris (Pan Books, 1972).
   A standard text book on transactional analysis – a study of how we communicate with (and manipulate) one another. Relevant to what I describe as 'our preferred way of communciating'.

Managing Assertively by Madelyn Burley-Allen (John Wiley, 1983).
   A comprehensive guide to behaving assertively in managerial situations packed with numerous self-analysis questionnaires.

100% Mind Power by Jack Ensign Addington (Excalibur Books, 1988).
A stimulating, if somewhat evangelical book on positive thinking.

What Do You Say After You Say Hallo? by Eric Berne (Corgi Books, 1978).
A mammoth account of how we can be affected by our early programming.

When I Say No, I Feel Guilty by Manuel J Smith (Bantam Books, 1975).
The standard text on assertiveness – entertainingly written too!

A Woman in Your Own Right by Anne Dickson (Quartet Books, 1982).
A professionally written book on assertiveness tailored to the needs of women.

INDEX

agreement *see* negative assertion
aggressive
  behaviour 13–15, 18–20
  managers 21, 66–7, 68, 70, 141–5, 179
  people 10–11, 75, 154–5, 189–90,
    205–7
  handling 118–28
assertive
  behaviour 13–14, 16–17, 18–21
  managers 21, 67, 68, 143–4
  mental attitude 228–9
  people 12, 97, 152
authority figures *see* parents

basic assertion 83, 85, 92, 97, 121, 126,
  139, 151, 166, 193, 199, 208
body language 10, 11, 12, 77, 88–92, 103,
  118
Bond, James 31
broken record 78–80, 84, 92, 97, 121,
  139, 158, 166, 193, 199, 219

childhood 28, 56, 116, 119, 227
  see also children
children 36–44, 50–1

  see also childhood
communicating, preferred way of 42–4,
  60
coaching 131, 180
conflict, resolving 147–53
coping mechanisms 5, 41
counselling 131
criticizing *see* reprimanding
criticism 73, 75, 76
  just 108–11
  unjust 111–13
  see also reprimanding

data banks 35–44, 72, 213, 228, 229
delegating 141–6
  see also tough targets
dysfunctional behaviour 69

early programming 35–45
emotional blackmail 53, 56
  see also manipulation techniques
empathy 83, 85, 92, 97, 208
empowering influence 37–9, 99
expectation 26–7, 101, 102
eyes *see* eye contact

eye contact 90
evaluative behaviour 131

face 90
fight or flight response 11, 41, 44, 64, 66, 78, 119, 211, 227–8
fogging 75–6, 83, 91, 121, 132, 139, 186, 193, 198, 208

gestures 90
giants *see* parents
group maintenance behaviours 69

Herzberg, Frederick 67
Hierarchy of needs *see* Maslow

interpretive behaviour 131

K.I.S.S. 158

life plan 42
logic 57–8, 221

macho management 99–100
manipulation techniques 41, 47, 58, 64, 67, 157, 172
Maslow 67–8
McGregor, Douglas 4, 60, 67
meetings
  importance of 189
  performing well in 189–94
mistakes 55
mind set 26
Montgomery, Field Marshall 105

negative assertion 72–5, 83, 91, 97, 166, 172, 193, 208

parents 36–44, 48, 50, 53, 66, 119
perception 227, 232
personal credibility 4–5, 93, 113, 231
Peters & Waterman 175
pointing out a consequence 81–2, 84, 92, 97, 121, 193
pointing out a discrepancy 80–1, 84, 92, 97, 193, 200
poor listeners, talking to 195–203
positive thinking 32
posture 89–90
praise
  being praised 183–8
  conditional 178, 185
  confusing 178–9, 186
  critical 177, 184–5

giving 175–82, 208
  ineffective 176–80
  plastic 176–7, 183–4
probing 76–8, 84, 91, 97, 121, 126, 132, 139, 151, 158, 180, 186, 193, 198, 200, 208
proximity 91
put-down 52, 118, 123–6

questions
  closed 78, 222–4
  open 77–8
  see also probing

recognition capability 25–6
red rag 103
reflective behaviour 132
reprimanding 99–106
refusing a request *see* saying 'No'
resentment, handling 136–40
restraining influence 37–9
restraint *see* restraining influence
rights 44, 46–65, 72, 100, 190, 214, 228, 229–30, 231
Rogers, Carl 131
rules 5, 36–44, 48, 56, 60, 67, 227

salespeople
  handling 217–26
  making assumptions 219–20
  pressure 218–19
saying 'No' 154–61
seeking guidance 204–10
self esteem 55, 67, 132
self disclosure 77, 84, 92, 97, 166, 186, 208
self image 42, 60, 62, 119, 163, 227
self talk 24–34, 100, 101, 102, 132, 136–7, 164, 214, 228
shaping behaviour 176
signposting 77, 84, 97, 151, 156, 158, 166, 186, 193, 199–200, 208
situational leadership *see* Tannenbaum & Schmidt
stress 211–16
  self-generated 214
  typical causes 212–13
stroking 180
submissive
  behaviour 13–14, 15, 18–20
  managers 21, 67, 68, 70, 142–3, 179
  people 11–12, 59, 75, 190
    handling 129–35
supportive behaviour 132

tactics 14
Tannenbaum & Schmidt 68–9
task behaviours 69
team building 68–70
teasing, persistent 113–16
techniques 72–94
theory x *see* McGregor
theory y *see* McGregor
tools 77, 82–5
tough targets 169–74
   see also delegating

Townsend, Robert

verbal
  aggression 118–23
  judo 73, 78, 151
voice 81–2, 88, 127

win-win outcome 83
workable compromise 83, 85, 92, 97,
   121, 158
work overload, handling 162–8

The Motivation Manual

Gisela Hagemann

Motivated staff produce the best results, but how do you ensure the motivation of your team?

Improved productivity, flexible work practices, low rates of absenteeism, commitment to quality, ever-higher standards of customer service – these are the benefits of a well-motivated workforce. In this prize-winning book the author takes modern motivational theory and shows how it can be practically applied to create shared vision, develop mutual trust and involve employees in the decision-making process.

The text is enlivened throughout by examples of the techniques described applied in practice.

- Includes a model questionnaire which can be used to find out what motivates and demotivates the staff in your organization
- 27 exercises cover topics such as active listening, giving and receiving positive and negative feedback, teamwork and organizational change
- Provides the tools needed to design an improvement programme in any organization.

The Motivation Manual is designed as a sourcebook of practical guidance on what is recognized as one of the keys to effective management. A European bestseller, it has already appeared in Czech, Finnish, German, Italian, Norwegian and Swedish. Beyond Europe, it has been published in Mexico, Indonesia and India.

Contents

Part I Motivation and Organizational Change • Part II Material Incentives • Part III Communication as a Motivator • Part IV Participation • Part V Practical Activities for Personal and Organizational Development.

1994   257 pages   0 566 07613 6

A Gower Paperback

Problem Solving in Groups
Second Edition

Mike Robson

Modern scientific research has demonstrated that groups are likely to solve problems more effectively than individuals. As most of us knew already, two heads (or more) are better than one. In organizations it makes sense to harness the power of the group both to deal with problems already identified and to generate ideas for enhancing effectiveness by reducing costs, increasing productivity and the like.

In this revised and updated edition of his successful book, Mike Robson first introduces the concepts and methods involved. Then, after setting out the advantages of the group approach, he examines in detail each of the eight key problem solving techniques. The final part of the book explains how to present proposed solutions, how to evaluate results and how to ensure that the group process runs smoothly.

With its practical tone, its down-to-earth style and lively visuals, this is a book that will appeal strongly to managers and trainers looking for ways of improving their organization's and their department's performance.

Contents

Part I: Introduction • The benefits of group problem solving• Problem-solving groups • Part II: Problem-Solving Techniques • The problem-solving process • Brainstorming • Defining problems clearly • Analysing problems • Collecting data • Interpreting data • Finding solutions • Cost-benefit analysis • Part III: Following Through • Presenting solutions • Working together • Dealing with problems in the group • Index.

1993   176 pages   0 566 07415 X

A Gower Paperback

The Skills of Leadership

John Adair

Leadership is an essential ingredient in successful management and every manager therefore needs to acquire or develop the skills of leadership. The aim of this book is to provide guidance to that end.

Skills cannot of course be learned from a book alone, and constant practice is vital. What the book does offer is an explanation of the concepts underlying the skills of leadership, supported by a wealth of practical hints, and enlivened by examples drawn from a wide variety of circumstances. The present text has been developed largely by condensing and combining the ideals contained in three of the author's earlier works, with new material added where appropriate. The result is a modern treatment of leadership, decision-making and communication which no manager with 'people problems' can afford to ignore.

Contents

Leadership The nature of leadership • Looking at leaders • Leadership selection • Developing leadership • **Decisions** The nature of thinking • Thinkers in action • Decision making • Problem solving • Creative thinking • **Communication** The nature of communication • Effective speaking • Better listening • Clear writing • Meetings - the leader as chairman • Communicating in large organisations • Action programme – how to improve your communication • Conclusion • Appendix • Notes and bibliography • Index.

1984   298 pages   0 7045 0555 X

A Gower Paperback